MOTHER VINCENT WHITTY

Mother Vincent Whitty

WOMAN AND EDUCATOR IN A MASCULINE SOCIETY

Sister Mary Xaverius O'Donoghue

MELBOURNE UNIVERSITY PRESS

First published 1972
Printed in Australia by
Wilke and Co. Ltd, Clayton, Victoria 3168 for
Melbourne University Press, Carlton, Victoria 3053
Great Britain and Europe: ISBS Inc., London
USA and Canada: ISBS Inc., Portland, Oregon 97208
Registered in Australia for transmission by post as a book

ISBN 0 522 84017 5
Dewey Decimal Classification Number 377.829430924

To Mother Mary Damian Duncombe

First President of

The Australian Federation of

Sisters of Mercy

ACKNOWLEDGMENTS

It is difficult to thank adequately the men and women in several countries who have assisted in the research for this work. Of the many, it is possible to mention only a few.

Mother M. Damian Duncombe, who was first Mother General of the Mercy Congregation of All Hallows', the oldest Queensland Community, generously provided the conditions that made research and writing possible, and thereby showed her sense of the continuity of history. Archbishop Sir James Duhig had permitted free access to the Archdiocesan Archives for a previous work; this permission was kindly renewed by his successor, Archbishop P. M. O'Donnell.

Cardinal Agagianian graciously granted access to the Archives of the Sacred Congregation for the Propagation of the Faith in Rome. To him and to Reverend Dr D. Murphy, C.S.Sp., who presented the writer to his Eminence and led to other valuable sources of research, grateful thanks are due. I am indebted also to Bishop Herlihy of Ferns, then Rector of the Irish College, Archbishop McQuaid of Dublin who gave entry to the Archdiocesan Archives, the Mother General of Carysfort Park, Mother Gabriel, and the nuns of Baggot Street, Carlow, Athy, Enniscorthy, Abbeyfeale, Tralee, St John's Wood in London and the Washington Motherhouse (U.S.A.), particularly Mother Stella Maris, for hospitality and the use of their archives. I wish also to thank Reverend Professor F. X. Martin of Dublin University College, Mr T. P. O'Neill of the National Library, and Father J. Broderick of the English Province of the Society of Jesus, and, nearer home, Monsignor C. Duffy, Archivist of St Mary's in Sydney, Mother Philomena, Mother General of the Monte Sant Angelo Congregation in Sydney and the Sisters of the Nicholson Street, Melbourne and Geelong convents for access to their records.

Dr Michael White of the University of Queensland Department

of External Studies guided the pattern and organization of this work. Reverend Dr T. P. Boland and Sister M. Anne McLay read the manuscript and merit thanks for their valuable comments. Thanks are due also to Father F. H. Douglas, Diocesan Chancellor, for his assistance over several years. Lastly, the sustained interest of Cambridge research student, Dr S. Gilley, and his suggestions as to content and style, have been deeply appreciated.

CONTENTS

ILLUSTRATIONS

INTRODUCTION

Firmly entrenched in the history of Australian education is the name of Bishop James Quinn. J. Murtagh[1] and R. Fogarty[2] rank him among the foremost architects of Catholic education in Australia. Yvonne McLay attributes to him the major role of guide and policy-maker in Queensland Catholic education and gives only brief mention to the co-founder of the system, Mother M. Vincent Whitty.[3] T. L. Suttor advances one step farther: 'the organization would have been a body without a soul were it not for the Mercy nuns', he reflected.[4]

This work began as an attempt to uncover as much as possible concerning Mother Vincent Whitty, Superior of the Sisters who accompanied Quinn from Dublin. Since almost two thousand women—Sisters and lay staff—carry on her work in present-day Queensland in schools and institutions dotted over thousands of square miles north and west of Brisbane, her personality invited scrutiny. To peel off the cloak of anonymity which for a century has hidden her personality, to discover what manner of woman she was, and what were her aims, methods and motives, was a necessary preliminary to an assessment of her place in Queensland's religious, cultural and social history.

A perusal of the Brisbane documents left unanswered many tantalizing questions. Mother Dominick, the Dublin archivist whose help was sought, had no doubt that Mother Vincent was among the really great women of the Institute, and declared that an Australian writer should uncover her name and fame as a United States biographer had already done for Mother Francis Warde, Mother Vincent's contemporary. To encourage an immediate start, she lent a sheaf of letters from Mother Vincent to the Dublin Head House. This batch left unproven Mother Dominick's judgment of greatness, and gave the impression that Mother Vincent had caught the eye of history because of the time, place and manner of her life. As an individual, she might well have been forgotten, but having joined an active religious community, she was caught up in a large historic movement which dragged her along and overshadowed her. It was impossible for her in mid-nineteenth-century Ireland with its great population exodus to live in a world apart, sufficient to herself alone. She was not of the calibre of Florence Nightingale.

Much travel and research modified that view. The durable solidity of the schools and hospitals which Mother Vincent established in Dublin testify to energy, zeal, and foresight; the vast projects of her spiritual descendants in the United States and in England perpetuate her dynamism, as do the Sisters of Mercy engaged in spiritual, educational and social works in Queensland. Through letters unearthed in Rome and elsewhere, it became possible to understand the past, to get closer to it by feeling with it, and Mother Vincent took flesh and form. Her photographs lost their remote dignity. She emerged as a happy nun, interest and intelligence in her eyes; sympathetic in manner, a good listener; quick in movement and decision, and occasionally fiery in temper; of a practical and rather unimaginative turn of mind, a doer rather than a thinker; a hard worker; ready to help with the problems of others but excessively reticent concerning her own; her driving aim was to bridge the discontinuity between the secular and the religious plane and promote unity among men of all classes and creeds.

Thus this ordinary-seeming Sister of Mercy appeared in mid-life when she left Ireland for the Queensland mission. The unsuspected depth, complexity and inconsistencies of personality which unfolded within her in her new life make her thirty years in Australia the most rewarding part of this study. For here she encountered four great challenges to her individual responsibility and freedom of action: state domination of education; the vastness, isolation and poverty of pioneering Queensland; episcopal control; and the threat to the Mercy ideal within her own religious community as well as in the wider society.

The first tension stemmed from conflicting goals in education. Politically organized society sought universal literacy through public schools alone, in the quasi-religious belief that thereby it would ensure unity and national salvation and security. Mother Vincent, on the other hand, wished to give primacy to the spiritual and moral formation of the individual, though secular knowledge was to have an essential place. Further, through the school she desired to establish deep and lasting links with the family, the home and the parish community. Whether the healthiest development of the state goal would necessarily inhibit Mother Vincent's is an open question, but beyond doubt subservience to political and social demands would destroy her educational ideals. The nineteenth-century state's increased involvement in education made ideological differences in aim inevitable. But whereas in Ireland the Board of National Education comprised Catholic, Anglican, and Presbyterian churchmen, in Queensland there was no such accommodation of religious policy; education was, in fact, a function of politics.

In the resulting dualism, Church and state had to solve as best they might the problems posed by a frontier existence—the vastness of a colony three times the size of France, without roads or navigable waterways; wide dispersion of population; poverty, and lack of material resources. Mother Vincent's decision made it possible for Church to follow state in establishing central control as a response to this challenge, so that Queensland's initial pattern of educational development is very different from that of other Australian colonies.

The third theme is Mother Vincent's individual responsibility in tension with episcopal control. Her wide experience, her vigour and broad talents in education should have found free scope in the new colony. At first sight, nothing was more surprising than that Bishop Quinn, whom she ranked high among her friends in Dublin, and who had gone to great lengths to secure her for Queensland, should then overstep his powers and encroach on affairs that were strictly her domain. All possible theories were explored to discover why. Was the difference between Brisbane and Dublin so overwhelming as to find Mother Vincent discouraged or incompetent to deal with new conditions? Her own reticence might have made it impossible to find a convincing answer. Her colleagues, more outspoken, reveal sources of friction about which she was silent. But the true key is provided by the character of the bishop. His relationship with the Fathers of the Assumption, with the Sisters of St Joseph and with his own clergy show that, for all his gifts of nature and grace, he found it impossible to allow others free initiative.

The degree of control which he exercised set up tension within Mother Vincent's own community between the rigidity of his spirituality and the Mercy ideal. Mother Mary of the Cross, who founded the Sisters of St Joseph, adopted a historic solution to a parallel problem with Bishop Quinn and his brother bishop in Bathurst. Mother Vincent, too, had to save the fabric of communal life from disintegration, but decided against withdrawal; that challenge once overcome, her supreme task was to preserve freedom of spirit. For a new legalism in the training of the novices, traceable to the bishop's bid for control, was implanted in the young sister, Mother M. Bridget Conlan, who had had no opportunity to absorb the Mercy ideal. To limit its effect, Mother Vincent's solution for the tension was a new understanding of free commitment, and she sought by personal influence on new nuns to counteract this tendency to autocracy.

These conflicts and the conclusions that flow from them form the central theme of the present work. Also implied is a methodological principle. Chapter 1 follows the chronological method, to recount the successive influences that went to shape the character and outlook of Mother Vincent. In the subsequent chapters, chronology gives way to an alternative procedure which permits greater flexibility in following through the conflict of authority and freedom.

The sheer mass and weight of her contribution to building, educational expansion and social work are less important than the ideas by which she lived. Thus though demographic, social, economic, political and cultural conditions fill out the main theme, they do not distract attention from it. In the clash of authority and freedom in education, generalizations can be misleading, obscuring nuances. A case-history has obvious limitations too, yet there is an advantage in portraying a trail-blazer's attempt to serve all three levels—state, episcopal, and internal—without losing sight of her basic aim.

1

MOTHER VINCENT'S IRISH BACKGROUND

Ellen Whitty was born in 1819 and died in 1892. She was educated at Enniscorthy and Dublin, and became a Sister of Mercy and a teacher. After some years in Ireland's capital as Reverend Mother of the Head House of the Order at Baggot Street, she set out to found a convent in the colony of Queensland, Australia. The following thirty years saw her busily spreading a network of schools and charitable homes from sub-tropical Brisbane to Mackay, well inside the Tropic of Capricorn.

This bald chronicle of her activity was all that was known until a few years ago. If her life was as colourless as the story implied, then her name would be adequately perpetuated by the slightly larger cross that marks her grave where she lies in Nudgee surrounded by hundreds of her spiritual children. These short and simple annals give no real notion of her worth. No ordinary woman, Mother Vincent Whitty surmounted difficulties of an unusual and perplexing kind; and the most formidable of them confronted her in the sunny land of the Southern Cross.

Ellen Whitty's remote preparation for her life work began in her Wexford home by the broad, island-dotted Slaney. The very day she was born, 1 March 1819, her devout parents had her christened in the Oylegate church near Enniscorthy. Father J. Dixon, who sixteen years before said the first Mass of which we have record in Australia,[1] was a frequent visitor at the Whitty home, and as Ellen grew up he told the children stories of the faraway southern land. Such encounters, along with the religious instruction and example in the home, and the unfailing regularity of family prayer in the evening, were in due time to turn the thoughts of more than one of the Whitty children to the service of God in Australia.

But as Ellen played marbles and skipping-rope with her brothers and sisters, or attended the local Catholic lay school to learn history and geography, reading, writing and arithmetic, Wexford seemed large enough for a lifetime. Her ancestors bore a proud Norman name, and the Whitty family cherished the memory of castles that had belonged to them in a happier past. Nevertheless, Ellen was so busy living in the present that she believed only old people talked about days gone by. She loved the river and the flocks of teal, ducks, geese, and wild swans which it attracted, and to the end of her days she recalled the bright arc of the salmon's leap.[2] But her practical grandmother would allow no day-dreaming and taught the girls the old arts of spinning and weaving, and trained them in household management. Ellen proved amenable and quick to learn, and could be relied on to see any task to its conclusion. In this she resembled Mary, the eldest, but differed from her younger sister Anne who tended to let ideas and projects trail away into inconclusiveness. At the age of twelve, Ellen differed from both in a remarkable unwillingness to tolerate conversation that could wound the reputation of an absent person.[3] If on such occasions the speaker was a younger member of her own family Ellen administered a reproof but, if it was an older person, she was so miserable that she sought any excuse to leave the company. Apart from this trait she was a perfectly normal girl who loved music and singing and the company of friends.

The orchard and farm produced enough to give the children a good education, and Ellen's father was determined that the boys should go to college. Robert, as an alumnus of Maynooth and Dunboyne, later joined the Westminster diocese and became Nicholas Cardinal Wiseman's Vicar-General and the Provost of Westminster Chapter, but in his forties joined the Society of Jesus and, after a period as Provincial of the English Jesuits, was called to Fiesole near Florence to become Assistant to the Father General. William also undertook studies for the priesthood, but died while a student at the English College, Rome. The only other son, Peter, achieved a high post in the civil service in Dublin at a time when Catholics were few in white-collar positions. Mary married a London Quaker, Edward Lucas, who became a Catholic as did his brother, the more famous Frederick, founder of the English Catholic paper, the *Tablet*. Anne became a Sister of Mercy in Dublin, nursed the wounded at the Crimea, and pioneered the Mercy Order in Buenos Aires.

To continue her education, Ellen went to Dublin where, at the academy of Miss Finn in Hardwick Place, she studied music, singing, French, embroidery, and the 'accomplishments' of the day.[4]

The contrast between wealth and poverty in the city was more pronounced than in Wexford. The fine Georgian mansions of Merrion Square and the glittering shops of Grafton Street made more appalling the dark and narrow lanes with their thousands of ragged urchins reared in ignorance and vice. Ellen had never seen nuns in Wexford county, and now she was astonished to see Sisters of Mercy walking through these lanes with baskets of food and clothing. On asking her brother Robert, then a student at Maynooth, about them, she learned that they gathered the children for lessons in the House of Mercy in Baggot Street, where Daniel O'Connell's daughters and other ladies assisted for a few hours daily.[5] Gradually, as the Sisters' manner of life was unfolded to her, she was drawn to consider whether she might join them, since for some time she had given thought to the religious life as the best means for her to love God, save her soul, and share the burdens of others. She visited their convent at Baggot Street and was surprised to note that, despite the nature of their work, they were joyous and lighthearted; they were in fact quite different from the normal world, and seemed to have rediscovered the secret land of the Gaelic Oisin:

> Where nobody gets old and crafty and wise . . .
> Where nobody gets old and bitter of tongue,
> And where kind tongues bring no captivity.

On 6 January 1839 Ellen Whitty presented herself to Catherine McAuley and asked permission to join the Order. That same night, as the winds were gathering force for a violent cyclone, Mother McAuley wrote a letter to Mother Frances Warde of Carlow, and serenely told her of the 'very pleasing and musical' girl who was to enter Baggot Street House on 15 January.[6] Ellen was 'rather below middle height, very graceful in her movements, but quick and energetic. Her face was handsome . . . calm, earnest and expressive; features regular, rather long than oval; her complexion of a pale olive tint; her large liquid eyes dark and beautifully set.'[7]

Ellen entered at a time particularly favourable to her religious formation. The whole of her novitiate of two years and nine months was spent with Mother Catherine McAuley who personally prepared the novices for their profession, the day on which they made their vows. With Ellen were six Birmingham girls destined to form a branch of the Institute in the industrialized Catholic section of England, and Fanny Gibson from Liverpool who was to be Superior of the first convent to be opened in her city since the Reformation. Ellen's closest friends were Fanny and Juliana Hardman of Birmingham. Welsh and Scottish Sisters in the Baggot Street convent helped to provide a catholic breadth which was to make the Order at home everywhere.

Gifted with intelligence and a lively manner, Ellen Whitty was normally assertive and sure of herself. Coming from a home with six children she was sensitive to the needs and feelings of others, and quick to help. She mixed easily, and strangers felt at ease in her presence. For friends she liked the stable-tempered rather than the mercurial. She was notably lacking in wit, and had no gift for verse-making, unlike many of her companions, but was loyal and trusting, and had a large capacity to give and receive love.

The strong bonds of friendship forged in the novitiate were to last through life, and Dr Robert Whitty often commented on the similarity of character that linked Sister M. Juliana Hardman, Sister M. Liguori Gibson, and his sister. On her part, Sister M. Juliana found Mother Vincent over again in her brother. 'We are delighted with him,' she wrote from Birmingham to Mother Vincent. 'I do not remember any Jesuit who seems to make such an impression and to stir you up to the love and service of Our Lord as he does. I could think I heard you speaking.'[8]

In Ellen, the Baggot Street Superiors had a disciple docile to spiritual teaching, but full of sane common sense. They provided room for her initiative, first in small ways, such as training choirs for which she arranged the music, to sing in Dublin, Birr, and other churches to which the Temperance preacher, Father Theobald Mathew, drew crowds. Immediately after her novitiate, when the foundress and the Mistress of Novices both went to Birmingham, Catherine McAuley placed the newly professed Sister M. Vincent Whitty in charge of the novices. Only twenty-two at the time, Sister Vincent felt the responsibility greatly, but acquitted herself well, and soon more tasks were entrusted to her. Conscientious and a hard worker, she expected her charges to be equally quick in response, and she demonstrated a certain irritability in her dealings with the tardy and negligent, even to the point of intimidating with a strap those she considered sluggish.[9] Yet when Sisters were ill, she sat by their bedsides all night to minister to them.

Her letters and spiritual notes written during her early years in the congregation reflect the novice's introspective glance at herself and her pursuit of true conversion of the heart. Certain devotional leanings may be discerned in the meditations and reflections jotted down in neat handwriting, chief of which sprang from appreciation of the Mass and of the Blessed Sacrament. It is noteworthy that in her earlier period in the religious life, references abound to the sorrowful Passion of Christ without the balancing thought of his glory after the Resurrection, so that one derives from Sister M. Vincent's notes an impression of the austere rather than the joyous. Moreover, the strong current of French spirituality still discernible in Maynooth was passed on to her through Robert Whitty but even more through her cousin, Dr Thomas Furlong, and Dr Miles Gaffney, with heavy doses of Francis de Sales and Fenelon. While credit must surely go to 'the devout de Sales' for helping Ellen to curb her temper, a touch of Jansenism tainted some of her reading, causing her to think of God as a Watchman 'on Heaven's high tower', who spies out all our actions 'even in darkest night'. However, in later years, when she came under the influence of Jesuit Father Robert St Leger, she emerged from the shadow of Jansenist influence.

From the biographer's point of view, it is a pity that Ellen needed to write so seldom to spiritual directors, to whom she spoke freely of herself; they lived close to Dublin, and she naturally found a personal interview more satisfactory. A numerous and varied collection of letters provides an insight of greatest value into character and motive, but Ellen's hasty missives prove limited in scope; they rarely reflect her delight in nature, never touch on the stirring events of her day, nor do they reveal a notable intellectual force or theological depth. Yet, to be chosen when quite young for responsible posts, she must have towered above her colleagues; their judgment, and her own actions, are the best guide to her character. Nevertheless, among her papers, there is one which, though brief, offers valuable clues to her preferences; it is an outline description of the person she most admired, the foundress of the Mercy Order, Catherine McAuley.

Ellen Whitty did not greatly feel the gap of years and the weight of experience which separated her from the sixty-year-old foundress, because a simple and happy interchange was encouraged among the Sisters. She found in Catherine the qualities she most prized—evenness of temper and openness to ideas. While she venerated the older woman for the manner in which she had begun a great work, she loved her as a friend who was 'so humble yet dignified, so playful and witty yet reserved and charitable.'[10] Nothing, Ellen believed, could convey a knowledge of Catherine

McAuley to others like the experience of living with her. Descriptions and stories of her deeds fell short of the impression gathered in her presence. Ellen came to know the members of Catherine's family and the profound affection and concern shown by Catherine for them. Similarly news of the wider religious family, shared at the evening recreation, showed Ellen the joys, trials and successes of the new foundations in Ireland and England.

For Ellen entered when the Order was only eight years old, and still so small that the concerns of one house were the concerns of all. Education was the main work Catherine had in mind when she launched the Institute of Our Lady of Mercy in 1831—the very year that the Stanley Irish National System was founded. But visitation of homes and relief of all forms of human distress were also among her aims. This social concern, and the fact that the Sisters were free to move about and enjoyed a government unimpeded by rigid central control, made the Order a valuable aid to the episcopacy.

Mother McAuley wished the spirit of charity and service to be the real bond in the new order rather than a tight centralization. Through her frequent visits and her much-sought counsel she preserved a loose federation between filial houses, which allowed easy exchange of Sisters and mutual help. Thus when English girls came to train for a London foundation, Mother McAuley sent them to the house in Cork; and as each recently founded branch felt strong enough to make an independent move to a new centre, the Superior first laid her plan before Mother McAuley as a matter of filial courtesy. However, Mother Catherine had only ten years in which to guide her Institute before she died.

Whether she would otherwise have modified her government to prevent the encroachments of bishops is a matter of conjecture. Indeed 'with further experience' she might well have followed the example of Brother Ignatius Rice, who on the suggestion of Archbishop Murray took steps to prevent a repetition of an upset in Cork city where a bishop became over-possessive of his community of Christian Brothers. On the death of the foundress, the loose federation lost its most precious link, and Mother M. de Pazzi, who succeeded Catherine as Reverend Mother of Baggot Street Head House, had neither the prestige nor the personality to act as liaison between houses now scattered over several counties in England and Ireland. Thus the pattern of new foundations followed the old monastic plan of frequently distinct and autonomous houses, some with no branch convents, others with one.

Ellen Whitty, as Reverend Mother in Australia, was to see the Order spread around her with its many branch convents all closely bound to the mother house.

Catherine McAuley's Order, despite fragmentation into multiple units, could no more lose its spiritual character than a woman can lose her personality. It is remarkable that to meet the critical times Nano Nagle, Mary Aikenhead, Frances Ball, Catherine McAuley and Margaret Aylward each represented in a unique and unforeseeable way the creative riches of the Church.

Catherine, like the others, based her work on the spiritual, intellectual, moral and institutional values of her day, but she nevertheless raised her eyes to countries beyond the sea where she personally hoped to serve, and she provided for the conservation and transmission down the centuries of her intentions through the disciples she sent forth rather than by her writings. Mother Clare Moore of London, Mother Frances Warde of the United States, Mother Ursula Frayne of Perth, and Mother Vincent Whitty of Brisbane, more truly carried the torch of Catherine's spirit than could the static word. To attempt to reduce to writing what Catherine McAuley so well conveyed by voice and eye, by gesture and action, by prayer and suffering and boundless charity was a task for which Mother Vincent felt herself quite unequal; words were too 'slow and imperfect' to describe one so greatly gifted.[11]

This is not to say that Mother McAuley's own writings do not reveal something of her spirit. But it must be understood that her concept of the active life was comparatively new. Mary Ward had shocked the episcopate three centuries earlier when she, a mere woman, had sought to found a religious Order of women who would be free to serve outside the cloister. Nano Nagle's similar wish had been foiled after her death when her Presentation nuns became cloister-bound. Catherine McAuley shared the responsible and mature outlook of these women, but was so hampered by the inertia of ideas that she first planned to serve God in the freedom of a laywoman. Wise and saintly clergy counselled otherwise, and to give the stability and permanence of religious life to her work she agreed to the normal novitiate training with the Presentation nuns before founding an Order more in accord with Nano Nagle's original idea. Then she moved cautiously in framing her Rule and Constitutions. She wished to maintain the solid basis common to all religious life, namely contemplation and penance; and for guidance she turned to existing Rules.

What was new was Catherine's accent on service, for her Sisters vowed devotion to the poor, sick and ignorant as well as the traditional chastity, poverty and obedience. The vow of service demanded more initiative than was provided for in the model Rules of the past; hence the tension in the written word of the foundress, between new and old, for which her own practice proved the best solvent. A new concept demanded a fresh theological framework, which could be evolved only with time and thought.

Mother McAuley sometimes perforce adopted a hand-me-down phraseology or formula which could have gravely misled, if she had not interpreted it in daily life for her followers. Thus, in order that unity in work would proceed from unity in judgment, Ellen Whitty heard bald exhortations impossible to fulfil, such as, 'We must have no opinion contrary to that of the superior, and above all entertain no wish to be listened to, despising our own sentiments.'[12]

Clearly Ellen Whitty did not take these words at face value, nor was she meant to, for in describing the most attractive traits of Catherine McAuley, she emphasized that the foundress was 'always ready to listen, to consider . . . whenever applied to.'[13] The lag between the letter and the spirit was as great as the distance between the rather doubtful asceticism of some pious manual and Mother McAuley's humane and practical holiness.

But if Mother Catherine failed to give clear definition to her personal understanding of obedience, she placed beyond doubt her interpretation of concord; and for Ellen Whitty both nature and training combined to make this religious quality the most attractive of virtues. Moreover, the spirit of unity and charity was at the core of the Mercy way of life, which, in the interest of the common good, expected members to sink personal ambition and the desire to shine. Self-effacement was to be the norm for the Sisters of Mercy. 'We should delight to be unknown, that we may the more resemble our blessed Saviour who was constantly labouring and doing great things for his Father and for our salvation without bringing himself into notice or being distinguished.'[14] When contradiction came from others, a mortified will enabled the novice to endure it 'humbly and sweetly' in order to sanctify the soul. Mother McAuley drove home her lessons by verse as well as by prose:

> Be glad to find a critic both truthful and severe.
> Whatever be the verdict, accept it as sincere.[15]

The 'Horarium' or distribution of the hours further reinforced the ideal of unity; work, prayer, and meals brought the Sisters together while allowing them to enjoy a certain privacy; at recreation they met as a single family. The tranquillity of order thus imposed was 'an image of Paradise.'[16] The net effect of theory and practice in the religious formation encouraged the individual to merge with the group so cohesively that, unlike the Christian Brothers, the Franciscans, the Cistercians, no Sisters of Mercy ever seceded to found an independent Order.

Strengthened by such steadfast unity of purpose, Ellen Whitty was undaunted by the social and moral conditions of mid-nineteenth-century Dublin; indeed, it was precisely as a response to these conditions that she had thrown in her lot with the group that gathered round Catherine McAuley. For to dispel the spiritual and physical misery of impoverished Irish Catholics was Ellen's key to a free Church in a free state. Many men besides Daniel O'Connell sought this goal through political unity,[17] but the Mercy nuns attempted to reach it through education.

While the Rule of the Order envisaged other services, primacy was given to the schools because, in the words of Catherine McAuley, 'no work of charity can be more productive of good to society or more conducive to the happiness of the poor than the careful instruction of women.' The basic assumption of Mercy Sisters, Ellen included, was that the strength of women could leaven society, 'since whatever be the station they are destined to fill, their example and advice will always possess influence; and wherever a religious woman presides, peace and good order are generally to be found.'[18] Hence, on the education of girls rested the whole grandiose scheme to re-create society.

Though religious, social and political conditions in Ireland were at a low ebb at the time of the Order's inception, they were to worsen steadily after Mother McAuley's death in 1841, for the mid-1840s brought the devastating Potato Famine which catapulted revolt, and emigration on a phenomenal scale, and filled with derelicts the prison-like workhouses of the towns. In the wake of the Famine, there was work to do for Ellen Whitty, chosen to fill Mother McAuley's role as head of the Order.

Called Sister Mary Vincent from 1840, Ellen Whitty began her teacher training by observing and participating in the work of the Dublin schools. The day began with twenty minutes of Christian doctrine, after which regular school work commenced, with occasional breaks for reflection or prayer. She learned to combine the pedagogical methods of the Presentation Sisters and of the Kildare Place Society, which resulted in a modified form of the Lancastrian system.[19] This meant that Sister M. Vincent assisted the presiding Sister in one room, in which monitors or pupil-teachers took sections of the work to be taught. Part of Sister M. Vincent's duty was to keep full records of names, ages and addresses of pupils and a register of the sacraments they had received. On her visits to the homes of the children, she saw how to adapt her illustrations and the trend of her teaching to their immediate needs. She used rewards and prizes to stimulate competition, and made sure that the poorest came to the annual Christmas dinner provided for them by Mother McAuley.

The very year in which Ellen Whitty had joined the Order, 1839, the Mercy schools were placed under the Stanley National Education Board because, as the foundress said, 'our children will improve much more when expecting examination.'[20] Archbishop Daniel Murray of Dublin approved of the Stanley plan, though other Irish prelates did not; notable among these was Archbishop John MacHale of Tuam who repudiated it after a short trial, on the ground that it was one more proselytizing agency.

During penal times, the English Protestant government had outlawed all non-Protestant forms of education, and tried to coerce Catholic children to attend 'approved' schools. When the notorious Chartist schools failed, other evangelizing bodies took their place. Even the best of these, the Kildare Place Society, lost the confidence of Catholics, because of its assaults on the conscience of children. At this point, an English Protestant Secretary of State, Lord Stanley, appeared with a humanitarian scheme to provide education for all for a nominal fee and in a form 'from which should be banished even the suspicion of proselytism.' Accordingly in 1831 the government grant was withdrawn from the Kildare Place Society and its administration was entrusted to a Board of Commissioners who were to superintend Stanley's new system of national education. Chairman of the Board was Anglican Archbishop Whately of Dublin, but other Churches were represented also, including the Catholics. Archbishop Murray (Catholic), agreed to become a member and because he was aware that his people could not provide schools out of their own resources, he grasped at an opportunity to guide the new policy which could. For the Stanley scheme would pay all approved teachers, and yet it allowed the safeguard of control of the schools and even their withdrawal altogether from the National System should there arise a threat to the faith of the children. Such withdrawal was made possible by the plan whereby schools could enjoy 'non-vested' status; that meant that the Church provided and maintained the building, but the Board paid the teachers. On the other hand, the school was 'vested' if it was owned and controlled by the Board. The open door provided by 'non-vested' status was a comfort to some bishops who had been harassed by the dilemma of no education or Protestant education. But other bishops would have no truck with government-controlled schools.

The sharp division among Irish hierarchy was to be reflected in Australia. There the Stanley system was adapted to suit the different colonies, though the basic principle remained the same: that children of different religious tenets might gather together in one school for combined secular education and have separate religious instruction from members of their own Church.

However, because in Dublin Archbishop Murray sat on the policy-making Board, Mother McAuley had no fear, and so Sister M. Vincent undertook her teacher training under Board regulations and in 1842 obtained her teacher's certificate.[21] The Sisters' Poor Schools, unlike the national schools, required no fee, and had a utilitarian curriculum suited to girls who had to work for their living. The literacy schools, however, were fee-charging, and their students provided the monitresses who gradually formed the nucleus of the Mercy Training College. The Board Normal Schools (that is, the teacher-training schools) in Dublin and elsewhere gave their teachers twenty weeks' annual training through lectures and practice but they were suspect as proselytizing agencies. Hence the anxiety of the Mercy Sisters to train their own girls, a work which they commenced in Baggot Street during the 1840s.

During her novitiate Sister M. Vincent was often excited by tales of missionaries, and repeatedly volunteered for some distant land. In June 1841 the famous Bishop John England of Charleston offered Mass in the convent chapel and in a most urgent and appealing manner told the novices about his vast diocese and its needs. But eleven Mercy foundations in a mere ten years had drained Baggot Street of its mature members, and as Catherine McAuley gazed at the young and eager faces turned towards the speaker, she had to refuse; her little company needed a breathing space and 'time to come to maturity, reduced to infancy again as we are.'[22] Sister M. Vincent's offer to accompany Bishop J. Pompallier to New Zealand was similarly refused.

The year 1841 was important in other ways. On 19 August she made her vows, in company with the Birminghahm girls, and in the presence of Archbishop D. Murray who brought Dr E. B. Pusey as guest to witness the ceremony. Immediately afterwards the foundation party left for Birmingham, accompanied by the foundress and the Novice Mistress Mother Cecilia Marmion, who was to remain in England for some months. When the foundress returned, she was fatally ill. For weeks Sister M. Vincent nursed her with loving attention to every detail, but not even her cooking could restore the failing appetite; and her only consolation was to listen to the infrequent words full of light and strength, of the woman who had accomplished so much, and write an account of events in Baggot Street for Mother Cecilia and the English nuns. Sister M. Vincent chronicled the comings and goings of Mother Elizabeth from Limerick and various other Superiors and the last words addressed to each, but she failed to mention the important role which the dying woman prophesied for her; others, however, noted down what Mother Catherine said, namely that Sister M. Vincent would do great work for God.[23] Nor did Sister M. Vincent's letters reveal that the foundress had specially asked her to remain up with her the night before she died, and that during the vigil Mother McAuley entrusted her with a final task, the secret and immediate disposal of her instruments of penance.[24] On the following day the young sister so recently professed, said the prayers at the moment of death for her whom she so profoundly esteemed and loved.

The death of Catherine did not check the rapid expansion of the Order, and Sister M. Vincent's desire to go on a mission was gratified when in August 1843 she was chosen for Liverpool with her close friend Fanny Gibson, now Sister M. Liguori. The foundation group was in the care of Reverend Mother M. de Pazzi Delaney and Father R. J. O'Hanlon, Superior of the Carmelites and confessor to Baggot Street; it included Sister M. Aloysius Consitt, Sister Martha Wallplate, Sister M. Baptist Geraghty and Sister M. Teresa French.[25] Liverpool was a strong centre of the old Catholics, few, staunch, and exclusive. But since the 1820s there had been considerable Irish immigration, for Liverpool was the gateway into England for the seasonal harvesters, and while Irish labourers helped build the docks, factory workers were absorbed by the industrial expansion of the cotton towns.[26] A single convent in Liverpool could not hope to serve a Catholic population estimated at 8,000 in 1840, and the nuns of St Ethelburga's in Mount Vernon quickly set up several schools in the city.

Help to staff them continued to come from Dublin, and Dr Robert Whitty, then in London, directed girls with vocations to the Liverpool Mercy novitiate; among them was Miss McQuoin, who as Mother M. Ignatius was to found Monte Sant' Angelo in Sydney. Dr Whitty was on the faculty of St Edmund's College, Ware, and closely resembled his sister in that each identified fully with the people among whom they worked; for both, God's work was everything, and nationality meant nothing. Through her brother, Mother Vincent first felt Newman's influence, for some inner sympathy drew the two men together. Newman found Whitty 'one of the most striking men I have seen . . . a more winning person I have not met, though an Irishman. I really seemed to form a sudden friendship with him.'[27] Newman's touch of condescension mirrors the low estimate Englishmen formed of the hordes of unkempt and uncultured labourers from John Bull's other island. Poles apart from the Oxford converts and from the reserved old Catholics, this proletarian flood was to bring a new and sturdy element to the English Catholic Church. Mother Vincent's Liverpool experience made her acquainted with both strands.

Recalled to Dublin, she was made Mother Bursar.[28] Her duty then was to become as familiar with business houses and the cost of living as any administrator, to supervise housekeeping and to help Sisters leaving for distant foundations. In such work, her practical bent found ample scope, and her contacts widened with men and women in all walks of life. She also provided 'the magnificent breakfasts we used to enjoy as only boys can', recalled an altar-boy who had been regaled after a liturgical function. 'I fancy I used to think that persons who could so dispense such good things must be warm-hearted, generous and unselfish, in a word very motherly, and that they rejoiced at seeing others happy, as you certainly in those days made me.'[29]

In 1844 Sister M. Vincent was appointed Mistress of Novices by the third of Baggot Street's Reverend Mothers, M. Cecilia Marmion. Ireland was then entering the distressing years of the Great Famine. In the resulting mass migration, which nearly halved the population,[30] Mother Cecilia and Mother Vincent were unable to refuse the urgent requests of bishops and priests for Sisters for England, America and Australia. They were forced to free for the missions young Sisters who had not enjoyed normal opportunities to deepen their spiritual life or perfect their training for the tasks ahead. Thus a pattern was established which saved the situation for the moment but created later difficulties. Bishops impatient to see Sisters in their schools expected that hasty novitiates should be the norm, and the fruits of over-compliance were curtailed training and diminished effectiveness.

Nevertheless, critical times evoked an astonishing response. Mother Vincent was cheered by the reports of the heroism and endurance of her young charges. From Perth, the most painful and impoverished of missions, she heard of their cheerfulness amid privations of an unparalleled kind.[31]

Nothing better illustrates the sort of mature and responsible tasks thrust on young Sisters than that Mother Vincent, at twenty-five years of age, should be expected to prepare Sisters for pioneering difficulties in new countries, and that one of her novices professed in 1844, Sister Anne Xavier, became Mother Assistant in Perth in 1846. Young as they were, both had the wisdom of spirit to understand that the essential point of Christianity is the release of love within us, and that, in the words of St Augustine, if the domain of charity is to be enlarged, the domain of the flesh must be restricted. Disaster and death struck at Perth's first missionary party and Bishop Brady was not the man to help in a grim situation. His unrealistic estimate of the colony's resources reduced the Sisters to such a state of want that their Dublin community sent them the money for their return passage; but Mother Anne Xavier agreed with Reverend Mother Ursula Frayne that the money should go into a building fund instead. Matching efficiency with pluck, they provided an acceptable education for the colonists and interested themselves in the Aboriginals. Their all-embracing service diminished sectarian hostility and Governor A. E. Kennedy's 'affection for the Sisters of Mercy and his sympathy for their work was well known in Perth.'[32]

The bond between Mother Vincent and her far-off children was all the stronger for the pain endured. 'Your beautiful kind letters', wrote Mother Anne Xavier, 'made us quite ashamed of ourselves. Surely anything we might have to endure is as nothing compared with what you must suffer in the midst of Ireland's afflictions and the sickness of our dear Sisters.'[33] A shortened novitiate had its disadvantages, yet the prayer recited in choir at Lauds was surely answered:

The faith that first must be possessed
Root deep within our inmost breast;
Then joyous hope in second place,
And charity, Thy greatest grace.

The highest testimony to Mother Vincent's standing in the eyes of her community was her election in 1849 as fourth Reverend Mother of the Head House of the Order. The choice implied confidence in the spiritual leadership of the thirty-year-old nun, for the Head House provided for five hundred inmates, made up of Sisters, teacher-trainees and girls in vocational training. It also showed approval of her practical sense; since the Dublin archdiocesan convents were directly dependent on Baggot Street, and it still had close relations with convents at home and abroad, she was entrusted with the highest administrative post in the congregation.

Such a weight of administration made her feel to a distressing extent the tension between the active and the contemplative life. She found it hard to strike the balance for herself and for her community. Robbed of the counsel of her old friend, Mother Cecilia Marmion, who had preceded her as Reverend Mother but died in the post-famine fever, Mother Vincent often lost her tranquillity in her dealings with characters very different from her own among Sisters and clerics. Her nervousness was ascribed to 'tantrums' by unsympathetic Sisters, but there was perhaps a streak of obstinacy and self-will in her insistence on having her own way. So at least one concludes from her two years' correspondence with Dean Walter Meyler, with whom she had a verbal battle over the appointment of a chaplain.[34] Her self-assured tone nettled the dean.

A few days after her installation as Reverend Mother, she purposefully took pen in hand to tackle him. She would not tolerate the erratic behaviour of the chaplain supplied by the dean. Must the five hundred women inmates of the Baggot Street convent be subjected to his eccentricities? Her persistence reminded the dean of 'the first Prioress', he said, recalling his parallel dispute with Mother McAuley.[35] Mother Vincent had real grounds for anxiety, because her charges were afraid to approach the sacraments. On the other hand, the dean appealed for compassion for the chaplain, who appears to have been an epileptic, but it was 'not easy to soften the hearts of Wexford nuns', he grumbled. It would be heartless to dismiss a sick man, he declared;

but in the same breath he promised to change the chaplain if Mother Vincent raised the stipend by £10. This she refused; the £10 'would be lost to the numerous poor that surround us.' Chaplains were also miserably poor, but Mother Vincent was obstinate. She next sought to deprive the dean of his right to appoint a chaplain to her convent. Dr Moriarty, President of All Hallows' College, or Dr James Quinn of St Laurence's would supply a chaplain with the dean's consent. This was an affront to his authority as Vicar Capitular, and the dispute threatened to drag on endlessly. Mother Vincent wrote to Archbishop Murray, but he was now old, and Meyler was his friend. She felt worn out from this inconclusive bickering. Finally, she asked Father Meagher to intervene. A senior priest of wide influence, he at last brought about a truce.

From this quarrel so early in her career, Mother Vincent learned a lesson. In future differences, she showed less obstinacy, and more readiness to meet the other person's point of view. Some would judge her, in later life, too docile to the will of superiors, but the Meyler incident revealed a native fire and tenacity which she deliberately controlled for the general good in subsequent experiences. That her community approved the change is shown by the fact that it repeatedly voted against Mother Vincent's decision to leave them to serve elsewhere.

For six years Mother Vincent made the decisions for the Mercy schools and the social work of the Dublin Archdiocese. She had to promote the spiritual and temporal welfare of her charges, find staff and finance, and meet the demands of outside missions. Towns in Ireland were quite as much in need of convents as any abroad. When Bishop C. Denvir asked her for Sisters for Belfast, there was not a single convent within miles. 'In a city so immense there is but one parish, which also encompasses an extensive tract of the nearby countryside, and . . . no more than five priests to look after the spiritual needs of the people.'[36] Mother Vincent could spare only three Sisters, and when she travelled north with them she met many who had never seen Sisters in their lives. The first years were difficult, and Baggot Street could give little help, for Mother Vincent had to see to the provision of convents and schools in other places in quick succession—Dundalk, Athy, and Loughrea in Ireland, and Clifford in England.

There were many requests she was obliged to refuse. Bishop W. B. Ullathorne from Derby and Reverend Hugh Gallagher from San Francisco could not prevail on her to give nuns;[37] she insisted

Mother Mary Vincent Whitty

The *Donald McKay,* which brought Mother Vincent to Australia

Mother Catherine McAuley

Bishop James Quinn

Archbishop Roger Vaughan

upon at least a minimal preparation for her novices. Yet it cost her a great deal to deny aid when she had listened to the descriptions and stories brought to her parlour by bishops and priests from far-away places. She followed with delight the accounts of the Cherokees and Choctaws of Arkansas when in the autumn of 1850 Bishop J. Byrne called to see her at Baggot Street. 'His earnest entreaties and eloquent exposition of the wants of his vast diocese touched her to the heart, and it was with deep regret that she found herself unable to respond to his pressing invitation.' Even though she had not a nun to spare for the work, she advised Byrne to see the Naas Sisters whom she persuaded to co-operate.[38]

Mother Vincent's ability to enlist the co-operation of houses not under her jurisdiction was again illustrated in the foundation which she made at Athy, County Kildare. In an anaemic state because local effort was inadequate to supplement the little that she could give, Athy tested her ingenuity to the utmost. While the convent building was ready by October 1852, there was no school building as such, and because Sisters and children were forced to use the church as school all through the icy winter, enrolment dropped from five hundred to three hundred. The following year, however, help came through one of the Mahers of Kildare who entered the Dublin novitiate, for Mother Vincent sent her to Athy, and Carlow convent lent two more Maher Sisters, and their father gave £10,000 to build a proper school for Athy. Mother Vincent's arrangement with the Carlow Superior for a loan of the Mahers was a sagacious move; the stuff of leadership was in that family, who were cousins of Archbishop Paul Cullen; and one of them as Reverend Mother of Athy Convent was later to train good members for Mother Vincent's Brisbane community.

In 1854 Reverend Mother Vincent made a departure from the norm which was quite unprecedented in Irish conventual history when she sent nuns into the arena of an international war. It was both a courageous and generous step, for her own sister, Anne Whitty, now called Sister M. Agnes, was among the volunteers. It is true that the initiative did not come from Mother Vincent, but from Henry Edward Manning, later to be England's first convert Cardinal, and from Mother Vincent's brother Robert, Provost of Westminster Cathedral and Vicar-General to Cardinal Wiseman; but the decision to accept or reject the offer of service to the wounded soldiers lay completely with Mother Vincent. Not even Archbishop (later Cardinal) Cullen would interfere with her freedom of decision and action, so that this phase of her life stands in marked contrast to the circumscribed role that was to be hers a decade later under Bishop James Quinn of Queensland.

Mother Vincent was busy on many projects, including extensions to the Baggot Street school, when in 1854 the Crimean War broke out. The fear of Russian preponderance in the Black Sea could not stir the martial feelings of Irishmen or the religious zeal of nuns, but the prospect of Russia's claim to bar the holy places in Jerusalem to Western Christians was motive enough for thousands to take up arms in a holy cause.

When Manning learned from Dr Robert Whitty that Mother Vincent had had members of her Order trained in Continental hospitals, he wrote to Dr J. H. Newman, then in Dublin as Rector of the Catholic University, to call on Mother Vincent on his behalf.[39] At the same time, Manning interested Monsignor William Yore, Dublin's Vicar-General, in his project of finding nuns to volunteer for the Crimea. Thus after both Newman and Yore had satisfied Mother Vincent that the cause was sufficiently urgent, she accepted the challenge, and wrote to the British War Office to ask that the Sisters might be allowed to serve gratuitously.[40]

However, to find the ten to twenty Sisters required proved a difficult task. From her own Baggot Street convent Mother Vincent could spare only two, Sister M. Anges Whitty, and Sister M. Elizabeth Hersey, sister of Lady Mary Clifford, whose brother held high rank in the British Army. Mother Vincent therefore wrote to Sisters in other Irish and English convents, and made the special point that one fruit of their efforts might well be a mitigation of the bitter sectarianism from which Catholics still suffered.

To expedite preparations, since Manning impatiently awaited her reply, she sent two Sisters accompanied by Dr James Quinn to the various dioceses. Quinn was to consult the bishops on behalf of Yore, while Mother Vincent's Sisters explained the type of equipment needed. Cork, Kinsale, Charleville and Carlow responded magnificently, and the ten volunteers from Irish convents were joined by three from Liverpool and one from Chelsea.[41] Other Sisters of Mercy from London had already decided to serve with Florence Nightingale.

On receiving a letter from Archbishop Paul Cullen, absent in Rome, expressing anxiety at the nuns' entry into an unaccustomed military environment, Mother Vincent gathered the Sisters together in Dublin for advice. Aware of the dangers, she directed the volunteers not to mix freely with the paid nurses, since few of these had professional standards, not to neglect prayer even under fire but, above all, to discuss religious topics only with Catholic soldiers so that there could be no charge of proselytism, and to direct to the chaplain any enquirers about the faith.

Mother Vincent attached much importance to the presence of a chaplain in the area where the Sisters were to work, and because Manning was experiencing difficulty in the appointing of a Catholic chaplain, Mother Vincent herself crossed to London to see the Secretary for War, Sidney Herbert, at his Belgrave Square residence. There, however, she learned of the strength of nonconformist prejudice which impeded such an appointment, and afterwards she conferred with Manning concerning this and other matters. Her report to Cullen showed Mother Vincent buoyed up with the conviction that religious tolerance was improving, because the Sisters had been permitted to appear in religious dress in the wards of St George's Hospital in London, 'a circumstance that would have provoked a serious outcry a few years back.'[42]

Soon the Sisters were on their way. A Whitty kinsman, Frederick Lucas, founder of the *Tablet*, conducted them to Chelsea convent where Dr Whitty gave them an inspiring farewell address. Two graves on the hills of Balaclava and a handful of medals are the only material legacies of the appearance of the Sisters in that sad war.

By 1854 Mother Vincent had already made nursing a normal part of the Community's service. She had been requested by the Board of the Jervis Street hospital, founded in 1728 by a group of medical men, to take over its management. A solid building with brick exterior, it included lecture accommodation, board room, and six wards for seventy patients. It had the backing of philanthropic merchants, and leading surgeons and physicians visited it, while a committee handled its funds and paid its domestic staff. Mother Vincent therefore found it an excellent opening for work which the Mercy foundress, Catherine McAuley, had prayed might one day be permanently open to the Sisters. The committee approved Mother Vincent's conditions for acceptance of her new responsibilities, and arrangements went into effect in 1854.[43]

However, Mother Vincent envisaged care of the sick in larger terms than the Jervis Street infirmary would permit. Shortly after she became Reverend Mother, a beautiful 15-acre site came on the market to the north-west of the city. By 1851 she had secured it through Dr David Moriarty of All Hallows' and had sent John Bourke, the architect, on a tour of inspection to Edinburgh and

London before he drew his plans. Mother Vincent consulted many people for ideas; the first Mater Misericordiae must be worthy of Mother McAuley. Care and forethought prevented a patchy product. 'It was built as it stands', the president of the Medical Board proudly proclaimed a century later, 'a complete hospital of its period, and it was not preceded by a temporary building.'[44] The first wing, the Eccles Street frontage, was planned for forty beds at a cost of £27,000, but the completed hospital was to accommodate five hundred, at a cost of £68,000. Considered in terms of income, that sum multiplied by fifteen would roughly give the present-day equivalent.

The surgeons and physicians already on the staff of the Jervis Street hospital were to form a core for the new venture, but the Catholic University provided much-needed assistance. The 1850s were a time of ferment and wide change in medicine, and in 1858 the first Medical Act to control standards went into effect. The poor people for whom the hospital was mainly intended were justified in the confidence they had always displayed in the Sisters since the dread cholera days. Said Lord Thomas O'Hagan, 'The hospital is open to people of all religions. Here the rights of conscience are respected; and when men come within these walls they find a care and a devotion which are not to be found in many institutions of this world.'[45]

The arduous task of fund-raising was part of Mother Vincent's life as Reverend Mother, and with it came financial anxiety. For, besides school extensions, help in the people's homes and in the almonries and care of the sick, she planned many other forms of social work. Men who could make large benefactions were few, while others, who could, were misers without a thought of the poor. Yet Mother Vincent's confidence that most men were generous, and that they would respond to a work good in itself, gave her courage to depend on public support. Charity sermons, house-to-house appeals, subscriptions and bazaars enabled her to extend the services of her community to thousands of adults as well as children. The bazaars were important social events patronized by all classes. Thus on 16 and 17 January there was a brilliant gathering 'at the Rotunda for the benefit of the new Mater Misericordiae Hospital' which 'the Lord Lieutenant, the Lord Mayor, the Catholic Archbishop of Dublin, and a large number of clergy, nobility, and laity attended.'[46]

Over-simplified accounts of the nineteenth century describe churches as if they were concerned only with 'souls', and social workers as if confronted daily only with ignorance and crime, while all groups were eager to use the schools as a panacea. But the Mercy Sister viewed the child as a unity, and the nun, philanthropist and social worker within her united in the effort to get to the root of the trouble.

Thus in 1855 Mother Vincent opened at Glasthule a home for unmarried mothers. She was opposed by nuns to whom any kind of rescue work appeared undignified. The majority of Sisters, however, recognized the image of Christ whom they served not only in the ignorant and the sick but in women destitute of all that the world values, and the home was only the first of a series of similar Mercy social works.

The next was for neglected children who had broken the law. For them Mother Vincent established an industrial school, providing a home where the Sisters could teach them manners, morals, letters, and an employment. According to their capacity, the children helped a little in their own support, and occasionally in the support of their families, by 'plain and fancy work, embroidery, knitting, netting, and that peculiar invention of the nineteenth century, crochet.'

This scheme led Mother Vincent's nuns to visit the prisons regularly; there they found young girls mixing with older and hardened types of criminals. They established the Refuge at Golden Bridge, to which selected women prisoners were directed on the basis of assessment by the nuns during their prison visits. Case histories of the girls in the Refuge were made available to Thackeray during his stay at Golden Bridge. He reported that the average number of inmates was sixty, and the regression only 4 per cent, and that the Refuge achieved good for society.[47] But Mother Vincent knew that prevention is better than cure, and she devoted far more thought, effort and care to the extension of schools than to any other form of social work.

'She was goodness, kindness, and sweetness all in one', wrote one of Mother Vincent's past pupils, and reflection on her former teacher led her to the conclusion that 'People make a great mistake when they try to gain happiness for themselves; they should try to forget themselves and live only for others, as you are all doing, dear Sister.'[48] These artless words point to the hidden power that generated the movement outward and upward of the submerged Church of the nineteenth century. The 'bright and energetic' Mother Vincent was possessed by one idea—to educate, to rescue from vice and crime, to save from suffering of mind and body; to restore to the human being no matter how poor, neglected or forsaken the dignity of the child of God. She thus contributed in no small way to the dramatic resurgence of Catholicism in Ireland which began under Archbishop Murray and continued under Archbishop Cullen.

Cullen moved to Dublin from Armagh during the first half of Mother Vincent's term as Reverend Mother, and she could not but be influenced by the strong leadership of this very Roman-minded Irishman, this passionate iceberg, so ardent for the concerns of the Church, so cold to national aspirations. Cullen could flout Lord John Russell and hold a national Synod without British permission, but he set his granite-like face against any show of rebellion.

His influence on Mother Vincent reinforced that of her friends among the Maynooth faculty, whose letters stressed above all the sufferings and forbearance of Christ.

Thus, though most of Mother Vincent's period of administration was wedged in between the Young Ireland rising of 1848 and the Fenian rising of 1867, the forces most proximate to her and most compelling tended towards acceptance of unavoidable ills. Dr D. Moriarty, an alumnus of Maynooth, was more downright than Cullen in opposition of the Fenians, and Dr James Quinn, whom Cullen appointed confessor to Baggot Street, was another Rome-trained man in the Cullen mould. Quinn thus had every opportunity to watch the growth in maturity that broadened the experience of the young Reverend Mother.

Meanwhile, Mother Vincent's guiding ideas further crystallized through life in community. Two retreats in a year, and the normal devotional life of all religious Orders, the Mass, the Blessed Eucharist, and the liturgy, developed in her that inwardness, recollection, and spirit of prayer which set in perspective the immediate and ultimate goals of life. Her position as Reverend Mother or as Mistress of Novices from 1844 to 1860 gave her not only a wide personal knowledge of administration but also afforded moments of quiet absorption to penetrate profoundly into the implications of the Rule and spirit of Mother McAuley. Her life with the foundress enabled her to interpret the law, the written word, so as to effect 'that liberty of spirit which raises us above the opinions of the world, human respect, self-love and worldly wisdom, while it enables the soul to see God intimately, to view all things in Him and through Him and subservient to Him.'[49]

Mother Vincent's own natural bent to social harmony, strong even as a child, was strengthened by the priority which Mother McAuley gave to fraternal charity; and to help smooth away the frictions of community life, she stressed the need for kindness to others. Mother McAuley considered that the faults which annoy the neighbour should be first eliminated, rather than the defects which trouble the owner most; and like the Saints, the Sisters should reflect the attractiveness of Christ by the sweetness, gentleness, and affectionate manner they show in community and to all whom they wish to serve. All mediate the grace of Christ to each other, and love has precedence over everything. Love rightly understood is strong and even demanding. Mother Vincent required strength in her Sisters when she transferred them from a beloved niche to a new and hard assignment. She expected them to be as ready to leave all as she was herself.

A Carmelite nun, Sister M. Angela of Warren Mount, considered that while Mother Vincent's achievement in Australia later was truly great, 'her previous work of forming so many young religious in the spirit of their vocation was almost greater.'[50] Scattered through America, England, Ireland and Australia, they recalled 'the noble, holy, happy and desirable goals she set before them, and with affection and deep gratitude' they remembered her charity and tenderness which was their inspiration.[51]

One of the best-known of her former novices was Sister M. Liguori Keenan, sister of Sir Patrick Keenan. Repeatedly elected Reverend Mother of Baggot Street after Mother Vincent's departure, her proudest boast was that she 'had the great privilege' of being formed in the religious life by Mother Vincent, who was widely acknowledged 'one of the most distinguished women in the Order, who had been specially beloved by the holy Foundress, and inherited much of her double spirit of sweetness and zeal.'[52]

Mother Vincent's many-sided gifts were appreciated outside as well as inside the cloister. Sir Patrick Keenan, a senior officer of the Education Department of Ireland, found her presence 'a balm and a comfort', while her schools were 'as proficient as critic or inspector could expect or desire them to be.'[53] The sincerity of her interest transformed even official relationships into enduring friendship. 'I shall never forget your present any more than your past goodness', wrote John Sheridan, a Marlboro' Street inspector. 'In my new capacity my influence extends all over Ireland, and I assure you, dear Mrs. Whitty, that it will always afford me the greatest pleasure to be of service to you.'[54]

Many sought her advice, including the Bishop of Ossory, the future Cardinal Moran.[55] Then too, Bishop Moriarty wished Mother Vincent to head a foundation of Sisters of Mercy in his diocese, but her community could not bear to part with her, for without her they would be 'miserably lonely' as she was 'such a necessary being and such a host in herself.'[56]

But where Moriarty failed, Dr James Quinn succeeded, by a simple expedient. He requested Archbishop Cullen to reverse the Community Chapter decision, and force Baggot Street to free Mother Vincent to accompany him to his new diocese of Queensland, Australia. The Archbishop's word carried weight in papal councils, but in Dublin it was law, and no religious house dared question it. Dr James Quinn made adroit use of his knowledge of the Archbishop's sway. A student under Cullen's rectorship in Rome, he owed him his appointment to the Queensland episcopacy. Quinn was astutely aware, too, that Mother Vincent could enhance his promotion by the prestige of her name, should he be able to secure her for his mission. He believed that in the eyes of her community he had some merit, since he had frequently escorted the Sisters whom Mother Vincent sent on long journeys; he even acted as their guide on the Continent where she sent them to study nursing methods. On his consecration in 1859, his first thought was to provide nuns for his diocese, and he turned to Mother Vincent for help.

'As to Brisbane', she wrote in a formal request for permission to go, 'I should like that sort of mission more than one in large towns such as Sydney or Melbourne. I have placed before my mind all the possible difficulties . . . and still they do not discourage me.'[57] Once again refused permission by the Community Chapter to leave Dublin for the missions,[58] she visited various convents in Ireland in search of volunteers for Quinn. However, although he was due to depart within three weeks, she could find no one to accompany him. It was at this point that Quinn invoked the Archbishop's authority.

On 27 November 1860 the Reverend Mother of Baggot Street received a hand-delivered letter, signed by Paul Cullen. 'Dr. Quinn', it ran, 'is anxious to secure Mrs. Whitty's assistance in establishing a house of Sisters in Brisbane. If Mrs. Whitty be willing to go, I am perfectly satisfied that she should go, and as she has so much experience, I think she would secure the success of the mission.' Further, Mother Vincent was to have one or two novices to accompany her. On a note of urgency the letter concluded 'Dr. Quinn sails in a few days so there can be no delay.'[59]

Thus Mother Vincent left in a whirl of preparation. There was no time to say good-bye to the foundations peculiarly hers—at Belfast, Loughrea, Athy, Clifford. The novices to accompany her were Sisters M. Benedict McDermot and Cecilia McAuliffe. Dr Quinn had found two young women to join them as postulants—Jane Townsend and Emily Conlan, and Mother Vincent hoped to find a volunteer in Liverpool. On 3 December they sailed from Ireland, and on 8 December they got under way from England with the hoped-for English nun, Sister M. Catherine Morgan, in the fast American clipper *Donald McKay* which within five months landed them in Australia.

2

THE EDUCATION QUESTION

Mother Vincent's combination of energy and experience, valuable in any field, was particularly so in the young colony of Queensland. Her Dublin schools provided a model on which to build, yet there was a fluidity in her concept of education which permitted adjustment to changing needs. This chapter takes note of three phases in her response to the demands of Christian education in her adopted country: namely, her six-year period of independence in which she had complete freedom to order her schools to her own ideas, followed by her fourteen years of limited alliance with the government Board of Education, and finally her adaptation to new conditions when the Education Act of 1875 took effect.

As joint founder with Bishop Quinn of the Catholic education system, Mother Vincent's was the less spectacular but more essential role. Victorian women in general, and nuns in particular, shrank from public debate. Hence when ideas had to be thrashed out and the Catholic position clarified Quinn, as Bishop of Queensland, was the natural spokesman. While this was the episcopal privilege everywhere in the Australian colonies, it was especially noticeable under the administration of Queensland's first bishop, for he held that there should be only one head, one organizer, for every venture, and that nuns, even in mission conditions, should adhere to cloister and remain as far as possible hidden from the world. Such a view suited Mother Vincent admirably, on the whole, for she was no publicity seeker, and she respected Quinn's educational experience.

This chapter, therefore, deals with the education controversy at two levels, namely the practical and the ideological. In the first, Mother Vincent demonstrated her own theory of education with its highly individual approach to the child and the family; the bishop advanced his views in the press, at public meetings, and before the Royal Commission on education in Queensland during the years 1874–5. Though Mother Vincent's ideas were basically similar to the bishop's, she showed a distinct preference for independent schools, like most of the Australian hierarchy. However, because the bishop was her ecclesiastical superior, Mother Vincent was prepared to forego some of her own most cherished plans in order to meet his wishes.

Thus she is remembered best not as a theorist, but for the essential and enduring contribution which she made to Queensland education in the form of a structure, an organization, that was to be self-perpetuating, and destined to carry forward into the future the educational ideal. Later chapters will attempt to show the rationale of her action by following it to the spiritual sources from which it derived; but here it must be stressed that, apart from contributing a structure, Mother Vincent's role in the education controversy was decisive, for even though she remained spiritually dependent on the hierarchy, and moreover chose to follow their lead in educational policy, without her active co-operation the first two bishops could have effected little. Furthermore, her school system was economically and functionally self-supporting, relying for handouts neither on state nor on diocese; this was the irreducible argument to prove that Catholic education would not be abolished by cutting the state purse-strings.

Mother Vincent's letters written to Dublin after her arrival show a lingering and meditative backward glance over her past experience, and an intuitive, forward look towards things to come. The bridge between education in the old country and in the new was the Stanley National System, but in its Queensland form it was an unreliable structure. For it had been built by men like G. W. Rusden and William Wilkins who proposed 'to dispel theological superstition' through a universal and secular education,[1] and it was administered by self-assured liberals who haggled over the degree of participation to be permitted to the Churches in the instruction of the young. The society which Mother Vincent had left behind in Dublin, dominated by the Establishment and the Ascendancy as it was, professed to live by Christian principle and to take the various Christian bodies into partnership, with the Catholic and Anglican Archbishops of Dublin on the Board. Yet even while in Ireland Mother Vincent had of late become disenchanted with the Stanley Board, because its opposition to religious symbols in the schools boded ill for educational freedom.

When on 10 May 1861 she stepped off the *Yarra Yarra* and into the life of the young colony, she found a Select Committee on Education wrangling over whether or not school buildings might be used for worship, and whether or not religion might be taught during school hours. She firmly declared that she wanted to be free of such galling restrictions; that she had no wish to 'contend with National schools' (that is, the government schools); that she desired above all to serve the spiritual interests of the children, many of whom 'in the bush . . . have very little means of education, and if they are not instructed, of course religion will suffer. Indeed after a few years there can be no religion in the country.'[2]

It is clear from Mother Vincent Whitty's letters that she had made her own the old monastic ideal, *vacare Deo,* to be open to God, to be dedicated to him in and for himself alone, and not for any self-preferred way of serving him. He was in charge, not the Board, not even the bishop, and as for the working out of educational ideals—'all such things are in God's hands'; hence the manner in which she was allowed to serve was of secondary importance, to be determined by circumstances. 'I do not think that I have any plans or notions for the future, or I may say for the present', she wrote, 'but just to live for the day and do and suffer God's will only for the day.'[3]

The tortuous course of the education controversy was matched in her imagination by the uncertainty of life itself in the new subtropical land. Fireballs ripped through school buildings, men died of sunstroke, fierce drenching downpours caused flash floods and loss of life, and such events filled her with foreboding of sudden death.[4] An urgent sense of the shortness of time spurred her on to immense efforts in the cause of education, despite the headaches and ear-trouble from which she suffered.

Thus while Anglican Bishop Tufnell engaged the Board of Education in spirited argument, and Quinn rode away on horseback to the farthest limits of his diocese, Mother Vincent visited the homes of her prospective pupils to create bonds with the parents. Such contact to her was essential, something to be enduringly maintained, so that religious tradition could be assimilated from the child's early experience, and not become something apart from association with the family. Through such visits she persuaded the older people to approach the sacraments more often, and improved school attendance.

Her preoccupation with religious values contrasted sharply with the approach of the Board of General Education, which was secularist and liberal. Sir Charles Nicholson, Randal McDonnell and their colleagues who helped Queensland in its infant years were not irreligious, but they accepted the liberal assumption that religious and philosophical beliefs were 'private affairs, of ultimate moment, perhaps, to the individual's salvation and his sense of the meaning of life',[5] but quite outside the ambit of state activity. But Mother Vincent saw life as a unity and could set no limits to her involvement and, until increasingly heavy administrative duties impeded her, she visited a number of homes every day.

At the same time she attended to the practical details of school organization. She visited St Stephen's Cathedral school, standing near the Pugin-designed old stone Gothic church of the same name, where seventy children were taught by a lay master and mistress.[6] She intended to commence her work here, because the Board had stopped salaries to teachers in denominational schools earlier in 1861 and the Church had no revenue on which to draw. For the same reason, she supplied Sisters to the Wickham Terrace denominational school (later moved to Fortitude Valley) in 1862. As finances improved, lay teachers would be extensively employed, but in each new centre Mother Vincent's nuns took charge.

The initiative for a foundation usually came from laymen. Thus a delegation of Catholic men came from the town of Ipswich a few days after Mother Vincent's arrival to ask her for Sisters for the existing school in that town.[7] She was unable to do so, however, until 1863, when Ipswich itself provided a postulant, Jane Gorry, the first Queenslander to join the Order. The Ipswich invitation was the first of many, and Mother Vincent found it impossible to meet all requests.

The St Stephen's school was much more adequate in size than most of the makeshift buildings available in the first few decades. For the eighty children present on the first day, Mother Vincent had only one room, 41 feet by 21 feet by 10 feet in height, but she made it 'clean and bright' and gay with Queensland flowers, 'the richest in the world'. As school supplies were unavailable in Brisbane, she promptly wrote home for great quantities of geography books, maps, charts—school equipment of every sort. It was a distinct advantage to have such good agents in the Sisters in Dublin, familiar with her needs and ready to dispatch goods quickly. For by 1863 she had 300 children to supply in two Brisbane schools, and 200 more in Ipswich.[8] She had brought with her a harmonium and piano, music being indispensable to her concept of education, and in each new school a piano was installed with the blackboards.

According to the custom observed elsewhere in Australian dioceses, Mother Vincent divided each of these three parish schools into two sections, the 'select' and the 'general'. Both portions were housed under the same roof, but the device was a concession to the class distinctions of the time, and was also an inducement to the better-off to help finance an unendowed venture.[9] Government schools also charged a weekly fee until 1869, but the poorer colonists, Catholic or Protestant, could not afford the sixpence. Thus the appeal to pride of status was a necessary plank of support. Press accounts of school functions show that uniforms were a luxury reserved for the 'select'. It was noted that 'the children, especially of the select schools, presented a very pretty appearance on Thursday, all being dressed in white, the seniors with blue sashes and fillets, and the little ones with the same ornaments in red.' The prestige enjoyed by the select would gradually extend to the general with improving social conditions. Primitive Brisbane society had to be levelled up, not down.

Mother Vincent's strong sense of organization prompted her to introduce uniforms and distinguishing badges for the different classes. There is something almost military in the precision and order of the schoolchildren who met the bishop when in 1864 he arrived in Ipswich for a religious function. 'Two hundred little girls . . . separated into miniature guilds of about fifty, each with special banners, all in white, with veils and wreaths' walked in procession accompanied by the Sisters.[10]

But in her classes, the impersonal value of order gave way to a personal approach to the child. Her government was mild, and she was at pains to break down the sense of awe felt by pupils in the unaccustomed presence of religious. Half a century after her death, her former protégées could still recall their enjoyment of her lessons, her skilful questions to induce thought, the familiar illustrations by which she made herself approachable to the most retiring.[11] Out of school she met the children on a still more intimate footing through treats and parties on the school grounds which celebrated events in their lives, and when any child returned after an illness at home, Mother Vincent took her to the refectory for a nourishing midday meal.[12] Such considerate touches, along with her knowledge of the family, made Mother Vincent in the children's eyes an extension of the home circle.

As the only member of the first group of Sisters to possess a certificate from the Irish National Board, it fell to Mother Vincent's lot to guide the young teachers in her schools, and she stressed the need for a similar interested and personal approach as she moved from one classroom to another. She counselled her Sisters not only to make learning as interesting as possible but to be liberal with small rewards for work well done. Coldness, formality and officialdom had no place in the Mercy schools; in the words of the *Queensland Times*: 'Judging from the kindness and gentleness of their demeanor towards the children, and the affectionate confidence manifested towards them by the latter, it is impossible to doubt that they are really the right ladies in the right place.'[13] Such praise gave Mother Vincent a quiet happiness. 'I believe the respect of all denominations for us is increasing', she wrote to her Dublin convent.

As to curriculum, she was content to adapt to the Queensland pattern. The 'ordinary branches of an English education' then comprised reading, writing, arithmetic, grammar, and geography. Mother Vincent supplemented these subjects which were taught in the national schools with music, singing, needlework and history. Music was so much a response to the popular demand that her letters repeatedly refer to the need for more Sisters who could teach piano-playing. In their absence, she had to employ lay music-teachers, even men, because music was 'the passion of the colony'. Otto Linden, well known at the time in Brisbane circles, taught singing at St Stephen's and at All Hallows'. Messrs Strachan and Parkes were music and singing masters at Ipswich,[14] while part-time elocution masters produced children's plays like Wiseman's 'Fabiola'. Because parents were mostly uninterested in education, Mother Vincent made 'exhibitions' a regular feature of school life.

The exhibition combined entertainment with a display of work. After each of the term examinations, parents were enticed to see their children perform on the stage and receive prizes. Bonds with the families were strengthened through such occasions, which also brought forth the children's best efforts. Prestige was nearly always lent to these displays by the presence of the bishop accompanied by some clergy, and awards, ribbons and insignia of merit for conduct were enhanced when conferred with all possible pomp and splendour. Moreover, the bishop reinforced the Sisters' efforts for the social betterment of the future citizens, for he never failed to tell the pupils that if 'they were only industrious and persevering, sooner or later they must succeed.'[15] Prizewinners' names were supplied to the local press, with an account of performances of vocal and instrumental items, dancing, drama, and work-display.

The embroidery taught was destined to be a leisure activity in later life directed not merely to personal and home adornment but to church service. Ecclesiastical vestments 'of rich material finished with extreme care, which the pupils had stitched', were often on show, and future loyal daughters of the Church would provide for the local altar in some little bush sanctuary, of poor materials and style, but decently and reverently kept.

There were social reasons for the inclusion of history in Mother Vincent's schools. A subsequent chapter will examine the impact of immigration more fully, and of Quinn's part in bringing impoverished Irish Catholics to Queensland. The movement snowballed, for 'it is well known that the Irish in leaving their unfortunate country never forget those relations they leave behind, but take the first opportunity of having them brought to their new but more prosperous country.'[16] When they encountered a strong sectarianism reinforced by imperial superiority, the newcomers were abashed and dismayed, but from the study of Irish history, Mother Vincent considered, their children would learn that 'they were descended from a people of whom they had no reason to be ashamed, but on the contrary in every way worthy of their imitation.'[17] The faith too was to be strengthened in a land of peace and prosperity by remembrance of ancestral heroism and martyrdom. But English history was also to be taught and a special episcopal prize was offered for 'this subject of greatest importance . . . to be given in succession for the history of different countries.' Irish and English history were still among the subjects examined at Nudgee in 1880 in the presence of His Excellency the Administrator of the Government, Mr Joshua Bell, the Chief Justice, Charles Lilley, the Colonial Secretary, the Hon. A. H. Palmer, Dr and Mrs H. Challinor and other eminent citizens.[18]

But while Catholic schools always stressed that they could not agree to a religionless Christianity or ignore completely the record of the past, they showed in every possible way that their faith demanded unity and integration with the rest of the community in all civil matters. A symbol was the conclusion of exhibitions with the lusty rendering of 'God Save the Queen', 'with solos and chorus, all present standing and joining in.'

Since religion was at the root of what the liberals claimed to be a divisive separateness, it is well to clarify Mother Vincent's personal attitude. She could only shudder at 'the dreadful government schools where no religion is taught', and she often referred

Archbishop Robert Dunne

Mother Mary Patrick Potter

Mother Mary Damian Duncombe

Miss Florence O'Reilly

G. W. Gray

Dr George Fullerton's house, purchased in 1863, became the nucleus of All Hallows'

to them as 'Protestant schools'.[19] Was her attitude to Protestants then one of hostility? Her words and her deeds disprove the notion. 'I have never in my life had so much to do with Protestants as I have had since I came on this mission', she wrote, 'and I find them so very good and simple.' As an instance, she told of the assistance of a Protestant minister who was among the first to offer help to the nuns at the time of a fire which threatened the Ipswich convent. Then, too, the Harris family and Mrs A. H. Palmer constantly supplied flowers for the altar, and Protestant gentlemen outnumbered Catholic laymen on the All Hallows' committee.

For her part, Mother Vincent freely admitted non-Catholics to her schools, but did not allow them to join the religious classes without their parents' consent and the written permission of the bishop.[20] Parents could thus rest assured that daughters 'would never be kidnapped into a religion different from their own. Catholics . . . respected too much the rights of parents to tamper with the faith of those entrusted to their charge.'[21]

Certainly Mother Vincent feared proselytism. She had seen too much of it in Ireland not to expect it also in Queensland. Thus she complained that Brisbane had only one school for teachers, the one controlled by the Board, and she lamented the comparatively privileged position of the Dublin Mercy convents which educated their own teachers. As a mark of her anxiety she included in the home mail a pamphlet setting forth the Queensland regulations for trainees. One cannot see, with twentieth-century eyes, the positive danger to the faith that Mother Vincent believed to be lurking there. The one real disadvantage involved for her girls was withdrawal from Catholic surroundings at an extremely early age and the consequent loss of the Christian formation that Mother Vincent so desired for them.

Against the background of incessant struggle to provide staff and finance, Mother Vincent's achievement by 1866 was unmatched anywhere in Australia. At no small cost to herself and to her Sisters, in physical effort and mental anxiety, she had built an independent system, with no ties whatever with the existing Board of Education. In the years 1861–6 she had founded six educational institutions:

1. St Stephen's, Elizabeth Street, 17 June, 1861;
2. St Patrick's, Fortitude Valley, 2 October 1862;
3. St Mary's, Ipswich, 7 April, 1863;
4. All Hallows', Ann Street, 21 November 1863;

5. St Mary's, South Brisbane, 2 April 1866;
6. St Vincent's Children's Home, 11 December 1866.[22]

That Mother Vincent could accomplish so much with a small staff and slender resources is proof of the value she set on a separate system. Sydney, so much older, better established and better provided through state grants to the Denominational Board, had only five schools under teaching Orders by the 1870s.[23] Mother Vincent had translated into reality what she conceived to be the best approach to education. In its emphasis on faith, family and person, her concept differed widely from the ideal of the framers of government school policy. Her sweep of action likewise exceeded theirs, for she had blazed a trail for independent schools at secondary as well as at primary level at a time when the state concerned itself only with elementary education.[24] She had proved that her concept fitted into the Queensland scene and was acceptable to the Catholic body. But 1866 was the moment when economic and philosophical arguments fused to melt away the separate ground on which she stood. Never again would her schools be quite so free.

It might be thought that in Bishop James Quinn Mother Vincent had a powerful ally to defend her point of view. This was not so. Her first letter showed that, alone among the Australian Catholic prelates, he sought an alliance with the Board of Education; he was even then determined to 'get his own way' in the end, but wanted some guarantee of success before he moved.[25] What were the grounds of his choice? To what extent was he prepared to accommodate to the National System? What forces in the community opposed or aided him? To answer these questions is to follow the sharp controversy of educational debate in Queensland during the 1860s.

Quinn was no novice in scholastic matters. His entire career up to his arrival in Queensland was concerned with colleges. After his graduation in Rome with a papal gold medal and doctorate, he was placed in charge of a Dublin school which prospered under his administration. Contact with Newman and the faculty of the Catholic University gave him insight into educational cross-currents, while his friendship with Gavan Duffy and the men of the *Nation* extended his influence and prestige. Twelve years of this background before his consecration in 1859 account for his unique role among the Australian hierarchy.[26]

Where Archbishop John Bede Polding of Sydney was cautious,

Bishop J. A. Goold of Melbourne sceptical, and Bishop B. Geoghegan of Adelaide openly critical of the Stanley System, Quinn on ideological grounds expressed a strong preference for non-vested status for his schools. To give due place to religion, but provide a meeting-ground for children of different faiths, was to him theologically desirable, since all baptized children belonged in spirit and essentially to the one true fold.[27] On a human level, such a school was the best promoter of harmony.[28] Moreover, those schools under the nuns afforded, in his opinion, an unmatched opportunity for personal and cultural enrichment, whose benefits he would wish to extend. These reasons alone justified submission to Board regulation.

But there were utilitarian reasons as well—the salary to teachers, the benefit of inspection by an outside body, and the sense of security to parents from an identical programme of studies in national and non-vested schools, with the bonus of religious formation in schools of their own choice. Catholic ownership of the buildings would protect the right to withdraw, at need, from Board tutelage. Finally, the right to nominate teachers gave the bishop virtual control of education in his schools.

The current of colonial thought ran counter to his scheme. Three decades earlier, liberal Governor Sir Richard Bourke had believed that he had the solution to the country's educational need in the Stanley Irish National System. In the interval, the conviction had grown that education must be available to all, that the onus lay with the government to provide it, and that the schools should promote tolerance.[29] Inter-denominational rivalries gave grounds for belief that the Churches hampered rather than helped the cause of harmony. Thus when Queensland swiftly passed its Education Act shortly after it became self-governing, some colonists experienced a sense of relief that there were no bishops yet in the colony to contest its clauses.

The empiricists who adapted the Stanley System to local needs had no explicit and articulate philosophy distinct from wisps of liberalism and utilitarianism, and for them the national system was an infallible norm; what existed in New South Wales should exist in Queensland, and the word 'national' carried value in itself.[30] Because some adjustments they made were not welcome to the Churches, Charles Lilley ascribed to clerical aloofness the slow advance of Board schools.[31] The prickly attitude was not one-sided, for the Board was reluctant to take the Churches into partnership even in a subordinate role.

When Bishop E. W. Tufnell arrived in 1860 and requested subsidy for Anglican schools, dissension broke out over the dual interpretation of the Education Act just passed. Some members of the Board, like chairman Robert Mackenzie, believed that the Act prepared the way for a purely secular state system, but others, like John Douglas and Colonel Maurice O'Connell, held that the Act did not exclude non-state schools. Bishop Quinn was an interested spectator of Tufnell's attempts to get a favourable judgment. He himself entered the lists to secure a Catholic Grammar School, but failed, and in 1863 he decided to join forces with Tufnell and have the Catholic and Anglican parochial schools connected with the Board.

At this point, the various non-episcopal Churches burst into active and virulent opposition, to the advantage of the dominant group among Board members. But the nonconformists allied themselves with the secular liberals, not from any dilution of theological principle, but from their inability to meet their educational needs out of their own resources when expansion of Anglican and Catholic schools seemed imminent. Dissenters resented the long domination of the Church of England over their ancestors, as they feared and hated Rome.

Their aggressiveness was inversely proportionate to their numbers, and they had powerful press organs to remedy their numerical weakness. When Quinn bought the *North Australian*, the *Queensland Guardian* described a plot to overthrow the Protestant religion. The mocking reply of Quinn's paper scarcely exaggerated the panic among Protestants who imagined 'that all our printers are Jesuits, that the Bishop writes our leading articles and corrects our proofs, that Cardinal Wiseman is our London correspondent, that we have petitioned His Holiness the Pope to come to Ipswich to live'.[32] The Protestant defence of government policy was all the more remarkable in that Irish nonconformists had worked the other way round: they had fought to make the National System denominational. With them on one side of the fence and Catholics and Anglicans on the other, it is impossible to interpret the education question in terms of the age-old conflict of Church and State.

The famous 'Bishops' Crusade' 1863–4, mocked in the Evangelical press, was derided also in government circles as an attempt to overthrow the National System of education. It suited the bishops' foes to misrepresent the prelates' views. Quinn and Tufnell therefore resolved to go to the people and jointly conduct meetings in the larger centres of south-east Queensland, at Dalby, Toowoomba, Drayton, Ipswich, and Brisbane.

The *North Australian* fully reported these meetings; as this journal has not been consulted by Queensland researchers till now, it is worth stating that, on the evidence of their speeches, the bishops did not suggest turning back the clock. They approved the National System for rural districts, but sought the substitution of the English Privy Council System in populous centres. The Board would then consist of members of the executive council, while heads of Churches would be *ex officio* members, and inspection and setting the curricula would remain Board prerogatives; but, whereas the National System aided only those schools established for the education of all classes and creeds within the one building, the Privy Council method of administration would grant aid to schools of various denominations. In short, Quinn and Tufnell applauded government control of standards, but resisted secularization and unfair taxation.

Only a small section of Queenslanders condemned religious teaching as such. Voices of Toowoomba hecklers reflected the views of G. W. Rusden, who had lectured in Queensland that if 'every priest, bible, church, and religious idea were to vanish from the earth', society out of its own resources could check immorality and crime.[33] Replace theology in the schools by geology, cried a few men at the bishops' meetings.[34] But those who equated law and morality were few, and those assailed by scientific doubt still fewer. Quinn asserted that the 'large and enthusiastic meetings' encountered during the 'crusade' were evidence of a widespread and powerful body of opinion in favour of the non-vested system and delayed execution of the scheme of the secularists.[35] Yet there can be no doubt that the crusade created bitterness and had little permanent value.

More ecumenical times view with approval joint efforts of Anglican and Catholic on behalf of Christian education; but in the context of nineteenth-century Queensland, the 'crusade' was a scandal. Governor Bowen declared that if Cardinal Wiseman and the Archbishop of Canterbury toured England together in the days following the uproar over Papal aggression, the agitation could not have been more intense, and Bowen disliked and feared religious excitement.

However Tufnell, for all his zeal and his Eton and Oxford background,[36] failed to exercise strong leadership in his own Church. Factions within it contested his episcopal authority and sought to introduce the democratic church-management of the nonconformists.[37] His position was further undermined by those Anglicans who proved reluctant either on grounds of economy or of social harmony to support his efforts for a distinct system of Anglican schools. Moreover, while Tufnell's co-religionists failed him through their lack of cohesion, the nonconformists branded him a tool of Quinn. Thus when, at the end of the crusade, the two bishops presented a series of petitions to parliament (then two-thirds Anglican in composition)[38] to reassert the claims they had made during the campaign, the petitions were tabled, printed, and consigned to oblivion.

Catholics were at the time politically insignificant. Hence, though in theory Tufnell and Quinn had a following of more than 60 per cent of the Queensland population, in actual fact greater influence was wielded by the combination of nonconformists and liberals, riding on the powerful currents earlier described —historical, philosophical, social and religious. Future controversy would be coloured by the fact that 'the Liberal party had come to be associated in mind if not necessarily in fact with a fairly rabid Protestantism.'[39]

By the end of 1864 Quinn was losing patience with unavailing constitutional procedures. Moreover, as Tufnell was soon to leave for a prolonged holiday in England, the Catholic bishop would then be without the support he so much needed. The strain told on him. Mother Vincent commented that 'you would scarcely know him, he has got so grey and old-looking.'[40] Under these circumstances, his radical weakness showed itself, a defect soon to create a wasteland round him through an unreasonable exercise of his authority. Mother Vincent and her Sisters, his clergy and laymen were to experience its effects.

This aspect of his character astonished the Governor, to whom Quinn announced that he and Tufnell intended to present a memorial directly to Bowen, since parliament had ignored the others. Bowen, a self-styled autocrat,[41] by such acts as the arbitrary nomination of his first Executive Council,[42] had given the bishops hope that he would override parliament in their educational struggle. But Bowen now hastened to tell Quinn that any attempt on the part of Secretary of State or Governor to *dictate* in any purely local matter to the legislature of a colony possessing parliamentary government, would undoubtedly be resisted as an act of constitutional aggression.

Rejecting the lesson on democratic method, the bishop proposed that since Bowen was not prepared to dictate, he might do well to refuse another term as Governor, and so gain the favour of Colonial Secretary Edward C. Cardwell, who had similarly resigned in Ireland as a mark of protest against the manner in which the Stanley System was administered. Though Bowen treated the suggestion lightly, his visitor was in deadly earnest, for, according to the vice-regal despatch, 'Bishop Quinn stated that if I could not be persuaded to carry out his views, "dreadful consequences" would follow.'[43]

Afterwards the Governor made public the implied threat, which the press and his immediate circle interpreted as a plot to secure the Catholic Sir John Pope Hennessy's appointment to replace Bowen.[44] To forestall such a move and lessen the combined episcopal power of Quinn and Tufnell, the Governor suggested to the London Office the advisability of a new post for the Anglican prelate, who was then, in Bowen's view, playing hind to Quinn's panther. A missionary bishop ought to be made of sterner stuff than Tufnell who, said the Governor, 'would be well suited for the Headship of a College at Oxford or Cambridge, for a curacy in an English Cathedral, or for the rectory of an English parish.'

It might appear at this point that Quinn's quest for non-vested status for the diocesan schools was doomed. The fact remains, however, that he left that well-publicized interview with a clear assurance from Governor Bowen that the Board of Education would be prepared henceforward 'to give aid to all non-vested schools on principles analogous to those in force in Ireland, where even the conventual schools received assistance from the Government.'[45]

Behind this decision lay the fact that the members of the Board had been forced to re-think their regulations in view of the recent marked population growth and the worsening economic depression. From 1859 to 1875 Queensland showed the greatest proportionate population increase among all the Australian colonies,[46] and the government found it impossible to meet the corresponding need for schools out of its own resources. Official attempts to enlist the aid of local authorities, who were asked to provide one-third of the costs of a new school,[47] met with little success. Thus the Board was at last forced to admit the Churches as allies in the field of education but, because the bond was economic pressure rather than principle, the durability of the partnership depended on the flux of circumstances.

Quinn had received the Governor's sanction to connect diocesan schools with the Board at the end of 1864, but for two more years Mother Vincent clung to her independence. During these two years, however, her troubles were multiplied, and the economic sickness of the colony, the physical sickness of her Sisters, and grave internal community troubles threatened the very existence of the congregation in Queensland.[48] Even before the depression struck and the banks failed, she had confessed that she had no money to pay badly needed monitresses.[49] She prayed and pleaded for help from houses in Dublin, Liverpool, Hull, and London. In her requests, Mother Vincent told her Sisters overseas of the children she had lost to 'religionless government schools' because she had insufficient teachers.

But for all her earnestness, the response from the home convents was meagre in help and even in letters. Sisters everywhere were preoccupied with immediate problems, but of these Mother Vincent had more than her share, and the most insurmountable was isolation. It was only in the deep of the night that she could find time to write letters, and frequently in those low hours before dawn, she felt alone and powerless. 'You might all be dead and buried for all I hear from you', she wrote to Dublin. Nor could she share her anxieties with the bishop, for, as she said, 'we see very little of him.'[50] The procrastination of overseas nuns in the matter or correspondence, combined with the fact that in 1865 a new Reverend Mother succeeded Mother Vincent's old friend, explains this short account of events between 1864 and 1866.

Yet though the reasons for Mother Vincent's surrender in 1866 of the independence she had enjoyed since 1861 are only sketchily outlined in her letters, one may deduce from her own words that shortage of finance and staff was not the sole cause. Her strong belief in the supernatural dimension of history had not diminished and, far from being unduly disturbed by adversity, she sought God's will in the circumstances of the moment, which included the orders of ecclesiastical superiors. 'I know God will direct me through you', she had written to Mother M. of Mercy Norris when offering herself for the Brisbane mission.[51] What she had held true in 1861, she believed equally in 1866 when Quinn, then her spiritual mentor, pressed for the submission of her schools to the Board of Education.

Apart from her belief that circumstances were the burning bush in which God revealed himself, Mother Vincent was supported by another principle, namely that there is a necessary and valuable *esprit de corps* to be fostered both within the religious community and in the wider Church. 'All worth is little worth in a religious', she considered, 'if she has not our humble, charitable and obedient spirit.'[52] Only such a disposition could have enabled Mother Vincent to place the general good before private satisfaction and personal predilection, even to the point of forgoing her own most cherished ideas. Through all the factions that were to trouble the Church in Queensland, and even through the time of her personal humiliation, Mother Vincent was to cling fast to the ideal of unity for, as she wrote on arrival in Brisbane, 'if the bishop, priests and nuns only work cordially together, there is no part of the world where more can be done for God' than in Australia.[53]

If Mother Vincent placed cohesiveness before the ideal of a separate system, there were many Catholics who did not. Some believed that she had, in fact, traduced Catholic principle by accepting a measure of state supervision and Board regulation. Her Sisters came under fire particularly for opening their doors to non-Catholic children and for mixing freely with Protestants. For the brassy secularism of the voices which had shouted during the public debate of the 1860s that 'not transubstantiation but mensuration' should be taught in schools, had deepened Catholic distrust of the new idea that human values should be cultivated by human energies without reference to divine assistance or guidance. To hold that inclusion of geology in the curriculum meant the exclusion of theology was to provoke a new conflict.

The reaction of one extreme group of Catholics was a spiritual withdrawal as complete as was consistent with living in society. Sons of the Church should, in this view, stand aloof in their diligent quest for the kingdom of God, whose coming is not upon this earth; to mix with those outside the fold was to endanger the faith. Thus Scottish Father Duncan MacNab complained to Archbishop Roger Bede Vaughan of Sydney that the presence of non-Catholic children in Mother Vincent's schools tended 'to vitiate, influence and corrupt the ideas, feelings and morals . . . and to render the school unsuitable for the religious education of Catholic girls.' Moreover, MacNab considered that the presence of non-Catholics prevented religious instruction during school hours.[54] He likewise disapproved of the musical entertainments at All Hallows', 'protracted until after midnight', where the elect Protestant society of Brisbane enjoyed concerts given by the girls.

Letters from a number of Catholic laymen also made their way to Vaughan's desk with similar criticism, for instance from F. N. Rosenstengel, and W. Crofton,[55] who was later to be editor of the

Age. However the prince of these epistle-writers was the tireless Denis O'Donovan, parliamentary librarian, whose monthly bulletins to Vaughan show beyond a doubt that, at least in O'Donovan's mind, the Mercy nuns were censured more for their loyalty to Quinn,[56] towards whom all the dissidents maintained an implacable hostility, than for the faults which MacNab saw in their educational system.

According to the extremists, the only real Catholic schools were those organized by the Sisters of St Joseph,[57] who began their work in Queensland in 1870. Their foundress refused to submit the Order to the Board's authority; she would not permit her Sisters to teach music, nor did she believe in higher learning, in uncompromising agreement with the Bishop P. B. Geoghegan of Adelaide: 'I say that, sooner than lose the faith by which every true Catholic should live, I would prefer that our children should be nescient of secular knowledge.'[58]

Mother Vincent's contrasting attitude in the work of the Mercy Sisters was illustrated both before and after the connection of her schools with the Board of Education; from the beginning she had accepted non-Catholics in her schools, and she had adopted the state curriculum, but enriched it through history, music and singing. Granted the freedom to provide a deeply religious content in education, she had no desire to crawl into a shell, but rather wished to draw all human institutions into the ambit of Christian influence. Also, to provide for the many-sided development of the child in harmony and proportion, each facet of knowledge, of vision and of values had its own special contribution to make to the creation of men and women truly seeking God. She was an incarnational humanist, who stressed that God so loved the world as to enter time and history as man.

Crudely expressed, the motto of MacNab and like-minded men was 'withdraw from the world', while Mother Vincent chose to mingle with it. The danger of the first attitude was to ignore the world because of heaven, and of the second to try to make a heaven on earth. The tension between these two attitudes was worked out in Queensland 1870–80, but the Catholics did not decide the issue among themselves. For a second sharp public controversy broke up the alliance between state and Church schools, and the Education Act of 1875 made inevitable the dual system of government and independent schools.

From one point of view the events of the mid-1870s flowed logically from the Education Act of 1860. After the parliamentary decision to undertake the responsibility of the primary education of all citizens, the next step was to build up the state's administrative machinery for the task. The Board, it was believed, should be more directly under a Minister responsible to the government.

That, however, was not the issue which sent Queenslanders to the polls, put Catholics once again on their mettle, and brought Orangemen and Evangelicals under the one flag to fight their old foes. At the heart of the freshly opened debate lay the liberal wish to have a single centralized authority in complete control of the schools.

With the discovery of gold in Gympie and an improved fiscal position, the temporary need for co-operation between the government and the Churches had diminished. Further, the conviction had strengthened that religion was not a government responsibility; increasingly the concept of the state was identified with promotion of the well-being of its citizens as men destined to live in the world, and the social good of universal education belonged in this sphere. Finally, Queensland tended to follow trends in New South Wales; and in that colony the 1866 Council of Education replaced the old dual Boards, national and denominational, with a unified administration.

While the hand of the government was thus strengthened, Pio Nono's *Syllabus of Errors* published in 1864 and the events of the Vatican Council of 1870 did nothing to enhance the Catholic position. Yet at the Second Provincial Council of Catholic Bishops in 1869, Polding of Sydney voiced the opinion of most of his prelates, namely that, although the government had discontinued subsidy in New South Wales, the bishops could not in conscience allow Catholic children to attend public schools. Thus, despite their contention that such taxation was a 'gross violation of common liberty of conscience',[59] they would have to organize unsubsidized Catholic schools while obliged to contribute to the upkeep of public schools.

The Queensland liberals were so far from agreement with Polding's views on justice that by 1873 they were prepared to cast off the comparatively small non-vested section. This they achieved in four steps.

First, in a circular to schools, the Board threatened that teachers who continued to impart religious instruction would have their salaries withdrawn.[60] This was a clear change of policy, since the first chairman of the Board had declared that any teacher might teach religion.[61] Attorney-General John Bramston held that the directive of the circular was illegal, but Charles Lilley supported it, and further claimed that the Board could at once pass regulations to cease aid to non-vested schools.[62]

This flank attack killed Tufnell's schools, because clergymen were not free to attend to religious instruction.[63] However, Mother Vincent overcame the difficulty by deploying her Sisters so that those who taught secular subjects in one city school walked to others to impart religious lessons. Under this arrangement, the Sisters kept the letter of the law, and no teacher of any school gave a formal religious lesson in that school. But, as compliance with the letter of the law entailed marathon walks and grave inconvenience,[64] it seemed only a matter of time before the Church-sponsored schools would wither away.

The second step was the introduction of 'Mr Lilley's Bill', an 1873 trial run for the 1875 Education Act, designed to set up a department under a Minister responsible to parliament and to end partnership with the Churches.[65] So lively was the opposition that education became an election issue. But, to the disappointment of Lilley and Griffith, chief framers of the later Act, the elections were favourable to the Church schools, even if only by a narrow margin.

Lilley was a genuine 'liberal' who helped the Catholics in the 1860s, and brought into parliament a champion of Catholic education, Dr K. I. O'Doherty. Lilley befriended the bishop, and was respected by Catholics, whose meetings he assiduously attended. Griffith, on the other hand, was the son of a Congregationalist minister who was, from 1882, president of the Orange Lodge. Griffith was not an Orangeman himself, but needed the political support which his father's connections gave him, and was therefore willing at times to appear so; in fact he was a zealous High Churchman. Griffith and Lilley represented two movements, one sectarian, Liberal and Orange, the other non-sectarian, and liberal in a truer sense; the first unconditionally opposed to Catholics, the latter only unwillingly hostile.[66]

In 1874 Griffith took the third step, with a Bill to abolish non-vested schools, which provided that, while no further aid should be extended to such schools, they could be conveyed to the Board at fair value.[67] In return for the Catholic vote in Ipswich, A. Macalister had promised to uphold non-vested schools, but made one of the 'famous recantations'[68] for which he has gone down in history. Nevertheless, his slippery support was insufficient for Griffith.

Thus the fourth and final step was the appointment of the Royal Commission on education announced in the Governor's speech in proroguing parliament. With Mr Justice Lilley as its chairman and Griffith a member, and the decision secured by their devoted followers who formed a majority in the Council, the report was predictably a one-sided expression of 'the Commissioners' own ideas, prejudices, and party affiliations',[69] and so the way was at last clear for the disendowment of Church schools.

H. Bryan claims that the 1875 'free, secular, and compulsory' Education Act was 'aimed quite definitely at Catholics'.[70] His interpretation restates C. M. H. Clark's argument that the marriage of the Rights of Man with Calvinism and fear of Catholic domination drove religion out of state-subsidized education.[71] In the sense that virtually only Catholic schools stood to lose, Bryan's judgment could be correct: the Act affected the one Anglican school which had survived the 1873 measure, and twenty Catholic schools,[72] or half the total number under Quinn's jurisdiction, of which only seven were Mother Vincent's.

Quinn's almost unobtrusive role in the debate of the 1870s contrasted sharply with the flamboyance of the public meetings of the 1860s. His paper, the *North Australian,* had been engulfed in the financial ruin of 1865. Then, too, his colleague, Bishop Tufnell, retired to England in 1874, and the Anglicans were leaderless. Moreover, petitions to parliament had proved fruitless, issues were now decided by the citizen at the ballot box, and only through it could the Church effect changes in the temporal order.

Despite his weakened position, Quinn did not falter in his claims for continued non-vested status for Catholic schools. The uniqueness of his attitude among the Australian hierarchy prompted the members of the Royal Commission on education to ask if he enjoyed a discretion quite independent of the policy of his Church the world over. He replied that in matters of faith there was everywhere consistency of belief, but in matters of discipline and custom, and education came under this head, he was free to act as he thought best. He considered non-vested schools 'in a certain sense preferable' since it was better to forgo for Catholic children 'some of the advantages they would enjoy in separate schools, in order to give to the other children . . . the before-mentioned advantages.'[73]

Closely questioned by Griffith on the ground of his objection to the single type of school planned under the foreshadowed Act, Quinn freely admitted that deprivation of the right to endorse teacher appointments lay at the core of his dissent, for approval of teachers carried with it for him the guarantee that the child's faith would be respected and that religion would provide the groundwork of morality.[74] Had the bishop conceded school property to the state, and Griffith allowed him approval of state-trained teachers, these two able men might have found the solution worked out in Scotland half a century later. They came close, but not close enough; the breach widened, and Church and state both lost.

Yet the careful reader of the evidence to the Royal Commission must admit that the inclusion of religion in public schools on a curricular basis presented an almost insuperable problem, since the dilemma was to make a single system cater for all. Even though Griffith and Lilley could not solve it, they found in Quinn a generous appraisal of their efforts. 'I approve of the secular education given in this colony', he declared in the presence of two thousand at the opening of the Christian Brothers' College at Gregory Terrace, 'because children of different denominations necessarily frequent the public schools, and no system of religion could be taught in them which would represent the tenets of the whole body of pupils.'[75]

Thus the bitterness of sectarian feuds found no echo in Quinn's words. He accepted reluctantly but with dignity the severance of his schools from the state system; and after Queensland law had abolished the non-vested status and abolished the subsidy, he still requested and was granted state inspection and the right to send Catholic pupils for state examinations. Principle and not choice forced him to return to Mother Vincent's ideal of independence.

Mother Vincent could only feel relieved at being freed from the Board restrictions which forbade the display of religious objects in classrooms and relegated religious lessons to periods before or after normal school hours. Certainly she had preserved the character of her schools by the witness of the Sisters' presence, the orientation of their lessons, and devices used to remind the pupils of the presence of God, such as the practice described by the bishop to the Royal Commission members: 'When the clock strikes', he said, 'there is silence for about a minute, no signal being given, which silence contributes greatly to the good order of the school. During that short silence, the children may if they wish say a little prayer in their own mind or make the sign of the cross or think of the presence of God.'[76]

Even in the face of Board regulation which rang the death-knell of the Anglican schools and severely threatened her own, Mother Vincent uttered no protest, but persevered indomitably at her task. Sisters freshly arrived from overseas noted the pallor of her hard-worked community, and how badly they needed rest and relaxation.[77] However, the peak of Mother Vincent's efforts to preserve Catholic schools by replacing lay teachers by religious occurred during the years 1875–80 for, by the end of this latter year, all government subsidy to non-state schools was to cease.

A strong conviction of the continuing need for separate religious schools provided the energy for this drive, for Mother Vincent could not share the optimism of those Protestants who assumed that, in the absence of denominational schools, parents would shoulder their responsibility to impart religious instruction where it is most effective. She agreed with Dr K. I. O'Doherty that 'in eight out of twelve of the ordinary families of labourers and artisans in this colony, there is no possibility of religious or moral instruction being given to the children in their homes.'[78]

Mother Vincent knew those homes intimately, and she perceived the need for spiritual regeneration, not through moral enlightenment or temperance movements, but through divine grace. All Catholics, whether prelate or farmer, layman or nun, whether English, Irish, French, German, Italian, Australian or otherwise, were united in faith as they read the words of the 1879 Joint Pastoral. They believed in the doctrine of original sin, in the interdependence of creed and conduct, and the need for that grace which can come only from the knowledge and love of God. On Christ's teachings must depend 'all civilisation and legislation, all morality, public, social, and private . . . Without these, man falls back into paganism and barbarism.'[79] Their common faith made the convent schools a matter of first concern to parents, clergy and Sisters alike.

But such principles entailed sacrifice from the Catholic population. However, parents had grown unaccustomed to delving deeply in their pockets for support of the schools during the years when the government had granted subsidy, and on the eve of the withdrawal of salaries, Mother Vincent outlined the position in a letter to the Bishop. 'In our schools which are under the Board there are thirty-eight pupil-teachers who receive salaries to the amount of £1,020 16s 10d . . . The places of these teachers must be supplied by nuns, and how are they to be supported?'[80] That the solution was left very much to her own ingenuity, the following chapter will show.

Silent as was Mother Vincent's voice in public controversy, she won the education debate by a stretch of ascetic virtue, by energy and dogged perseverance. Cut off from state support in the 1880s, hers was virtually the only teaching Order in the whole of Queensland, for the Christian Brothers, late arrivals, had still only two schools. It was a situation unparalleled anywhere else in Australia that a whole diocese (after Quinn's death two dioceses) should have the schools staffed by one Order of women operating from the capital city. Indeed, long before Vaughan voiced his scheme for manning diocesan schools, Mother Vincent had shown how it could be done.

She created her own pattern, and fits uneasily into the design by which historians seek to explain the development of the Catholic education. Thus Austin sees the resolution of the 1869 National Council of Bishops as an instance of the Catholic assault on the late-nineteenth-century liberal ethos inspired by the 1864 Papal Encyclical, *Quanta Cura*. According to Austin, the hierarchy were to 'create an independent system of Catholic schools',[81] which was a direct challenge to the prevailing concept of the National System.

But Mother Vincent needed no impetus from the hierarchy, and long before *Quanta Cura* was written she had shown a clear preference for independent schools even when Quinn, her ecclesiastical superior, sought connection with the National System. On his insistence, she accepted affiliation with the Board of Education in 1866, two years after the publication of *Quanta Cura*. The Sisters of St Joseph refused to concede to the Board, and this action was one of the reasons for their departure from Queensland in 1879. Mother Vincent's were the most numerous and most typical Catholic schools in this colony; but they afford scant evidence of the 'head-on clash' which Austin discovers as part of the Australian pattern, for to concede everything but a religious principle is hardly to assault the liberal ethos.

The Governor of Queensland, William Wellington Cairns, set the high seal of approval on Mother Vincent's efforts. The nuns were, he declared, 'par excellence the ladies capable of imparting the moral virtues of obedience, self-denial and modesty, the essentials in forming the character of a gentlewoman.' At the same time Cairns delivered a mortal blow to the Protestant champions of a religionless school by adding that the convent 'was the only establishment in Brisbane in which the daughters of Protestants could receive a religious and moral education.'[82] The subsequent dissatisfaction of Anglicans and Protestants with the inadequate provision for religious education in the state system resulted in the partial revival of independent schools, and in the movement to have the Bible included in the curriculum of the state schools.[83] Thus Mother Vincent's steadfastness was tacitly, if tardily, approved by other religious bodies.

On the death of Quinn in 1881, Robert Dunne succeeded to the See of Brisbane. He too was a man deeply interested in education, but by the time of his appointment the ideological debate was over, and his task was not controversy but the promotion of social harmony and the improvement of scholastic standards. In his eyes Mother Vincent's schools were unsurpassed, their pupils were the only 'living poems', and she herself was pre-eminently a peace-maker, 'a little bottle of patent diamond cement'[84] who sent abroad her Sisters as 'the real apostles of the nineteenth century'.

The first bishop had nullified Mother Vincent's plans for separate schools; the triumphant state policy had defeated her adaptation to non-vested status. It required stamina of a high order and vast courage to persevere in her task, as well as tact and skill to guide her young and hard-worked Sisters. But in the end both Church and state gave their benediction and turned defeat into victory.

3

THE CHALLENGE OF VASTNESS AND ISOLATION

Queensland, the north-eastern shoulder of the Australian continent, is 13,000 miles by sea from the British Isles, the major source in the nineteenth century of its population, ideas, institutions, equipment and manufactured products. In size it exceeds any country in Europe except Russia, and could easily contain the combined areas of the British Isles, France, Germany and Italy. Its 667,000 square miles, almost one-fourth of the total area of the continent, straddles the Tropic of Capricorn; 54 per cent of the area is within the tropics.

When Queensland became a separate colony in 1859 it had a population of 27,000. By the end of Mother Vincent's lifespan, despite steady increase, it could still boast only half of what had been the population figure for County Cork fifty years earlier. Though most of its people were concentrated in the south-east corner, the land-settlement policy fostered by the first two bishops, the opening up of the north after the discovery of goldfields, and the construction of roads and railways, dispersed Catholics over distances beyond the imagination of Mother Vincent's friends in Europe. The absence of navigable rivers made the vastness of Queensland a formidable challenge. The coastal margin attracted more settlers than the dry interior, and many could be reached by the steamships using the Cape York route. But a voyage of a couple of hundred miles to Maryborough took forty hours; and for inland journeys, horseback was the fastest mode of travel until in the 1870s Brisbane and Roma were connected by rail. The tiny settlements were separated by so many hundreds of miles that Bishop Quinn, on his pastoral rounds, was often compelled, at the onset of night, to tether his horse in the trackless bush and seek rest on the bare ground. Distance discouraged women from moving out into the country and was a factor in making Queensland a masculine society.

Mother Vincent had to meet the educational needs of a diocese coextensive with the colony. How was she to bring education to families sparsely scattered over thousands of square miles? How was she to attract teachers to the remotest frontier of a continent at the edge of the world? How achieve and maintain high academic standards in a society where the labour shortage reduced school attendance?

Mother Vincent had been in Queensland only a few months when she thought out an answer to the first problem, distance. Her plan involved a radical departure from the accepted organization of her Order. In consultation with Quinn she decided that new convents and schools should be controlled from Brisbane, and not become autonomous.[1]

Flexibility had been the keynote to Mother McAuley's arrangements for her Order in Ireland. As it penetrated new dioceses, it gave local autonomy. Bishops undertook to preserve its Constitutions, but because it fostered their work of education and charity, they actively interested themselves in finding new members. The diocesan ecclesiastical structure was only one reason for decentralization. Another was the monastic tradition of the Benedictines which was still widely influential with active Orders of women. New offshoots, while sharing the spirit and interests of the parent body, were expected to draw their sap from the ground in which they were planted.

The very different physical geography of Queensland, and the complete absence of fostering dioceses, made necessary a different organizational approach. It is noteworthy that, just as state followed Church in Ireland and England in promoting education with the help of local effort, so Church followed state in Queensland and in Australia generally in concluding that the only viable mode was centralization.

On her arrival, Mother Vincent was quick to conclude that what was feasible in Ireland was impossible in Queensland. For in the early 1860s the whole gigantic colony was not only one diocese, it was virtually a single parish. Thus the Ipswich convent established in 1863 was the first of a large number of branch houses which shared staff and finance, the stronger centres assisting the weaker.

Mother Vincent's first letter home stressed that as many as ten groups of nuns, if available, could be set to work at once.[2] The upsurge of the population from both immigration and natural increase, and the swift advance of the frontiers to the north and west called for a carefully planned disposal of slender resources, and also for a generous co-operation from the locality where schools were to be established.

Organizations centred on Brisbane, both state and Church, encountered resistance in some local areas. For instance, when the Board of General Education required local governments to supply one-third of the cost of new schools, the mayor of Toowoomba, W. H. Groom, M.L.A., opposed the measure on the ground that the municipality was already well served with two denominational schools.[3] Lack of finance was likewise the main reason for resistance which the bishop encountered to the spread of the centralized Catholic system in the Darling Downs. He expected the parishes to provide buildings and the minimum equipment. However the clergy, faced with the poverty and the cultural indifference of their flocks, and the fact that comparatively few of the farmers, pastoralists and labourers scattered over thousands of square miles could reach the parish school, were reluctant to change their existing arrangements. Fathers Robert Dunne of Toowoomba, Denis Byrne of Dalby and Dermot McDonough of Warwick were the patrons of the non-vested lay Catholic schools in their towns. They chose the teachers who, when approved by the Board, were granted a government salary according to classification. Teachers were thus no charge on the parish.

But the bishop foresaw a not-distant day when all subsidy would cease for Catholic schools. There was no future for them, in his view, unless they could be staffed or at least supervised by religious. His policy was therefore to send some Sisters to the non-vested schools connected with the Board, whose salaries should be put by to pay lay teachers when government subsidy was withdrawn. The onus for maintaining the Sisters thus devolved on the parish, a cost which, though small because of the frugality of the nuns' lives, was still a matter of concern to the pastor.

If that were the only reason for reluctance to establish church schools, however, the men of Dalby would not have taken the matter into their own hands and sent a delegation to Brisbane to ask for nuns.[4] Even then, it required a strongly worded letter from the bishop to make Father Byrne set to work. His procrastination, the bishop charged, was 'a serious injustice' to his people.[5]

In their masculine and independent world, the clergy were jealous of their rights. It was galling that the staff for their schools should be appointed from All Hallows' and recalled at the whim of a Reverend Mother. Again, the threats of episcopal sanctions or interference with the internal affairs of their parish, even with the school organization, evoked sharp protest. Hence Father Robert Dunne, Vicar-General and leader inland from the Dividing Range, laid down the following terms on which he would accept nuns in his Toowoomba school: 'I will . . . allow no programme of studies, no distribution of time, no alteration of classes between teachers or pupil-teachers, or no division or amalgamation of drafts or classes without my written consent for each act.' He would not permit any teacher to be withdrawn or otherwise removed without due notice to him, nor should any teacher be sent to his school without his written acceptance. Sisters, if appointed, should act exactly like the lay teachers in Warwick, Dalby and Toowoomba.[6]

A similar lordly manner marked ecclesiastical correspondence with the Education Department. So Father Andrew Horan of Ipswich informed the secretary that he had 'appointed' Miss Margaret O'Brien as assistant to the convent school,[7] earning the retort that 'no salary should be paid, as no knowledge is possessed in this office of the teacher's fitness for her duties.'[8] A similar note went to Father Denis Byrne of Dalby who, like Horan, had taken the appointment of a lay teacher into his own hands. Indeed, the Department officially ruled that 'in future all teachers seeking admission to the Board's service must forward application in their own handwriting.'[9]

Left to herself, Mother Vincent would certainly not have attempted to found schools on the Darling Downs under these circumstances. When she had gone to Belfast in the heart of Protestant Ulster, she did so because the Catholics of that city had petitioned Bishop C. Denvir for a foundation of Sisters of Mercy, and the bishop had applied to her for help.[10] It was a rule that such invitations should come from the district and the undertaking have ecclesiastical sanction. But while the Sisters in Queensland were selected and furnished with their mandate by Bishop Quinn, the long negotiations with the local pastors, and the false starts, gave them the impression that they were not wanted. This was particularly true of the situation on the Darling Downs.

Dunne's opposition on the Darling Downs was partly to the authority of the bishop, partly to the autonomy of the Sisters, and partly to the idea of centralization. However, it can be properly understood only in the light of events described in the following two chapters. Nevertheless it is for present purposes essential to show the profound mistrust, the pessimism even, with which Robert Dunne confronted the concept of conventual education, a decade before he was to become Queensland's second bishop.

Mother Vincent was not Reverend Mother at the time of the Downs foundations. Largely for the sake of imposing a strong central system, the bishop had taken over supreme command of the Order; Dunne saw in Mother Bridget, who had replaced Mother Vincent, his inflexible foe. His letters to her argued that her insistence on centralization threatened his fostering role, and the efficiency of the school. 'You say that the Sisters were going to Toowoomba as "nuns sent" ', he complained, 'and subject to the bishop and local superior, without stipulation—the local superior meaning, I presume, the Sister in charge. Your words convey that I am to have nothing to say to them as far as subjection is concerned.'[11]

But Dunne had taken a pride in building up the school, and he had deepened the professional competence of the lay teachers by prescribing special courses of study in which he set examinations.[12] He feared that should Sisters be sent to his school the proximity of Brisbane would mean instability of staff. Rockhampton, much farther away, was safe from interference, but 'four trains a day between Ipswich and Toowoomba,[13] steamers, coaches etc. make a difference.'[14]

With the bishop, Dunne used still another line of reasoning. To hand over the Catholic education of children to a religious community, he contended, was 'a very questionable course'[15] because children so brought up were apt to fall away from the practice of their religion in after-school years. With lay teachers approved by himself, however, Dunne considered that he was in closer contact with boys and girls than he could be in schools staffed by religious. Then, too, lay teachers were, in his view. better placed to give youth the guidance needed for success in life. He did not approve, indeed, he positively discouraged, girls from entering religious orders. Quinn found incomprehensible these 'eccentric views', and the 'spiritual poison which they diffused' was the basis of correspondence between them for thirteen months prior to the establishment of the convent in Toowoomba.[16]

Nowhere did the Sisters feel unwelcome except on the Downs; indeed, in Gympie, they were received by a procession led by a band. But Father Dunne made it clear to the Sisters that he accepted them under protest. He appointed a lay teacher, Kate

Reordan, an All Hallows' past pupil, over them as headmistress, but she turned the fruits of victory to ashes in his mouth by resigning her position to join the Order, and Mother Vincent took her to Rockhampton to found a much-besought convent.

Centralization, despite initial opposition, was eventually accepted as a necessary device to pool resources under Queensland's conditions. However, from the first months of her life in Queensland, Mother Vincent found that boarding schools were equally necessary for families living well away from parish centres. Hence, when in 1861 country people asked her to take their daughters as boarders, she purchased some extra cottages near St Stephen's, her first school in Brisbane, and there Sisters and girls resided until Dr George Fullerton's home, Adderton, at Petrie Bight, was put up for sale. At the end of 1863 the new site with its pleasant acres perched over the river was ready.

Adderton was re-named All Hallows', partly because Mother Vincent took possession of it on All Hallows' Day, 1 November, and partly also because of the associations of the name of the great seminary in Dublin, built on the site of an earlier thirteenth-century priory called All Hallows'. The latter, in its turn, was named after one of the earliest churches in England, seventh-century All Hallows' by the Tower. In Australia, a country without significant historical associations and canonized saints, Mother Vincent liked richly reminiscent titles.

The boarding school also had to become a select school. The need for such establishments was stressed by two young ladies who visited Mother Vincent a few days after her arrival in Brisbane. They had been obliged to go far afield, they told her, for a better education and a more thorough knowledge of Catholic doctrine than they could receive at home; one had just returned from the Benedictine school at Subiaco, Sydney, and the other from Stanbrook Abbey in England.[17]

Clearly the rising class of pastoralists, business and professional men had already created a demand for an education beyond the simple rudiments supplied by the ordinary primary school. Indeed, when at Ipswich Mother Vincent accepted girls of seventeen and eighteen years who had never received a sacrament,[18] she was convinced of the need to extend boarding-school facilities. The girls of mature years who remained until their late teens were catered for first through the accomplishments valued in Victorian times, and in this way Mother Vincent gradually adapted the curriculum to give it a secondary bent. The boarding schools which she subsequently founded were dotted along the coastal rim and through the populous centres of the south-east, at Gympie, Maryborough, Rockhampton, Mackay, Townsville, Charters Towers, and Toowoomba, Dalby, Roma, Warwick and Stanthorpe (see map). Thus they were within reach of most families.

The status of the schools made them attractive to pastoralists situated on distant stations, Protestant as well as Catholic. Apart from the Brisbane Girls' Grammar School, established in 1869, there were no girls' boarding schools in the colony. Other Churches did not move into the secondary field until the close of the century, partly because 'the Roman Catholic Church was the only one whose people were willing to give sufficient money to set up worthwhile secondary schools',[19] but partly also because qualified women teachers and supervisors were virtually unobtainable outside the religious orders introduced from overseas. Even colonial governments, faced with the problem of reaching remote settlers and having experienced the unsatisfactoriness of itinerant teachers, had to reject as impracticable the proposal to establish subsidized boarding schools for children of primary-school age.[20]

Thus only Mother Vincent's convents and the grammar schools accommodated boarders and, in addition, only these schools offered a secondary education to Queensland children, for the government did not establish state high schools during Mother Vincent's lifetime; the Education Department might have met with stiff resistance from taxpayers had it attempted to do so,[21] for there was no widespread demand for schooling beyond the rudiments. Indeed, the *Courier*, reflecting popular opinion at the time, declared that secondary schools would only create distaste for manual labour when, in point of fact, a man with a trade was independent, while 'the genteel professions and occupations' were overcrowded and underpaid. This most influential of Queensland's papers went on to argue that with sobriety and intelligence, manual labour would lead to a competence, if not to ultimate wealth in this new country.[22] Such was the attitude of a masculine pioneering society where men could not be spared from nation-building. In the circumstances, girls rather than boys were given a higher education, which became a status symbol in the family. Thus prestige fostered Mother Vincent's boarding schools among Protestants, while the inaccessibility of the hinterland made them welcome to Catholics as centres of religious and cultural formation.

And so, to All Hallows', first and most popular boarding school for young ladies in Brisbane, came girls from the most remote

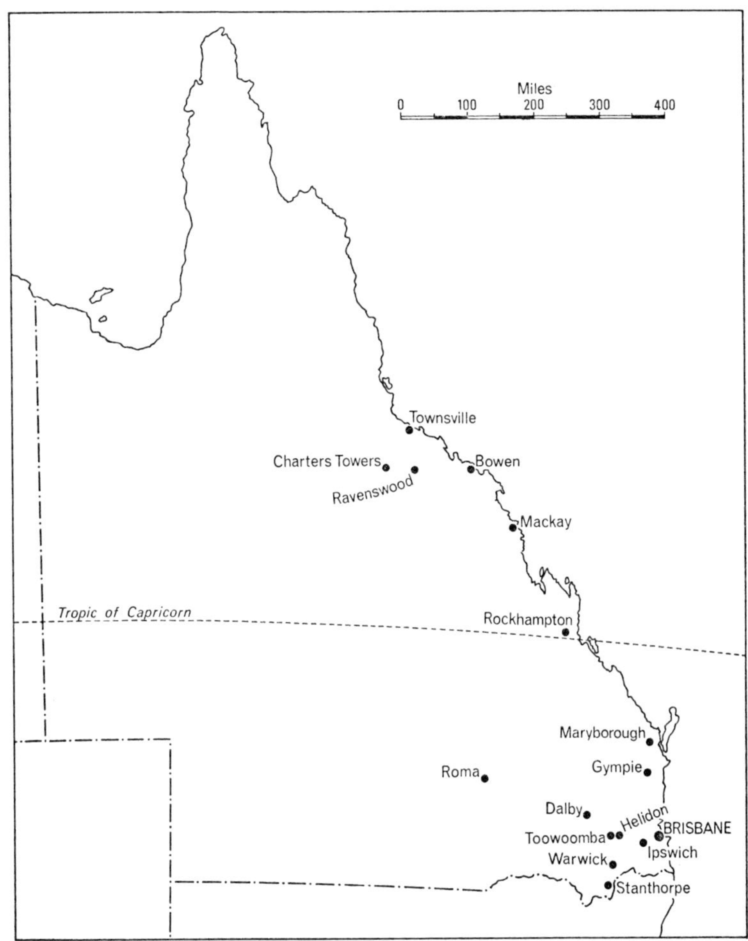

Map of Queensland, 1892. Brisbane had eight Mercy schools, and Rockhampton three; all other towns shown had one.

corners of north and west Queensland and New South Wales, many of them to remain in residence for years on end owing to the difficulties of travel. School activities of the 1860s included instrumental music, singing, drawing, dancing, languages and painting,[23] which comprised the types of accomplishment suited to a leisurely, examination-free age. The music belonged to the broad European tradition: Rossini's Overture to 'Tancredi' played by the All Hallows' girls opened the public concert in honour of the Duke of Edinburgh in 1868,[24] while an extant programme, printed on white satin, lists Mozart, Czerny, Donizetti, Glover, Handel and Cimarosa as offerings to their Lordships of Maitland, Goulburn and Bathurst. Although in most convent schools music was counted an 'extra', many girls studied it; but in All Hallows' to omit it was unthinkable.

Samples of the art-work of nineteenth-century All Hallows' pupils still bedeck the walls of many Queensland homes. In these water-colours or oil paintings of landscapes and seascapes, animal and still-life studies, one detects the lingering influence of the Romantic movement untouched by the Impressionists astir in France. The first art-master was the noted entomologist, Silvester Diggles,[25] while Godfrey Rivers[26] was among the teachers who helped to give the school a name and fame.

But while culture served to attract students, Mother Vincent did not forget their need for religious regeneration. Indeed, she deplored their thirst for 'showy accomplishments'[27] at the expense of the religious sense which gave life its true purpose. For the first few years she was much discouraged to find that everyone in the colony seemed to require money for services rendered.[28] Clearly, she had to build up among her charges an ideal of free community service which she described in an 1863 letter. Mother Vincent was to see the fruits of her efforts, for in the years after they left school many of her pupils became auxiliaries in districts beyond the Sisters' reach, ready to gather the children together and teach them the basic tenets of religion, prepare them for the sacraments, and lead them in parish activities.

Not all young ladies accepted readily this ideal of application and service, and some required a stern reminder that All Hallows' was no dream-world wherein to indulge fantasies of social aspiration. On the other hand, girls of great promise and prospects decided to throw in their lot with the Sisters in a way that rejoiced the heart of the bishop, who told his Vicar-General, Cani, that 'we ought to be most grateful to God for the fine spirit that is among our people here. All are fervent, and most brilliant girls are candidates for the veil.'[29] This generosity, he considered, was 'a tangible and wonderful result of prayer'.

Quinn was satisfied that Mother Vincent was striking a balance between moral and academic development. The Roman Catholics of Queensland, he said, were justly proud of the schools conducted by the Sisters of Mercy, 'for in these they find that perfect and complete education for their children which fits them equally for this workday world and for a higher and better one.'[30] But the parents who were his audience on that first All Hallows' speech-day in 1864 knew nothing of the tension between immanence and transcendence which exercised theologians and educators. Hard-headed men with feet on the ground, the pastoralists and business-men were content to hear that 'the programme of studies shows the extent, variety, and practical nature of the branches taught in the school, and [that] the results reflect the greatest credit on the industry and talents of the teachers.'

In order to dispel the apathy of most parents, Mother Vincent proved herself an active leader of her group of teachers in seeking every opportunity for contact with the common man. Her constant trips between the Brisbane and Ipswich schools brought her into touch, on the river steamer *Settler*, with men and women from far up the country. Some of these adhered to no particular church, mostly through lack of opportunity. Among the patients at the Ipswich hospital, she met a Catholic who had not received the sacraments in forty-one years.[31] From such encounters she derived an exceptionally wide grasp of varied human types.

Also, as part of her community programme, Mother Vincent discovered new avenues of service. In the Benevolent Asylum attached to the old George Street hospital, for example, she found a group of orphans whom she decided to care for and educate.[32] Her first offer was rejected by the authorities,[33] although later, the government came to realize that the Church 'in taking orphans under its own care, would be relieving the Government of an unwelcome responsibility.'[34] Thus by December 1866 the forty-seven children confided to Mother Vincent were cared for at Cairncross New Farm, until in 1867 some buildings were ready at Nudgee on a property which Quinn had acquired and given in trust to the Sisters for their new work.[35] Later the number of children under care increased to 300. Often the victims of a tragedy were brought down from the far north: thus the two children of the Corbett family sailed with their uncle in the *Black*

Swan after their mother had died in Normanton in the Gulf country and their father had been speared by the Aboriginals.[36]

Mother Vincent, in considering the distress of families so affected, saw that the lonely stretches of the north needed a refuge closer than Nudgee. She therefore established a second children's home at Mackay, which was later removed to Rockhampton because of the difficulty of sending goods so far.

Just as Mother Vincent pioneered secondary education for girls, so she began Church-sponsored care of homeless children in Queensland. As the Anglican Rayner says, 'at a time when other Churches were unable or unready to help orphans and others in need, the Roman Catholic Church was making admirable efforts to fulfil what it regarded as its duty towards those in distress.'[37] Mother Vincent initiated this venture in 1863 on the feast of her patron, St Vincent de Paul, lover of the afflicted, and by 1890 her two homes cared for 600 children, 'or almost half of all those in institutions in the colony'.[38]

In view of the fact that Mother Vincent's homes were thought of primarily as Catholic, this disproportionate percentage could be evidence of the high Irish mortality rates, the fruit of poverty; or it could in part stem from the fact that the Sisters kept open house for children of any faith who needed them, and for Aboriginals. But the high percentage resulted also from the Sisters' wish to shelter children beyond the age when the state institutions ceased their tutelage, because Mother Vincent and her nuns were reluctant to see ten-year-old boys cast on the world to fend for themselves, often at the hard work of stations and farms.

For this reason, the Sisters enlisted the help of Sir Maurice O'Connell to have the law amended so that boys could stay at the home until they were twelve years old and girls until they were fourteen.[39] Then, in order to have a half-way house between the child's dependence on the home and actual working conditions on discharge, Mother Vincent and Bishop Quinn established a vocational school at St Anne's in Ann Street, Brisbane.

Employment for girls who learned dressmaking there was found at firms like Finney Isles and in the large drapery stores in the major towns.[40] For the boys, different industries were tried at Nudgee to provide a trade, sericulture, leather-work, vegetable-growing and care of stock. But for such industries to thrive a capable and experienced manager was needed, and in Mother

Vincent's time none of that calibre could be secured for the home. Printing and book-binding absorbed a few boys when in 1878 the *Australian* was launched, but Mother Vincent never arrived at a satisfactory solution to the problem of vocational training for boys.

Yet the anti-Catholic *Courier* had praise for the atmosphere of care which she and her Sisters provided in the 'excellent and well-managed establishment' at Nudgee. The good work done there was obvious to the most careless visitor. 'It is not only that so many little waifs and strays of society are gathered under comfortable roofs, well fed and cared for and well taught; all this might be done and the place yet be cheerless enough.' The journal further claimed that to the nuns belonged the credit of having converted the homeless little ones 'into as bright, happy, and intelligent a community of children as could be found in a similar station of life in any part of the world.'[41] It helped that each of the schools attached to the homes catered for the education of local children with the orphans, and that country fee-paying boarders among them preserved contact with normal life, for in this way the homes were boarding schools with a difference.

A group united by agreement as to the things they love can take discomfort lightly in pursuit of their goals. Thus we find Mother Vincent and her Sisters on their first night in Brisbane stumbling along in the light of lanterns in search of a house. When they reached it, there was no water, furniture, or crockery; it was unprotected, and they were afraid of 'the blacks'. This experience was a prelude to a pioneering existence which demanded their skill and ingenuity, their cheerfulness and adaptability, to make the best of what was available and add a touch of beauty and brightness wherever possible.

Mother Vincent discovered immediately the effect of distance from Europe on the cost of living. 'I only wish I had accepted dearest Mother M. Rose's offer of blankets', she wrote to her Dublin convent. 'They and all sorts of manufactured goods are exorbitantly dear.'[42] Freight costs from Europe were heavy, and the huge waves in the latitudes of the roaring forties broke over the clippers and rusted the strings of her pianos. Freight inland was just as expensive and the slow-moving bullock teams which became bogged down in roads over unbridged creeks were hardly safer than the sailing ships for fragile goods. Moreover, demand exceeded supply for household items. 'Fresh arrivals by every week's packet have made it difficult to procure a regular set of delf or china,'[43] Mother Vincent told her Sisters in Dublin.

Apart from the expense of goods, the Sisters discovered that living conditions were primitive. On arrival Mother Vincent described the only schoolrooms available, wooden buildings, 'where the rain comes in now and then, still they look clean and bright.'[44] She was happy, nevertheless, that they had so much to do; the Brisbane Sisters, she declared, had more children to teach, and more converts to instruct than the Sisters in either Melbourne or Geelong.[45] 'It is a pleasure to be employed thus amongst the poor', she wrote reassuringly to the Dublin Reverend Mother who feared that the new missioners might be in want. 'God will provide enough. I love that saying of our Blessed Lord's—"Seek first the Kingdom of God." '[46]

Only during the blackness of the mid-1860s depression did Mother Vincent doubt whether she and her Sisters could cling on when good men advised them to return home. But having survived that crisis, Mother Vincent might well worry about her Sisters in the clammy cold of a Toowoomba winter. The Superior of that convent wrote to her of their needs, mentioning that Sisters had given their beds to three new boarders. 'We have not sufficient of our own or cash to buy more, and the weather is too severe now for any Sister to have only a mattress under her. It was the way we managed before. One had the mattress of a bed and a blanket, and another had the remainder.'[47]

A spirit of mutual consideration made lighter the shared hardship; while lack of sympathy made it onerous. Earlier reference to Father Robert Dunne's parsimoniousness and his unwillingness to accept the centralized convent system, explain his unavailability when the Superior, Mother M. Rose, wanted to see him about providing certain essentials for the school. 'With reference to seeing me—I have not much time,' he wrote to her, 'and am scrupulous both as to time and money in a mission like this—but anything you write to me about shall have my earliest attention.'[48]

The convent was a considerable distance from the school, which was also the church, and Mother Rose sought his permission to set up an annexe for a staff retiring-room, a place where the Sisters could change drenched clothes or have a cup of tea. Dunne's letters make his attitude difficult to understand. To Dr Cani, whom the Sisters revered as the kindliest of priests, he had promised to find a more convenient house for his staff, and showed that he clearly understood the need when he wrote:

> All Sunday and today I have been worrying myself with the thought of how impossible it would be for the Sisters to get down from that house to the church or school in weather such as all through yesterday. I would sink down to the ground with very shame at seeing them attempt it.[49]

Yet he was to let them do so for seven years, although, apart from the rent he paid for the house, they maintained themselves at their own expense.[50] More surprisingly, though for two years he refused to build a retiring-room, he had qualms about what he described as 'the frequent journeyings between the school and the convent each day', which had been 'the subject of comment even among hard-working men in the Smithys by the roadside', and among the pupils. 'It had been freezing hard all night and the streets and paddocks were white with frost as a tablecloth', he wrote on one occasion, 'when the Sisters came down for 7 o'clock Mass.' Back for breakfast, four hours' teaching, back for lunch, then down again until late afternoon. He was mortified that one of them became so faint one day that 'a neighbouring woman came to here aid.' With the grounds to be cleaned, and pews to be stacked in preparation for Mass the following morning, there were many demands on their energy apart from teaching. When Father Dunne went overseas, the Sisters, at the bishop's direction, moved into his house.[51]

Catholic and Protestant families were thoughtful and often sent the Sisters gifts of food. But laymen deplored the effects on them of malnutrition and poor housing. True, a dissident Catholic's letter to Rome about 1879 described convents as 'in most cases miserable wooden huts, without lining or ceiling, such as are built here for the occupation of a labourer's family.'[52] In the century temperatures of Dalby when the convent ran out of tank water, and the only shelter was a corrugated iron roof, a Sister died of fever, probably typhoid. But even more devastating was tuberculosis.

Between 1868 and 1888, twenty-seven young Sisters broke down and died. The bishop mourned Mother Rose when she was 'booked for Heaven'. 'Her age is about thirty-four', he wrote, 'and she is the oldest but one of twelve whom we have interred within the last ten years. This dozen included some of the most gifted and saintly women that have ever come to Queensland.'[53] Mother Rose had pioneered Toowoomba and Dalby, and Robert Dunne at last came to repent his earlier intransigence. As bishop after Quinn's death, he watched over the Sisters' health and scolded them for imprudence. 'You nuns, at least the best of you, are like fire or steam; if you are let go your own way you'll burn or explode yourselves out in no time, destroying yourselves and doing no end of heartbreak to those in charge of you.'[54]

Education, never an easy avocation, was made more difficult by the poverty of the people. Through frequent home visits, Mother Vincent and her Sisters did all they could to encourage regular school attendance, and provided clothing when the parents were reluctant to send children to school in shabby dress. But because the nuns were unable to reach all absentees, 'a thick and extensive stratum' of children who avoided both government and church schools was a fertile source of trouble in the streets.[55] The Sisters accepted the common nineteenth-century assumption that there was a close connection between poverty and crime, and they did everything possible to make education a bridge to a better life.

It was difficult to finance the schools in the impoverished condition of Church and people. The limitation of revenue may be gauged from Dunne's suggestion for the agenda of the 1885 Plenary Synod, 'to consider that practically not ten per cent of lay Catholics contribute to the support of public worship; and whether a means can be adopted to equalize the burden to all.'[56] The financing of the schools was discussed at an earlier Brisbane Synod when in 1880 the government subsidy was withdrawn, and it was decided that 30 per cent of Church revenue was to be set aside for boys' schools, supplemented by door-to-door collections and rent from pews.[57]

This decision followed on an abortive attempt to form a 'Catholic Union', which was 'to enable the Catholic community to provide every requisite in the matter of elementary education without any aid from the Government.'[58] The method was to create a permanent school fund by dividing Brisbane and other towns into zones each responsible for a contribution. Pew rents, favoured by the bishop, were unpopular, since to the clergy they were 'a source of scandal',[59] and to the people 'an awful thing, most unchristian, and a Yankee notion'.[60] Thus boys' schools were financed mainly by door-to-door collections.

The nuns' schools, claimed a letter submitted by the priests of Synod, caused little anxiety, for they were 'self supporting, independent of State aid, and for the future, with school fees, they will be in a still better position. Nevertheless, if required, one or two collections annually might be made for the Sisters.'[61] However, there were no nuns present in Synod to share the priestly optimism.

In a brief review of their resources, we may first consider salaries paid by the government to convent teachers. Of the eighteen schools under Mother Vincent and her Sisters in 1880, seven had been connected with the Board of Education before the 1875 law which abolished non-vested schools (see table). The average duration of their connection was 9.2 years; and during those years Sisters were salaried according to classification. There were usually two or three nuns to a school, assisted by lay pupil-teachers. Taking the Toowoomba school as sample of salary scale, the head teacher received £136 per annum, the assistant £60, and four pupil-teachers from £16 to £30.[62]

After the 1875 Act, however, a pinchpenny government policy distinguished between salaries for non-vested and for state schools. Thus Alice Byrne of Dalby on passing her promotion examination expected the usual £10 extra.[63] But when she applied to the Secretary of the Education Department, she was informed that despite her distinguished pass there could be no increase, 'because the full amount available for the payment of salaries to the Dalby Roman Catholic School is already apportioned. You should apply to the Local Patron, who will no doubt provide for the balance of salary to which your rank in a state school would entitle you.'[64] The Dalby head teacher's salary was then £60.[65]

The government's periodic shortages of money for education were partly due to the fact that only Queensland of all the colonies

Mercy schools in Queensland connected with the Board of Education, showing the year of their approval, the year in which each school came under the Sisters' management, and the duration of its connection with the Board thereafter.[66]

School	Approved	Came under Sisters	Duration of connection years
Cathedral	1866	1861	14
Fortitude Valley	1866	1862	14
Ipswich	1866	1863	14
Toowoomba	1870	1873	7
Rockhampton	1870	1873	7
Dalby	1870	1877	3
Warwick	1871	1874	6

persisted in its policy of assisting migrants to the turn of the century; it spent half of Australia's total for immigration.[67] Variations in amounts appropriated for salaries fluctuated from year to year and from place to place. Assuming, however, that the salaries from the seven schools for any one year amounted to £1,000, then over a nine-year period the Sisters' savings represented a substantial sum. But not a penny of this was used for their support, but was forwarded to a central fund which was to be used to pay lay teachers when the government subsidy was finally withdrawn, and to expand the schools.[68] The Sister at the head of the administration in All Hallows' usually purchased the site for a convent and the parish built convent and school.[69]

The nuns, then, did not support themselves through their salaries, and the resolution of the 1880 Synod to revert to school fees was difficult to implement, because fee-paying had been discontinued in government schools since 1869,[70] while children in Catholic parish schools had never been expected to pay.[71] During Synod proceedings, the bishop referred to middle schools and parochial schools. Housed in the same building, there was little difference between the children of the two, except that the middle schools were made up of middle-class children who could afford to pay fees. But during the years when the Sisters were salaried, the custom of paying fees had fallen into abeyance even for those who could pay, and was so difficult to revive that even by 1882 no fees came from St Stephen's school.

After the abolition of non-vested schools, the first convent to be opened was at Stanthorpe. As the school was not to be connected with the Board, the bishop decreed that the Stanthorpe parishioners should show others the way to meet the altered situation. This centre was to test the clerical theory that the Sisters would be better off than before.

But so discouraged was the convent Superior after a two years' struggle that she prayed to be relieved of her responsibility, because the buildings were wretched, inadequate and full of holes; each Sister taught two classes; no doctor was available for nuns requiring medical attention; there was 'not the slightest chance' that the people would exert themselves to provide the extra room needed;[72] and the pastor, Father Davadi, a mild Italian more interested in vine-growing than in building, was not the man to help.

The parishioners were unaware that the school fees did not even suffice to pay the pupil-teachers until, many years later, a threat to withdraw the Sisters from the district brought action to remedy the situation. In a vigorously worded letter, which Father Davadi was directed to read from the pulpit, Archbishop Dunne told the men of Stanthorpe how far £36 a year went towards the upkeep of the school. 'It appears very plain to me', he wrote, 'that the people for whose sole benefit the Sisters are in the place, should provide them with reasonable shelter.' The Mercy nuns were not a cloistered Order 'spending their time in personal prayer and devotion.' If the people for whom they worked gratuitously were not prepared to provide such shelter from the rain and frost as shearers enjoy in the wildest parts of Australia, the archbishop resolved that he would send them to a parish that would care for them.[73]

In his drive to shore up the tottering parochial finances Dunne blamed the Sisters almost as much as the laymen for not taking positive action; the Sisters were, he complained, 'too proud' to ask for fees from those who could afford to pay. For all five metropolitan parishes—the Valley, Kangaroo Point, South Brisbane, Red Hill and St Stephen's—were like Stanthorpe in that school fees fell short of the lay teachers' salaries, and the Parochial School Fund, drawn on for water-rates and running expenses as well, was never used for the Sisters' maintenance.

In a colony that was 'mad about music', as Mother Vincent often noted, the piano was more than a part of culture; it was the main means of subsistence for the nuns. Mother Vincent's earliest letters pleaded for more and more trained music-teachers. Mother Cecilia McAuliffe, who accompanied her from Dublin, had such a beautiful singing voice that she attracted to the cathedral Protestants as well as crowds of Catholics. Like later Sisters, she taught music to adults as well as schoolgirls. A music-Sister was regarded as essential for every school, for public concerts were a way of training children in poise, and a perennial source of funds.

Sister M. Claver, who had a first-class certificate from the Irish National Board and was also a gifted organist, preserved a pathetic note from the bishop: 'Dr. Mullen, I suppose you know, wants to get up an oratorio to pay the plumber', Quinn wrote. 'He and a few other gentlemen will sell tickets.'[74] It was literally true that the Sisters could not live without music.

Another means for convent maintenance was care of boarders. The small margin of profit from boarders' pensions helped with the living expenses of Sisters engaged in parochial schools. Thus All Hallows' supported all the nuns who taught in the other five metropolitan schools. 'It should not be so', Archbishop Dunne told Mother Vincent,[75] for he intended to make the parishes more able to depend on themselves. Mother Vincent was then endeavouring to pay for the first wing of the recently built school, after having finally paid off the £6,000 purchase money plus interest on the convent and grounds.[76]

She was thoroughly supported in her efforts by Dunne, who was well aware of her long struggle. 'You seem to have a semi-scruple', he remarked, 'about utilizing the public charity in bazaars, drawings, etc., for the building of All Hallows' School. I have none whatever. It is for me the greatest charity of all.'[77] For it supported not only the Sisters who resided there and taught elsewhere, but many a struggling country convent as well. Boarding schools elsewhere contributed according to their means to All Hallows' for the training of the novices of the Order.

Revenue from land might have provided a durable building fund if the first venture had proved successful. Mother Vincent hoped for a steady endowment for education from the Johnstone River sugar-cane farms during the 1880s. T. H. Fitzgerald, surveyor and engineer as well as parliamentarian, interested her in a project to grow and crush cane, and at the bishop's suggestion she and eight nuns took up 5,000 acres.[78] A benefactor living with the Sisters in All Hallows', Miss Florence O'Reilly, provided capital. But the rosy prospect of a future free from the necessity of organizing bazaars faded when disease struck the cane, and there was nothing for it but to sell the land. At £5 an acre it helped to tide the schools over the needs of the moment;[79] but it was a pity that the types of cane suited to Queensland had not been sufficiently studied.

When government subsidy was due to close, Catholics cast about desperately for other means of maintaining and extending the schools. They were supported by the *Telegraph* when in August 1879 they boldly put forward the idea of payment by results. 'According to this method,' the bishop's journal declared, 'while no creed is subsidised, each section of the community receives equal assistance with others, according to ascertained results [by government inspection] of secular teaching.'[80]

The idea was the basis of a series of meetings between the Sisters of Mercy and the Christian Brothers, to discuss the kind of action required 'to obtain for Catholics a just share of the State grant for education.'[81] The notion stemmed from the practice adopted a short time before in Ireland with the introduction of the intermediate examination. It was aired in the press, it was put forward confidently by Quinn at a meeting of 2,000 Catholics on the occasion of the opening of Gregory Terrace College, where influential men were present, including Dr K. I. O'Doherty, M.L.A., J. M. Macrossan, Minister for Public Works, Patrick Perkins, Minister for Lands, and a number of others.[82] But nothing came of it.

The Nudgee Home for Children was set up as a public charity but, despite the small government per capita grants, the nuns had insufficient from public money to pay even for the orphans' food. When they applied the pension from paying boarders for this purpose, Dunne was angry. With what funds then, he asked heatedly, were they to build, or repair existing buildings, or care for a sick Sister or bury her? 'Sir Samuel Griffith or Sir Thomas McIlwraith', he scolded, 'might as well take public money and build a hospital on the Volga' and be as reasonable as the Reverend Mother when she gave away what was intended for the corporal and spiritual maintenance of the Sisters to 'suck the very life-blood out of the unfortunate community'.[83] Public charities, he told them, were to be maintained by public appeals.

It had always been Mother Vincent's wish to free herself as much as possible from the material needs of the works of the Church. She longed to be able to pass over to another with a gift and taste for administration the minutiae which diverted her attention from the more spiritual care of children and parents. Thus, on arrival in Queensland she enlisted the help of capable laymen. A letter in the 1865 *Queensland Times* showed that through three trustees, leading Ipswich Catholics, the Ipswich convent funds had been lodged in the Bank of Queensland. 'According to the rules for all our charitable institutions', said the Sister's letter, a statement of receipts and expenses was to be published through these trustees.[84] If that practice had been continued, it would have avoided a situation so embarrassing for the men of Stanthorpe who were reproached for not knowing what they could not well have known, the state of the school finances.

However, the bishop felt bound to take warning from trustee troubles in the American Church, and in 1866 he limited the action of laymen. 'The suggestion of the committee considered in itself seemed to me prudent, but', he argued, 'having given that subject mature consideration before nominating trustees, I deemed it better to pursue the ordinary course, and to confine the trust to the members of the [religious] community.'[85] That decision gave Mother Vincent the heavy responsibility of raising funds.

She had the consolation of the support of the nameless thousands who kept their schools going week by week. Whenever she announced a new project, there were men and women who at once, unbidden, sent help for it, since Sisters and people were in tune and in sympathy, and there was neither caste nor class distinction. The workers and the poor became thoroughly identified with their Church through their schools.

The difficulty of attracting teachers to nineteenth-century Queensland was proportionate to the distance from Ireland and England and the expense of the long voyage, as Dr R. Whitty recognized while recruiting teachers for Mother Vincent in England.[86] Having attracted them the problem was to keep them despite a fluid population and pioneering circumstances. Bolton points out that Queensland showed a 'high turnover' even in the ministry in all denominations. Thus Herberton had thirteen Anglican rectors in fourteen years.[87] Teachers tended to move about even more, and Mother Vincent found that even many Sisters returned.

Yet England and even more so Ireland remained her chief source of supply for nuns and lay teachers. Professed Sisters who volunteered for Queensland were often allowed to transfer the dowry they had paid on entering the convent.[88] Nuns always travelled cabin class, for which the fare was £50.[89] Even though assisted migrants could come for about half that cost and the Queensland government paid them a subsidy of about fourteen guineas,[90] lay teachers too disliked the lack of privacy in the barn-like sleeping quarters where a rail only 1 foot high separated family from family. Though the *Congregation de Fide* and private benefactors overseas helped to finance the passages of staff for the schools, the expense to All Hallows' may be gauged by the figures for 1879–80. During those years fifty-nine Sisters came to Brisbane at a total cost of £3,757.[91]

On a recruiting tour 1870–2, Mother Vincent made arrangements with Irish and English training colleges and novitiates for the reception and training of girls for Brisbane. Her personal sway and her method of providing a constant flow of Sisters were illustrated in her visit to Tralee. Here she was in the territory of her old friend, Bishop David Moriarty of Kerry. The Annals of St John's record her visit.

> All the Sisters were delighted to meet her, especially those who had known her in Baggot Street convent. One could not but see the impress of the perfect nun portrayed on her calm features. She looked as if nothing could now disturb the inward peace of a heart over which the storms of passion could never have any influence.

Mother Vincent told the Kerry nuns about Queensland 'with interest and love', asked for volunteers, and proposed that a basket should be hung before the statue of the Mother of God to receive the names. The results were gratifying, for 'on the following morning fifteen billets were found in the basket'. In the interests of his own diocese, however, Moriarty, generous as he was, had to limit the number of recruits to three.

Mother Vincent was as deeply impressed with the spirit of St John's as its nuns were with her, and she arranged to send future postulants to their excellent training centre. 'In the course of five years, thirteen subjects for the Brisbane mission were trained and despatched from St. John's to far-distant Australia.'[92] The arrangement continued during Mother Vincent's lifetime, as did a similar agreement with Newtownforbes.

From England less help was expected or received, since the convents there had their own gigantic problem of meeting the needs of an expanding Catholic population. Nevertheless Mother Vincent's old friend, Mother Liguori Gibson of Liverpool, provided some English and Scottish postulants. Mother Vincent also sought help from Sister M. of St Philip Lescher, who in 1856 had founded the Notre Dame Training College at Mount Pleasant, Liverpool, and Brisbane received a promise of future postulants and teachers.[93] In the All Hallows' archives rest parchments from the Irish National Board and the English Privy Council of Education; some of these classification and testimonial papers bear the signature of a man who returned to England after he had been for some time the stormy petrel of New South Wales educational politics, the 'most illiberal liberal', Robert Lowe.

When Sisters entered All Hallows' without previous teacher training, they studied and took examinations, under the guidance of veterans, according to the Queensland system. Mr J. W. Long, the well-known headmaster of St James's (a model school for boys training for the non-vested system)[94] was their mentor for many years. With a first-class certificate from the Irish National Board, Long was held in high esteem by the Queensland Board and by Chief Inspector Randal McDonnell.[95]

While he prepared Sisters in All Hallows', however, others studied in the branch convents through the pupil-teacher method. Only the Sister in charge of a school required a teacher's certificate,[96] but most were not worried by the reasonable Departmental requirements, and the qualification of a certificate was general.

Lay teachers brought out by the diocese needed a certificate, and were salaried according to classification, but on a lower scale than the government schools.[97] In Catholic schools not under the Board, men received £100 to £120 a year,[98] and women up to £110.[99] Thus a young woman, Miss A. O'Byrne, who taught for some time at Nudgee Home, with a classification of 'second of third' from the Irish National Board, and teaching experience in England where she received a certificate of the same rank, received '£80 a year plus £29 compensation fees'. The bishop described her accomplishments, typical of the time. 'She plays the harmonium and piano fairly well and teaches Hullah's system of singing well. She is very agreeable, industrious and painstaking. She is twenty-three years of age.'[1]

Meanwhile, All Hallows' included a model school for training lay teachers. Dean Henri Brun of Ipswich, whose parish extended to the foot of the Darling Range on the one side and to the Gympie border on the other, Dean Charles Murlay of Rockhampton, with as extensive a territory, Père P. Bucas of Bowen—priests everywhere depended mainly on convent-trained girls for their schools in outlying areas. An 1867 memorandum concerning All Hallows' shows that even then the school was concerned with more than music and art, that the course of studies was 'as solid and extensive, and at the same time as practical and useful as possible.'[2]

Mother Vincent had selected as staff Sisters who had studied the Irish National and English Privy Council Systems of education, and they adopted 'the best advice they can procure and all modern improvements which come within their reach.' The full course of studies provided by the staff involved examinations conducted under the direction of the head inspector of the Board of General Education, which accepted that

> the Sisters regard the Teacher's Certificate as the best proof that can be given of the pupils' success in the various branches of

> education. They also regard it as advantageous to the pupils as it qualifies them to take charge of schools under the Board of Education should they hereafter find themselves called upon to do so.[3]

Here we have two clearly stated motives: the first, to set a goal for colonial girls unaccustomed to strenuous academic effort; the second, to provide a profession in case of need, and a means of social mobility for poorer families. The requirements for a second class certificate included Latin, ancient and British history, geometry and algebra, as well as school management, arithmetic and geography. The first-class certificate included English literature and a modern language.[4] Boulogne-reared Sister M. Claver and Sister M. Antonia Kendrick, educated in Liege and Cologne, and according to Dunne 'perfect at French and German',[5] were valued members of the staff in Mother Vincent's time.

Inspector R. G. Anderson 'spoke warmly' of the girls trained in All Hallows'.[6] The non-vested school files bear further testimony, such as the following comment on Lucy Lalor, typical of many:

> The writer left the service in December 1876 to become a nun. Had she remained in the service she would ere this have been recommended for the position of first Assistant in a state school, her attainments, status and success as a teacher warranting such promotion.[7]

The magnet of better salary naturally attracted many teachers from the non-vested to the government schools, to such a degree that the numbers of Catholics in the state service brought a growl from the *Queensland Evangelical Standard*.[8] That the percentage was disproportionate can be concluded from the figures collected by A. H. Palmer. No fewer than 'fifty-five Headteachers and fifty-seven Assistant teachers in the State Schools' were Roman Catholics, i.e., 25 per cent of the first group and 30 per cent of the second group.[9]

The drift to government schools represented a certain loss of labour and expense to Mother Vincent and her community, yet they did not demur about a move so obviously to the social and economic advantage of their protégées. Their departure, however, left her with a critical problem on her hands. How was she to meet Dunne's demand to employ more secular teachers and save the nuns? The ideal, according to him, was to have two supervisory school Sisters and one music-nun to each centre, under whom lay teachers taught most classes.[10] To spread the Sisters' work more broadly and so extend their schools was his aim. Refusal to employ more lay teachers was, he claimed, 'killing the individual nuns and killing the Catholic school organization too'.[11] But Mother Vincent found this dilemma beyond solution.

Her schools were confronted by the same problems that militated against high scholastic standards in all colonies, in state and independent schools, though perhaps less noticeably in more urban and opulent areas. In raw pioneering conditions it was possible to rise economically and socially without schooling. An Ipswich self-made man could boast, 'I have never had a day's schooling in my life, and I can show ten pounds for every shilling that some of these cleverly educated men have got . . . We want men that have made money and got property in the town, and a little commonsense—never mind the learning.'[12]

The general body of Catholic working-class society were not affected by this crass acquisitiveness, but were apathetic about education beyond the rudiments. Alan Barcan, describing conditions in New South Wales, maintains that they were less concerned with education as such than any other denomination, and that free selectors as well as workers in mines and towns preferred to keep the children at home for their labour rather than send them to school.[13]

Another attitude tending to make for low standards is alluded to by Geoffrey Blainey who, in discussing educational problems in early Australia generally, claims that the persistent dearth of women in rural areas flavoured society in countless ways, one of them being the growth of the concept of mateship inimical to educational improvement. Mateship regarded the ambition to rise above one's station as treachery to friends. Men should be loyal to the companions with whom they worked and lived and not seek to break away from the class. Blainey concludes that 'in the equalitarian bushman's society of the nineteenth century, education was often seen as a form of snobbery and a way of social advancement which broke up the camaraderie of working men.'[14]

The attitudes of society were reflected in education, more especially in the education of boys. Yet there was one further reason to explain why male education was the Achilles' heel of the Catholic system in Queensland, the absence of a religious Order of men until the Christian Brothers came in 1875. Even then it was many years before the Brothers could establish a boarding school to accommodate a few wealthy Catholics able to benefit from a full secondary education. Sisters were restricted in their intake of boys by both civil and religious authority. In the non-vested schools, boys on attaining the age of eight were 'not to remain with the girls and infants', the Education Department directed, but were to attend the boys' school.[15] In other convent schools such as Townsville, boys remained until the completion of their primary schooling, at twelve years.[16] Thus the Sisters reached comparatively few through elementary education.

For secondary education before the Brothers came the Sisters thought of an unconventional beginning for boys. They asked Quinn's permission to set aside a room at All Hallows' for a civil service class.[17] Mother Vincent's Sisters from the 1860s had engaged male teachers for art, German, gymnastics, and choral singing. The nuns wished to permit boys as well as girls to have the advantage of their teaching. But the plan did not meet the bishop's approval. He held rather strict ideas concerning enclosure for nuns, which he only gradually modified to meet Queensland's circumstances. For several years he pertinaciously refused to allow them to raise funds by bazaars, which would involve them with the public.[18] They might not have a picnic outside school grounds, nor might they allow men to sing in their choirs in church. To teach boys in their teens was likewise against the bishop's notion of cloister. On Dunne's accession to the episcopacy, the petition was renewed. But he was no more receptive to the idea than Quinn, and even refused a request for 'men from the army' to conduct school drill classes.[19]

As late as 1893, Brother J. J. Barrett, Superior of the Christian Brothers, worried about the lag in male education. His Brothers were still so few that there were only 1,260 out of a total of 8,000 Catholic boys of school age receiving a Catholic education. Appealing for help to the home country, he wrote: 'But for the work of the Sisters of Mercy, it is to be feared that Catholicity—at least Catholic education (and are not the two practically the same?) would be but a shadow in this colony.'[20] The nuns were then teaching 6,200 girls and infants, 'or about sixty percent of those Catholics in Queensland.'[21] However, at the time, Mother Vincent and her nuns could do nothing to bring secondary education to boys.

But at least Mother Vincent was fortunate in that the pupil–teacher ratio remained reasonable in her classes, since in no one place was there a dense concentration of Catholic population. For instance in the year of her death, 1892, there were 130 Catholic teachers in Brisbane for a total enrolment of 3,434, giving an average of 26.42 pupils per teacher. Numbers in country schools were no larger.

With small classes, the pastoral care of the Sisters was at its best. Concern for and understanding of the pupils was directed above all towards assisting them to realize those qualities most valued in good women and good mothers. They were encouraged to *become* such, rather than to fulfil a set of requirements; the curriculum was an aid, not a master.

Academic standards in the nineteenth-century state or convent schools were the minimum normally needed for economic and social advancement. There is no evidence to prove that, except in the secondary field, Catholic teachers showed more initiative or were less dependent on rule and precedent than state-school teachers. Yet the struggle of the 1870s had left an aftermath of watchful rivalry between the two systems. It was a serious but, in retrospect, comical case of the pot and the kettle. The government schools had the advantage of commanding the purse strings, and Catholics whistled in the dark and told themselves that money was not the key to scholarship.

Bearing in mind the frequent press taunts that Catholic schools concentrated on 'frills' such as 'petitpoint and flowers on silk', the *Australian* proclaimed that 'familiarity with state education in its mature development had failed to establish it as the one thing needful to make a nation great, virtuous and happy.'[22] Further, the paper charged that the state's claim to offer universal education was a hollow boast; in many places children were not provided with the bare rudiments, and even in towns there was lack of accommodation. In the best metropolitan state schools, 'your children at twelve to fourteen, the age at which they quit public schools to fend for themselves, are able to read their mother tongue very indifferently. Correct English they cannot write.' Their arithmetic and geography were poor, history was not taught.[23] It must be admitted that arithmetic in the Sisters' schools was also chronically weak. The schoolrooms were often too small for the size of the class. But the prestige lost through such deficiencies was regained through school tone and proficiency elsewhere.

Mother Vincent did not allow the Queensland state schools to be the sole criterion for hers. On several occasions she went south to Sydney and Melbourne on inspection tours. Overseas, she gained insight into the way the Forster law was affecting English education. She also discussed school systems with visitors to

Queensland, and gained fresh ideas from the Sisters trained in overseas colleges and novitiates. Thus she did much to counteract the harmful effect of an inbred and isolated system.

A few years before her death, she received a high tribute from the man who had at one time been the greatest foe of her schools—Robert Dunne. After he had visited, in company with an inspector of the Victorian Education Department, the main schools of Paris and its environs (avoiding the convents) and had also seen many English schools, 280 in all,[24] he told Mother Vincent that her primary schools were 'not surpassed under any administration or in any country on the face of the earth.'[25] He had in mind scholastic standards, but he could have been prejudiced by his growing affection for All Hallows' and its associations, 'that shrine of all goodness', which he found hard to leave even for a short visit to Europe. 'God bless and keep All Hallows'. I'll never, *Deo volente,* come away from it again.'[26]

More impersonally, the *Courier* a couple of years earlier bore high testimony to the Mercy Sisters' teaching. It regularly published the gradings of state and independent schools, which were run on the same lines, inspected by the same government inspectors, and reported on the same form.[27] An 1887 issue placed a Catholic school at the head of the list of the metropolitan state and non-state schools, and eight of the eleven Catholic schools ranked among the top twelve.[28] As this was not an isolated success, it was a striking proof of the validity of the dual system.

Mother Vincent had worked indefatigably to lay the foundations well. She was no genius, no profound thinker, no striking theorist. Though she lived with and for education, and tackled its problems with rare courage and pertinacity, she was a pioneer rather than a perfectionist. Yet if Queensland's vastness proved so overwhelming that she could reach only 60 per cent of its Catholic schoolgirls, if chronic shortage of funds and teachers distracted her from her central task, if primitive conditions imposed grave cultural limitations, it is still true that her schools emerged from crisis after crisis able to hold their own. Mother Vincent had the solid support of most Queenslanders in her work, or she could not have seen 222 Sisters caring for twenty-six schools and institutions[29] with 6,254 schoolchildren at the end of her thirty-year life-span in the colony.

Her achievement represented no small measure of conquest of the obstacles of time and place. She shrank from considering the victory uniquely hers: rather she considered that it belonged equally to all who participated with her. For the secret which she passed on to the Sisters to lead the children upwards, she herself first applied to her colleagues and friends. It was to find the talent that God had given to each one, foster it, and through it draw them to God. Translated into everyday schoolroom practice, this meant that love would make children progress quickly where restraint would kill.

The women whom Mother Vincent had taught were impressed with a dimension beyond the statistical or the academic. Her 'unbounded charity . . . untiring exertions and self-sacrificing pains' were 'a labour of love with her' for the children of Queensland.[30]

4

EPISCOPAL CONTROL: FIRST PHASE

Bishop Goold of Melbourne held that Quinn had been 'inoculated with strange views' on state aid and education.[1] Mother Vincent only complied with Quinn's wish to connect her schools with the Board because, like him, she set a high value on social harmony and saw the schools as a way of breaking down prejudice and winning Protestant friends. As a bishop, he had a measure of control over education, but neither the Sisters of St Joseph who began teaching in Queensland in 1870 nor the Christian Brothers who came five years later, would assent to his wish for co-ordination with the government schools.

Thus Mother Vincent was prepared to agree with Quinn up to a point. Occasionally, however, principle made it impossible for her to give way. Her greatest difficulty with the bishop arose from their different attitude to authority, how she should exercise it in her community, and how far he should control her and her community. They both sought the same end, active and fervent service of God in harmony within the Church and in alliance with non-Catholic men of good will. They differed on the means.

For the bishop believed that 'there must be one head for success in all undertakings',[2] one policy-maker, to whom obedience was due as to a monarch, an unswerving obedience in the spirit of the Light Brigade. He was a bishop of the Church, deriving his strength from the certitude of a mission high and sacred. His zeal for the episcopal office was intended to vindicate the Bishop of Rome, soon to be despoiled of his temporal power: 'I hope the respect shown to the Church in the unworthy person of the Bishop of this diocese, without any external possessions or official insignia, will be a consolation to the Holy See', he wrote to a member of the Vatican Curia.[3]

A man and an idea. A sacred concept and a fallible human being. It was not to satisfy personal vanity but to bring honour to the Church that he set great store on protocol and precedence, on approval from social notabilities for his undertakings, in the form of laudatory speeches, addresses and testimonials. In democratic Australia, spiritual and temporal powers had been too recently separated for either to feel sure of itself. It took time for the idea to crystallize that the Church has a right to live freely in the world, and that the world has a right to live its own life. In this uncertainty over roles, Bishop Quinn guarded too closely episcopal rights.

His obsession was shown quite early in an incident at Ipswich. A few days after her arrival in Queensland, Mother Vincent received a citizens' delegation requesting a few teaching Sisters.[4] The Ipswich Catholics offered to provide a convent, for which they had collected over £1,000. The bishop, however, desired to control all diocesan finances, and asked Father McGinty, who had been resident in Ipswich for ten years, to have his trustees hand over the sum collected along with monies destined for other parish purposes.[5] This was the episcopal prerogative, but the manner in which Quinn imposed his will embroiled him in a protracted quarrel with priest and laymen.

Fresh to Queensland, the bishop had yet to learn the fighting style of Ipswich, where many of John Dunmore Lang's radical and energetic migrants had settled. With great zest and energy these Evangelicals threw themselves into the anti-squatter campaign, and when in 1860 Tufnell arrived as first Anglican bishop, they greeted him with noisy public meetings where they sought to teach him to adapt democracy to running his Church.[6] The many Ipswich Catholics could not fail to be affected by such radicalism and independence, and the Ipswich press, controlled by Evangelicals, naturally took Father W. McGinty's side against the bishop.

Catholic excitement was exacerbated by the character and position of the lay trustees, Patrick O'Sullivan and, to a lesser extent, Christopher Gorry (who later became an alderman). O'Sullivan, a Kerryman, was Queensland's first Catholic member of parliament, and belonged to the long tradition of Irish laymen who had exercised responsibility for the welfare of the Church, like the Irish 'erenaghs' of old,[7] where priests could not. His was the lone voice in parliament upholding Catholic education before the bishop's arrival. A worthy man and a witty speaker, he kept independent as a 'friend of Ministers and private members alike, and had a strong aversion to leaning up against anyone or anything.'[8]

Sir George Bowen

Sir Charles Lilley

Sir Samuel Griffith

Cardinal Moran and Archbishop Dunne

In the McGinty dispute, O'Sullivan held that funds collected for a specific parish purpose, particularly as Protestants were generous donors, should be left in the parish and, with a touch of borrowed Evangelical aggressiveness, he snorted at 'new chum priests who attempted to interfere with the civil liberties of their flocks.'[9] The situation called for tact, flexibility, and lightness of touch. Quinn flatly replied that his was the whole responsibility for the good government of his diocese. Prayerfully and with the advice of his clergy he would regulate ecclesiastical affairs. He told his people to pray that he might be guided by divine counsel, then leave him to his task.[10] Confronted by Bishop Tufnell the year before, Anglican laymen had repudiated this 'pray and pay' role. Now Patrick O'Sullivan reinforced his argument by appealing to the layman's responsibility in the troublous Irish penal centuries.

Rational discussion of the Ipswich affair was impossible because of McGinty's defiance and the strong-arm tactics of Father Scully, a Vincentian whom the bishop appointed his temporary Vicar-General. Once Quinn had made his decision he as bishop had a right to obedience from priest and flock. His was a high and magnificent design, the simultaneous establishment of the Church throughout the vast colony of Queensland. The vision of the Ipswich disputants did not extend beyond their own town, but McGinty should have understood that he had no right to earmark funds for local purposes before a just provision had been made for the diocese. Quinn was in the unenviable position of being responsible for Church extension without the help of the only parish outside Brisbane; and the Brisbane church was already encumbered with a £1,000 debt incurred before his arrival. His mistake lay in ignoring local opinion and in the old appeal to the secular arm; as Polding said, he was 'right in the main, but wrong in the manner'.

Quinn disciplined McGinty by having parliament stop the subsidy which the priests had been receiving under the 1836 Church Act; and he publicly suspended him. He then required the lay trustees to sign over the parish money. Characteristically, Quinn identified his human judgment with his ecclesiastical office. 'I am a sacred person', he declared. 'I have been ordained and received the Holy Ghost; anyone attacking my character commits a most gross and sacriligious act.'[11] After his suspension at Ipswich, McGinty served in the north until his death in 1871. O'Sullivan and Gorry apologized, and as a peace-offering the bishop presented the M.L.A. with two volumes of Irish history.[12]

The press of the day, 'completely under the control of the Protestant sects',[13] found fair game in the bishop. His every word came under its scrutiny and judgment. Thus the various journals took an extraordinary interest in the Ipswich affair, the grammar-school controversy, the Queensland immigration scheme, claims for Catholic primary education, Quinn's alleged speculation in land, his purchase of the *North Australian*, factionalism both clerical and lay, and Quinn's later clashes with the Sisters of St Joseph.

But of his differences with the Sisters of Mercy there was never a word. Suttor, reading through the back files, concluded that 'with Quinn, who had been their confessor for years past in Dublin, these nuns had a sort of deep unspoken understanding that their Sisters did not enjoy under Brady and Serra, or even Goold and Polding.'[14] With the full sources before him, he might well have continued the Shakespearean analogies of the early chapters of his book. For the tale of Quinn's relationship with his nuns was one of conflict, through which Mother Vincent Whitty remained loyal to her bishop despite every provocation to defy him.

Yet, when the full truth is known, it must be concluded that she had more cause than any other for disquiet, recrimination, and even withdrawal from Queensland.

Two very different concepts of spiritual leadership caused the tension in the first phase of relationships between Mother Vincent and Quinn. How authoritarian should a superior be? To what extent could episcopal control order conventual arrangements and supersede the Rule of the foundress, Catherine McAuley? To these questions the Reverend Mother of the Mercy Sisters and her ecclesiastical superior had different answers.

An autocrat is supremely self-righteous. Mother Vincent, however, was conscious of her many limitations as Mother Superior, a position of considerable power in the Mercy Order. Repeatedly she declared that one Sister or another would have made a better Reverend Mother than she, a better supervisor of schools, a more inspired guide to the young, or a more competent teacher. Further, she often requested that other Sisters might be sent out to relieve her of the many duties which diffused her energies.

But Mother Vincent's declarations implied no lack of confidence in 'the strength of God's arm' to aid her, and she was determined to do the task assigned. Indeed, the many Sisters who were to join the Order in Brisbane found her an ideal Mother Superior; not only was her experience impressive, but there was a remarkable directness and simplicity in her spiritual approach. A good listener, Mother Vincent drew people easily into conversation and gave them her full attention, encouraging them with a quiet informality, eschewing the note of authority.

On the other hand, the bishop believed that Mother Vincent's relationship with her Sisters should parallel his own with the parish clergy and the people generally. In his view, she should be aloof and polite, impose strict order and discipline, and exact obedience to the last detail. But such autocracy was not for Mother Vincent. Living in community, she best exemplified her unspoken theory of authority in intimate companionship, where the problems of daily life were shared, along with news, views, and laughter. Mother Vincent's influence was a strength of presence rather than a power which dominated and controlled. She lived *with* rather than above her Sisters, making no pretence to play the central presiding figure except on such ceremonial occasions as prayer in choir, or in giving the necessary orders for stable community life. Co-worker and Sister, Mother Vincent set an example of efficiency in the task in hand, but then at the evening recreation she cast off authority and was happy with the young.

The nuns' sincerity of love for her transcended the sentimental Victorian phrases in which it was expressed, and emerged too in the Gaelic idiom of this phrase—'Oh how she did work . . . without food or rest, and then the lovely sweet face of her in the evening.'[15] When all foregathered for recreation at dusk, Mother Vincent would invite Sister M. Cecilia McAuliffe to sing for them arias from the operas or folk songs, and she herself would often play the piano.

Nevertheless, when carelessness or negligence had to be rebuked, Mother Vincent did not shirk her duty. Nor did the dire need in Queensland for more Sisters ever diminish her selectivity. In explaining the dismissal of Sister Jane Townsend, Mother Vincent declared her readiness to suffer any privation rather than 'receive a Sister without a genuine religious spirit'.[16] Her outward mildness held a strength to guide which had to be experienced to be understood. 'Father Byrne thinks you have the kindest and mildest of hearts', wrote a Sister who had benefited by her counsel. 'He thinks you can't give a good scolding at all, but I'll never forget one you gave me—it terrified me.'[17] A few hours later,

Mother Vincent sought the chastened Sister to enquire, 'Well, dear, how are you now?' and to dispel any trace of hurt or resentment.

Such methods, in Quinn's eyes, betokened weakness and ineffectiveness. To be strong was to be stern; to exercise authority was to demand obedience. Incontrovertible proof of Mother Vincent's failure was the departure within eighteen months after arrival of Sister M. Catherine Morgan, the English Sister who had joined Mother Vincent's group in England. By alleging lack of strict discipline under Mother Vincent's regime to explain her departure from Queensland, Sister M. Catherine gave Quinn a trump card to justify a course of action that accorded well with his deepest wishes. To Archbishop Cullen, to the Baggot Street mother house, and to Mother Vincent's Liverpool friends, he could quote Sister M. Catherine when he demoted Mother Vincent in order to rule in her stead.

Mother Vincent interpreted Sister M. Catherine's motives for leaving in a very different light. Aware that the English nun had held the position of Bursar in Liverpool, Mother Vincent had planned to send her to establish the new foundation in Ipswich with the help of Sisters from Hull and elsewhere in Britain, believing that the expected arrivals would feel happiest under an English superior.[18]

However, the health and temperament of Sister M. Catherine aborted this plan. She was unsuited to raw missionary conditions, whilst bouts of illness kept her away from school. The cramped cottage at St Stephen's, the bustle and noise from the church-goers milling around in the yard, the constant proximity of romping children, the pressure of work on every Sister, made Sister M. Catherine long for the ordered ways of old-established houses. She was, in fact, emotionally unstable, a condition that could be only accentuated in the colonies.

Mother Vincent felt compassion for Sister M. Catherine, but no bitterness, when in September 1862 the English Sister travelled south. Her words show misgiving, but also a scrupulous desire to be fair. 'She has many good points,' Mother Vincent wrote to Dublin, 'but I did not know her ways, that is all. God is the best judge of everything, and she may yet do great things for Him in Australia.'[19]

Mother Vincent was not one to damn with faint praise, and events were to prove that Sister M. Catherine's quest for the perfect life was foredoomed to failure. It is more than likely that

Quinn also perceived her weakness, but it suited him to use her departure from Brisbane to discredit Mother Vincent Whitty and assume the authority of Superior himself.

Not that relations between the Reverend Mother and the bishop were always, or even often, hostile, for in both temporal and spiritual matters, Mother Vincent was grateful for the bishop's guidance. Far from being aggressive or self-assertive, she looked to him with trust and respect as the Sisters' only protection in the sometimes hostile environment of Brisbane in the 1860s. Thus when the *Queensland Guardian* concocted a fine story about nuns in politics,[20] the bishop's paper rushed to defend them from this 'unjust and unmanly' attack. Accusing the *Guardian* of being the government organ, the *North Australian* asked rhetorically what reason or foundation there was 'for thus dragging from their religious seclusion into the arena of politics these devoted Ladies, who renouncing home, family and friends, have given themselves to the service of the poor, and waste the oil of life in feeding the lamp of charity?'[21]

Mother Vincent also agreed to the bishop's request for the Sisters' land-orders (then available to all who paid their passage to Queensland) so that he could acquire a substantial block. Thus, up to a point the two were in complete accord and Mother Vincent did not object to administrative control.

However, when Quinn attempted to go farther and intrude upon the Constitutions of the Order, Mother Vincent could not but contest the degree of authority he desired. For she was the duly-appointed custodian of the Rule of Life to be observed by the Sisters of Mercy in Queensland; and she held in reverential awe the written word of the Constitutions concerning the novitiate. Postulants had a six-month apprenticeship before they were allowed to receive the white veil of the novice. Then they had to complete two years in a novitiate before pronouncing the vows. Emily Conlan, a postulant on board the *Donald McKay*, was known to the bishop, her spiritual director in Dublin for some years, as a pious and intelligent young woman. Shipboard life is hardly an ideal novitiate training, but the bishop decided to waive the normal canon law, and give her the veil then and there, and the name Sister Mary Bridget.

In explaining this strange event, Mother Vincent said that the bishop had implied that the Dublin Reverend Mother agreed to such a move before the party left Ireland. Quinn was apparently mistaken in assuming such consent, and when he later curtailed the two years' novitiate of Sister Bridget, Dublin sent a sharp remonstrance to Mother Vincent. In her reply she quoted the psalmist, that 'to be without correction is the most deplorable of all afflictions', and thanked her monitor with sincere humility. But she showed also how unavailing had been her protests to Quinn, since he had invoked a point in the Constitutions never very clearly defined, namely that until there were seven professed in Community the bishop had a greater voice in internal arrangements.[22]

There followed an earnest request from Mother Vincent for more Sisters. However, Dublin had many commitments, and Brisbane was not under its jurisdiction, the foundress of the Mercy nuns having expanded her Order on the basis of a loose federation rather than a tight central control. Thus, the Queensland Community of Mercy was bound to Dublin only by ties of affection and loyalty, and by the common Rule and interests, but not by any legal bond. Dublin could therefore only deplore infringements of the Constitutions; but it had no means of enforcing observance of the compact between bishops and the foundress. Hence in Queensland, Mother Vincent had to strive alone to preserve the Rule of her religious Order.

By 1863 she had a community of eleven Sisters, but only four had made their vows.[23] However, as her efforts to increase to seven the number of professed from the home convents did not succeed, the bishop once again seized the initiative and nominated three councillors to Mother Vincent; Sister M. Benedict was to be her Assistant (second in command), Sister M. Cecilia Bursar, and Sister M. Bridget Conlan Mistress of Novices. Thus the shipboard novice who could say, 'I had no Novice-Mistress but a very strict Novice-Master'[24] and who never had a chance to imbibe the Mercy spirit, was placed in the position of guide of the new members.

'If you were surprised at her Profession, you will be doubly surprised at her getting the novices so soon after it', Mother Vincent wrote.[25] She was disturbed, Mother Vincent told Dublin, by Sister M. Bridget's lack of knowledge of the Rule and of the basic ideals of religious life. Nevertheless, Mother Vincent hastened to point out what the bishop found valuable in his choice: Sister M. Bridget was 'the most punctual religious' she had ever met, 'extremely pious and orderly, with a great love for religious discipline.'[26] Brave as were these words, Mother Vincent felt anxiety for the impressionable novices,[27] for now through Mother Bridget the bishop would be able to channel his own interpretation of authority, which would involve control, conformity, and the suspension of initiative and freedom.

Charged with guiding her community according to the traditions and spirit of the congregation, Mother Vincent could not but feel ill at ease with another new arrangement; for while Quinn could influence the novices through Mother Bridget, he later tried to reach others through the confessional. As their bishop in Brisbane, his assumption of the duties of sole confessor to the nuns gave just grounds for complaint; not only was it against the Constitutions of the Order, it was also against canon law itself.[28]

The fact was that after his experience with Père Cusse, the bishop would trust nobody else to act in the capacity of community confessor. René Cusse, 'a saintly old French priest',[29] had officiated as confessor after the arrival of the missionary party. One of the three Augustinians of the Assumption who had accompanied Quinn to Brisbane, he remained only a year, at the end of which he joined forces with a faction hostile to Quinn, centre of which was McGinty of Ipswich, and he forwarded a complaint to Rome about Quinn's paper, the *North Australian*.

The bishop lodged a counter-complaint against Cusse, charging that he had 'refused to obey'.[30] Cusse left Queensland in mid-1862, and was appointed parish priest of Newcastle by Archbishop Polding, who received him with open arms.[31] When Sister M. Catherine Morgan left for Sydney two months later, Quinn decided that the Sisters should have no further contact with dissident priests, and took over their spiritual guidance completely.

This placed Mother Vincent in an anxious and perplexing situation[32] which, as she well knew, could jeopardize freedom of conscience for herself and her charges. Young and intense, Mother Cecilia immediately protested. Privately to Mother Vincent she declared that the bishop was inconsistent in stressing the value of the sacrament, while refusing her request for a different confessor on the ground that no other was available, when to her knowledge there were then in Brisbane at least two priests.

When Mother Cecilia refused to present herself to the bishop as her confessor, Quinn blamed Mother Vincent for not compelling her to do so, and bade her command Mother Cecilia to come 'in virtue of holy obedience'. This is a grave formula, scarcely ever used, for it demands compliance under pain of sin, whereas the ideal is obedience freely given as a voluntary act of worship.

Mother Vincent told the Sister that she was passing on the bishop's message, and would leave the rest to her. In reply, Mother Cecilia conceded that she would see him in the parlour, but not as confessor, since she believed that he had no power to give such a command, in proof of which she pointed to chapter 11 of her Rule Book.[33]

By such methods, Quinn in effect drove a wedge between Mother Vincent and her Sisters. She was increasingly estranged from her old Dublin companions, Mothers Benedict and Cecilia, her strength and comfort in the first years of the mission,[34] and she would align herself neither on their side against the bishop, nor on the bishop's side against them. Her impartiality provoked Mother Benedict to accuse her of 'acting a part'.[35] Only Mother Vincent's brother, Dr Whitty, gauged something of her anguish. 'You remember my telling you that you went out to suffer as well as to do', he consoled. 'And I mentioned one sort of mental suffering and perplexity from which you said you shrank, and yet perhaps this is the very cross God had selected for you.'[36]

In her mental and spiritual isolation, Mother Vincent sought strength in meditation before the Blessed Sacrament, where Christ's divinity lay concealed, just as it was hidden in his human form, a theme which she found developed in Abbé Boudon's *Vie Cachée en Dieu*. If the person of Christ lay mostly undiscovered, she reflected, may not the same mystery recur in his followers? May not there be an inwardness in each which it is impossible to reveal?

Her reflections gave her the faith to endure her relations with the bishop. Though she said of him, 'I think it is his way never to be satisfied with Superiors or their doings',[37] she could still recognize in him a quality of greatness; 'He is certainly a most holy man. The life he leads out here is wonderful, so rigid and regular.' His surface blemishes, his grumbling, she could understand, but not his inexplicable demand for control of the Sisters' lives. She could only strive to protect the freedom of her nuns and the integrity of the Rule. When rebuffed, she told her Dublin friends that though he was 'not oversweet in words', she intended to 'go on and not mind anyone's sayings'. In profound faith she sought God's plan behind all mystery, resolving to meet the incomprehensible with 'forgiving love, forbearing love, enduring love'.

But how was she to explain all this to impetuous young women bristling with resentment at invasions of their freedom? Mother Vincent found it impossible to discuss the question with them objectively as one might discuss the weather. While spiritual dignity kept her silent with her companions, in an explosive situation her silence was misunderstood by them.

She undramatically thwarted the efforts of Mother M. of Mercy in Dublin to draw from her confirmation of certain disturbing rumours concerning the bishop's infringement of the Constitutions. To tell her troubles would serve no useful purpose, she said, but might well augment them. 'Life would not be life without grievances, and heaven would not be valued unless we had them to wean us from the things of this world.'[38] Compared with the service of God in others, whatever the Brisbane Sisters had to endure was a mere trifle. The uncertainties of the day-to-day events made one wary of placing trust 'in anyone or anything' save the strong arm of God.[39] But with 'a great field for permanent good to be done in this diocese', she continued, it would be a vast pity if single-minded Sisters were prevented from coming; 'do not, I beg of you, dearest Rev. Mother, refuse to permit them to come . . . God's work in the salvation of souls is to be done here. Send them for that, and only that.'[40]

Insistently, Mother Vincent's letters reverted to the theme that God's work was 'the only thing worth thinking of' in life.[41] It was precisely to gain elasticity in charitable endeavour that Mother McAuley had accorded her Sisters a freedom of movement which had not been previously given to religious Orders. But Quinn, in keeping with the old ideas of cloister appropriate to a bygone day and to other Orders, required the Sisters to kneel behind a rood screen in St Stephen's, and curtailed their contact with laymen and laywomen.

Mother Vincent found his rigid notions particularly inconvenient when her Sisters became ill through overwork, poor fare and housing. She sought permission to take a house at the seaside for some weeks when Sister M. Benedict's stomach would not retain food and Sister M. Cecilia grew thin and pale and the doctor ordered rest, but the bishop would not even permit a few drives to take the air. In reporting this to Dublin, Mother Vincent tried to submit her judgment, declaring that they would 'yet feel the benefit of his strictness in these matters.'[42]

Womanlike, she expressed her exasperation more over petty obstruction than over more sweeping domination. Thus her patience snapped when the bishop extended his control to household details. On one occasion, she ordered a washing machine from Dublin through Mother M. of Mercy, and was about to send the money for it when Quinn told her to let his brother Matthew, his agent in Dublin, pay. More correspondence and no machine. Left to herself, Mother Vincent would have had the laundry quickly, but after months of helpless frustration, she cried, 'I must get very angry.'[43] However, in the larger purchases of the Community, the bishop often took the initiative. Thus at the end of 1863, as mentioned before, he acquired the home of Dr George Fullerton, Adderton, which Mother Vincent re-named All Hallows'.

The next crisis in authority arose when Mother Vincent attempted to return to Ireland to gather more nuns for Queensland. By 1864 there were about six hundred children in the Brisbane and Ipswich schools, and Mother Vincent was thinking of commencing a home for orphans. But for such work she needed more nuns, who could not be induced to come by her request in letters; hence her decision to make a personal appeal.

Setting out on 2 January 1865,[44] she rested at Subiaco in Sydney, where she conferred with the Benedictine nuns who had hospitably welcomed her and her party in 1861. She also revisited Melbourne and Geelong, and was refreshed with the sight of Mothers Ursula Frayne and Xavier Maguire;[45] then she crossed to Hobart[46] to join Bishop Willson for the voyage to England on the *Percy*. She looked forward to the journey with joy, to meeting her Sisters and family, to delivering messages from the Australian houses, showing off Jane, first fruits of Queensland, and gathering counsel, fortitude and forces for the time ahead.

But in this she was doomed to disappointment. On the eve of boarding the *Percy*, she was summoned back to Brisbane, not by telegram, but by the bishop's personal messenger, Father Robert Dunne. With Mother Vincent gone, the bishop had tightened his control to crisis point, and two Sisters next in command to Mother Vincent, Mothers Benedict and Cecilia, had taken the extraordinary step of stealing away to Sydney to consult Archbishop Polding.

In the letters which the two nuns wrote on the steamer to Father Michael Renehan, they complained of the pressures that drove them to flight. Their life had been a constant struggle, they averred, since they came on the mission, and the bishop made it impossible for them to keep their Rule.[47] Mother Benedict mentioned that, before setting out for Ireland, Mother Vincent had appointed her to act as Superior at All Hallows', but the bishop had sent her to Ipswich. Resentment, emotional stress, and conscientious anxiety were blended in almost equal parts in the Sisters' statement of motive. They intended to return to Ireland, but would first consult Polding.

Quinn could not divine the unhappiness which drove them to this step. As he saw it, 'they had left their convent without a shadow of reason.' That they should turn to Polding was altogether intolerable, since in 1862 the archbishop had honourably received the insubordinate Cusse, while in 1864 he had lent an ear to the exaggerations of Thomas Keating.[48] These circumstances made all the more alarming the journey south of the two nuns. Quinn sent Robert Dunne in pursuit to induce their return, in which task, after much persuasion, he succeeded.

For all the expeditious travelling of Quinn's courier, Mother Vincent did not hurry back, because she wished to inspect orphanages and other institutions. In her three weeks' consultation with the Charity Sisters of Hobart, with various Mercy groups—at Geelong, Melbourne and Goulburn—and with the Benedictine nuns, she had the opportunity to ponder on the ways of colonial bishops with their religious. Polding, for all his saintliness, had played havoc with the autonomy of every Order under his jurisdiction: Sisters of Charity, Passionists, Christian Brothers, and even his own Benedictine nuns. Not one of the five Sisters of Charity in the foundation group of 1838 remained in New South Wales. The men religious simply left the colony.[49]

Mother Vincent arrived back in All Hallows' on 8 March to learn that the bishop held her responsible for his inability to force Mothers Benedict and Cecilia to submit to his authority. Mother Vincent's own letters make no mention of what happened between Quinn and herself, but the Chapter Book records that with due form and ceremony, assisted by Dr Robert Dunne, Bishop Quinn publicly removed her from the office of Reverend Mother, and deprived her for a year of her right to speak on the affairs of the congregation.[50]

A strange sickness hung over Queensland. There had been a long drought, and winds from the west brought dust and searing temperatures. Miasmas rising from the gutters infected the air with fevers and typhoid.[51] There was a general feeling of malaise, almost as if external conditions reflected the inner turmoil of the cloister.

However, even the bishop could not stop protests in the convent against Mother Vincent's demotion. Sisters M. de Sales Gorry, Joseph Murphy, and Agnes White, outstanding religious who all later proved their worth, voiced their opinion, and like Mother Vincent were deprived of the right to speak in Chapter. Now there was a strange vacuum, with no visible Community head. The bishop intended to keep authority to himself, but after three months he appointed Mother Benedict as figurehead. To make it perfectly obvious that all power was vested in himself, he sent her to reside in the Ipswich branch house, and accorded her permission to visit her headquarters once a month, but strictly forbade her to alter any of his arrangements there.[52]

Meantime, Sister M. Vincent Whitty discouraged displays of loyalty to herself; there were to be no factions, no cliques. 'My soul is happy', she had written when things were worst, when she had been the bishop's spokesman. Now she was free of that onerous duty. She could give herself to the one absorbing thought of her life, 'Christ, her rich portion'. Rejected by human authority, she still felt needed by a divine one.

5

EPISCOPAL CONTROL: SECOND PHASE

Not even theology, says Newman, though it comes from heaven, is excluded from that imperfection 'which must ever attend the abstract when it would determine the concrete.'[1] The abstract, in the present context, was a principle; the concrete meant friends and allies alienated by Quinn's application of the ruthless logic of an idea.

The first phase has shown the bishop and Mother Vincent, in a conflict confined to the one area of interpretation of a principle. In the second phase, during the period 1866 to 1870, the conflict continued and broadened. Moreover, Bishop Quinn's attempts to extend his control at the time led to the departure of some of Mother Vincent's Sisters and many clergy. However, there were also dangers of another sort, for financial disaster threatened to sweep away the last traces of Mother Vincent's work in Queensland.

'The present looks very gloomy', wrote Father Patrick Dunne in mid-1866.[2] The £6,000 due for All Hallows' had to be paid to Dr Fullerton that year, 'and I firmly believe', Dunne continued, 'that if you were to turn out the pockets of every Catholic in Queensland at the present moment, you would not find six hundred, much less six thousand pounds.'[3] Moreover, propping up the failing *North Australian* had placed the bishop in debt for £1,600 to the Bank of Queensland, which now served him with a writ for the whole amount. Other debts made the position grave, and Dunne suggested to Archdeacon John McEncroe, Polding's Vicar-General, that 'if the worst should come', if the nuns were evicted, they 'should find a home with you'. Dunne noted 'a great want of confidence among the people about the collection of moneys for any Catholic or charitable purpose'[4] arising from the Ipswich affair and the bishop's land deals.

Meanwhile McEncroe had heard the complaints sent to Rome

against Quinn's administration, and was slow to send financial help. Quinn himself wrote to him, saying that the deeds for the convent were held by the bank as security for the £2,000 advanced as a second mortgage.[5] At the same bank he had another debt for £3,700 for which the bank held security value for about £15,000. 'Can you do anything for me under the circumstances?' McEncroe advised him to sell some of the land he had bought. 'I would willingly follow your advice,' Quinn replied, 'but at present there is no buying. Things are quite at a stand still here.'[6] The bank would take two months to wind up its own affairs, and would then close its doors. 'If within that time we cannot clear off our liability . . . the property belonging to us which the bank holds as security will be sold, and will not bring a tenth of its value, as things are now.'

As for McEncroe's account of the rumours about him, Quinn claimed that he was grossly misrepresented in New South Wales. 'How I have incurred the ill will of these people I am at a loss to know.' Even at this point, his immense confidence in his own righteousness did not forsake him. However he was unable to communicate this confidence to Patrick Dunne who informed McEncroe that 'Dr. Quinn has kindly offered me a mission here but I am certain I could not lay myself to work as I ought in this diocese.'[7]

Retrenchment of expenses through the closing of the Brisbane and Warwick boys' schools[8] (lay-taught) still left Church finances in a perilous state. 'I fear that a catastrophe will befall us sooner or later', Père Brun of Ipswich wrote to his Nîmes Superior. 'Nevertheless I persist in believing that in the interest of the souls confided to our care, we must remain here.'[9]

Ipswich Catholics also foresaw imminent disaster. A deputation led by Dr Kevin O'Doherty and Randal McDonnell (formerly of the *North Australian*) came to Sister M. Vincent, whom they still regarded as head of the Mercy community, to advise her to return to Dublin with her Sisters. 'The proposition staggered her for a moment.'[10] Here was the opportunity to retire honourably from the field if, as Dr Dunne once asserted, she was 'irritated with things in Brisbane and anxious to get to Victoria.'[11] She was in any case sure of receiving a warm welcome there from Mother Ursula Frayne who had told her that if ever she had reason to regret coming to Brisbane, she should consider Melbourne her home.[12]

Some such thought crossed her mind, because Mother Bridget noted in her a moment of irresolution. It passed, and Sister M.

Vincent decided to stay. 'The difficulty', she firmly told O'Doherty and McDonnell 'could be overcome by *prayer*, and a public appeal combined with energetic action.'[13]

Her expressed belief in the future of Queensland was verified the following year by the discovery of gold at Gympie. Charged with a new optimism and energy by her resoluteness, McDonnell volunteered to work gratuitously on a scheme to liquidate the debt on All Hallows',[14] and O'Doherty became one of a committee for organizing an appeal and plan of campaign.

The bishop at last agreed to let Sister M. Vincent use her initiative, and it was at once evident that she had a way of enlisting the sympathy and support of men of business, who went to extraordinary lengths to help her; Randal McDonnell conducted direct appeals on horseback among the squatters up to Gayndah and all over the Downs. Moreover, seeking to aid the committee by her vigour, she prevailed on the bishop to let her do what he had repeatedly refused until now: organize a bazaar. His desire to return the Sisters to a pre-McAuley cloister had to give way to the demands of the moment.

For the event, Sister M. Vincent enlisted the help of her friends overseas. Dr Whitty spoke to the Marchioness of Lothian, Lord Henry Kerr, and the Duchess of Buccleugh; this last he described as 'quite as generous as our own mother, and as like her in character of mind and devotion as any Duchess could be.'[15] Sisters in Hull, Liverpool, Birmingham, Edinburgh, London, Dublin and Loughrea made articles for sale, and her own family was generous.

'The day dawned when Sister M. Vincent's Grand Drawing and Bazaar took place and three thousand pounds was realized by the first effort at a time of unusual depression.'[16] Wrote Quinn: 'The success of the Grand Drawing surpassed immeasurably the most sanguine expectations. Nothing of the kind here (and old colonists say anywhere in Australia) created such a general commotion.'[17] Not a gracious word did he say of Sister M. Vincent, still under a cloud, though she had put her heart and soul into the effort.[18] There was still a debt on the convent of about £4,000 with interest. However, that first bazaar had set the tone for future efforts, which became important social events, attended by the governors and their wives, and by the many friends of the Sisters from all classes and denominations.

Even though the bishop appeared to assume responsibility for the Sisters' indebtedness, the onus of loan repayment lay entirely with them. 'From start to finish the community had to find the interest as well as the principal, which difficult work was from time to time facilitated by temporary accommodation loans from kind friends.'[19] The burden was lightened by a lucky Gympie fossicker, Patrick Lillis, who took over the debt and asked only 6 per cent interest instead of the 10 per cent required by the bank. Even that 6 per cent absorbed the entire annual income, and it was moreover a temporary accommodation. In the 1870s, however, Miss Florence O'Reilly paid the remaining £4,000 to the bank and took only 3 per cent.[20] Thus with the help of friends and with unremitting effort, All Hallows' convent and school were secured for the work of education.

During the depression period, the Queensland population was in a constant state of flux. Settlers moved to the greater security of the south, and some Sisters and many priests also departed from the Queensland diocese. The names of Fathers Scully, Larkin, Corly, Moynihan, Duhig, Golden, O'Donohue and Shimmick, for example, appeared briefly in the newspapers and then were heard no more.

In the matter of departures of religious, the bishop's attitude was of paramount interest. The ambivalence of his words concerning Sister M. Elizabeth Hersey shows a quality which made him to many an enigmatic and formidable figure. Sister M. Elizabeth, the first recruit from Baggot Street, arrived in 1865. An Englishwoman, she was the sister of Lady Mary Clifford and was Sister M. Vincent's personal friend. Coming out on the *Golden Land* with Sister M. Rose, she had no inkling of what had befallen Sister M. Vincent. She was thus distressed on arrival by the discovery that the bishop had taken over the function of community governor, and still more saddened that his Lordship refused to receive her officially as a member of the Brisbane Mercy community, and so she requested his permission to join the Sisters of Mercy newly arrived in Sydney.

A rare note of contrition marked Quinn's reply:

> I very deeply regret my own shortcomings in endeavouring to make you happy, though I cannot say I am surprised at my failings as they are an everyday occurrence. In your charity pray that God may enlighten and sanctify me, and also teach me how to be kind, since kindness is a debt I owe to all.[21]

To his brother Andrew he showed less humility; she had left, he claimed, because of foiled ambition.[22]

The All Hallows' chapel from the altar

All Hallows', 1890s, with Mother Claver and Mother Patrick

Sister M. Elizabeth's dismay was shared by nuns in Irish convents to whose ears rumours had come that the bishop was in virtual control of every aspect of the life of the Sisters. Quinn's pleas to his brother Andrew show that he knew about the impression he had created, but believed it totally unjustified, for he wrote optimistically, 'The reports, whatever they may have been, which so frightened Mrs. Maher you will be able, I am sure, easily to refute.'[23] Mother Teresa Maher was the Superior of the Athy convent which Sister M. Vincent had founded from Dublin, two of whose professed members withdrew their offer to come to Brisbane because of Quinn.

Yet the bishop gave his brother Matthew a glowing report of the success of his own regime:

> The discipline of the house [All Hallows'] is now in thorough good order, and all are most intent on their business . . . Sister M. Vincent Whitty is in the best dispositions. Her removal from office was conductive to her spiritual and temporal welfare, and also to the spiritual and temporal welfare of the community.[24]

'Authority is not a notably objective critic of itself',[25] however, and the bishop failed to see the weakness of externally imposed restraint, command and control. Even the loyal support of the Quinn dynasty could not ward off the consequences. For though Father Andrew exerted himself on his brother's behalf in Ireland, and Bishop Matthew Quinn, newly appointed to the See of Bathurst, defended him in Rome,[26] the volume of protest grew, until in the 1870s it erupted into faction.

Alienation of clerical sympathy from Bishop James Quinn may be deduced from Bishop Matthew Quinn's twelve-page refutation of charges lodged against his brother by Father Michael Renehan, the only Irishman in James Quinn's original missionary party.[27] Renehan, unenlightened because of his bishop's secretiveness, failed to see why a poor mission should spend £2,000 on a newspaper, when the education of boys was neglected. Moreover, the regulations of the diocese discouraged easy relationships between bishop and clergy. Quinn's prohibition of smoking as 'unclerical' was a trifle beside the ruling that weekly financial returns had to be on the bishop's desk on Monday morning or a priest was *ipso facto* suspended. Apart from the shortage of priests, only twenty-three to serve the whole of Queensland, suspension was a grave embarrassment to priest and people, because while it lasted there could be no Mass or sacraments. Bishops normally use this sanction sparingly, only for incorrigibility after a serious lapse.

Not surprisingly, therefore, the 1866 re-organization of diocesan finances[28] which entailed such dread consequences filled the clergy with alarm. Several of those in distant stations resolved to seek an interview with the bishop, but when they rode in from their respective missions, 'they learned with surprise . . . that he had left for Sydney.'[29] Led by Father M. Renehan, they sat down to compose a memorial in which they listed their complaints. But when, on Quinn's return, the memorial was submitted to a court of three, chief of whom was Vicar-General Robert Dunne, the court decided that there should be no alteration in the existing diocesan regulations.

The dissatisfied priests thereupon asked for permission to leave the diocese, and when Quinn refused, six of them departed in 1867: Fathers M. P. Renehan, J. Sheehan, W. N. Walsh, T. J. Hogan and J. J. McGahan.[30] It was a 'moral impossibility', they declared in self-extenuation to the Roman authorities, to carry out the diocesan regulations.[31] When their case was heard in Rome, efforts were made to negotiate a truce between the rebels and their bishop, but James Quinn was not one for compromise. His biographer writes that on this occasion the bishop showed himself 'stern, hard, inflexible—not one iota would he yield—back they should go, and before he would treat with them [they] should make full, entire, abject submission.'[32] At Rome, the priests were required to make a retreat with the Passionist Fathers, and then allowed to serve in the United States.

The letters to the Sacred Congregation during the 1860s from these and other disappointed priests and from Archbishop John Bede Polding of Sydney who was in sympathy with them, are rich in church history; but while they are often biased and hot-headed, they prove that the bishop was too impetuous, too eager, and too masterful in his efforts to meet the vast demands of his diocese. Certainly his office called for strength and a degree of authority unnecessary in a secure and established diocese. The uncertainty of the colony's economy, the restlessness of the gold-rush years, all accentuated his problems. Robert Dunne understood Quinn's impatient drive towards great accomplishment, having been with him, one way or another, since he was eleven years old. He stood by him, but discouraged his excesses, and, in particular, his concentration on one aspect of the institutional Church to the exclusion of others, namely 'the collection of money, now for schools, now for churches or convents, while the motto of the apostles—*Ministros Christi et dispensatores mysteriorum Dei*—seems comparatively lost sight of . . . It seems to me that someone will be sadly responsible some day for this great mistake.'[33]

Dunne was soon to re-echo these words in his protest at the episcopal treatment of the Sisters of Mercy. It is true that by 1867 there were signs of a thaw in Quinn's relations with Sister M. Vincent. He could even acknowledge her part in saving All Hallows' from the creditors. 'Finding that she has let mail slip without sending my message, I grumbled in thorough English style', he wrote to her Hull friends soon to join the Brisbane community. 'She has had very heavy business in hand in connection with the Grand Drawing and Bazaar, and has acquitted herself admirably . . . The sum realized, through her principally, exceeded over four thousand pounds—within a year, and that a year of great distress both here and elsewhere.'[34]

This graciousness was shattered by the disintegration of the conventual 'discipline' which he had imposed upon the community. Having made himself head of the congregation, he had a three-year term to test his authority. But he was too insensitive to detect the undercurrents of resistance, though Reverend Mother Benedict's words, had he heeded them, might have saved him much embarrassment. With open simplicity she repeatedly protested against his assumption of the duties of a Reverend Mother; hers was 'not a community with its own head and rules', she told him, because everything was done from outside.[35] She, 'nominally Rev. Mother . . . always found that when she came down from Ipswich, things had been quite arranged and settled with another Sister', to wit, Sister M. Bridget, Quinn's protégée since Sister M. Vincent's demotion.

The bishop had assured Mother Benedict that 'she was as much Rev. Mother as anyone would ever be' under him.[36] Mother Benedict was soon to test this statement by pointing out to Sister M. Bridget where she, Sister M. Bridget, had obeyed the bishop by disobeying the Rule, only to have the Rule Book handed back to her by Sister M. Bridget with the comment: 'The Bishop is my Rule'.

It was useless to show the bishop the conflict between the Rule and his will, for Mother Benedict was always rebuffed; it was for him, Quinn claimed, to interpret the Rule. She therefore asked for permission to return to Baggot Street or to go to some other convent. He refused. However, since Mother Benedict could not resign herself to this 'heartless iron domination', she told Quinn that she and Mother Cecilia 'would face the chances of getting shelter elsewhere and a quiet way to save their souls.' He answered that they might apply to Baggot Street, but implied that he could easily quash their application.[37]

These interchanges with Mother Benedict should have revealed to Quinn the tension beneath his iron hand yet, when the two took ship for Sydney vowing never to return, he informed Cardinal Cullen that there was 'no apparent reason for this strange act, and I believe no reason amounting to a tangible grievance of any kind arises.'[38] He said nothing of Mother Benedict's inescapable logic, and attributed their flight to jealousy of other Sisters.

Yet he described an interview with Mother Benedict on 7 January when she spoke of her decision to leave. Before she had finished he had cut her short, 'alleging want of time, but fearing really that she would give way to the strong excitement under which she was labouring.'[39] In other words, just as he went to Sydney when the priests had asked for discussion of their grievances, so he avoided settlement with Mothers Benedict and Cecilia. But he could not have failed to know of their unhappiness; Father Robert Dunne had told him unequivocally that in 'all this there is nothing new to your Lordship. They are statements you have often heard.'[40] But to acknowledge the flight of the nuns would be a lesser trial than to confess to the Cardinal a lack of discipline. In the words of Quinn: 'It would seem from this unusual occurrence that all must be confusion here. The contrary is the case. Here is perfect order—so far as perfection is compatible with the circumstances and individuals . . . the same order is among the priests, through a few observe it reluctantly.'[41]

The bishop was more than anxious that Mother Cecilia particularly should return without delay. For that year, 1868, the visit of Prince Alfred, Duke of Edinburgh, was about to take place. Melbourne had already given him a wildly enthusiastic reception with glittering illuminations and triumphal arches. Also, Sydney had outdone itself. The enthusiasm of the other cities, therefore, made Brisbane all the more eager to prove its loyalty. But there was little to show the Duke in the way of man's achievements in this youngest capital, and much thought and planning went into the entertainment, particularly the concert in his honour. The bishop set great store by Catholic participation in the concert, and was delighted that the main orchestral item was to be supplied by Mother Cecilia's musicians. 'She is highly gifted,' he explained to his brother, 'and able in that capacity to produce results that exceed credibility . . . All the principal ladies in Brisbane, married or single, are her pupils. Her disposition is as well known as that of any public character.' The Colonial Secretary had conferred with her on the programme, and 'her word was law with him'.[42]

Mother Cecilia and Mother Benedict left on 17 January however, long before the concert was due. Hence, to induce Mother Cecilia to return, Quinn's first letter to Sydney was mild. She could depart later if she wished, he said, but he wanted her 'as a special favour to prepare the children for the Prince's concert'. Appealing to her compassion for convicts, he added that the 'poor prisoners in the jail will be glad to see you a few times more, and I am sure after the concert the Prince will liberate two or three of them at the request of some of the young performers.' She would surely make any sacrifice in her power for these young fellows. 'Come back . . . All shall be perfectly right.'[43] However, unable to restrain his impatience, Quinn followed this appeal, two days later, with a telegram addressed to both Sisters, commanding them 'in virtue of holy obedience' to return without delay.[44]

When there was no answer, the bishop sent Father Robert Dunne, his trouble-shooter on the occasion of their previous flight in 1865, to bring them once again. Quinn desired to cloak the whole episode in secrecy, but Dunne pointed out to him that the fugitives had disclosed to friends on the wharf their plan to return to Ireland, while he had it from the Sydney archbishop's 'own lips'[45] that Mother Cecilia's sister had bespoken Polding's protection for the pair and had sent their passage money.

Not only the archbishop but several of his most eminent clergy were sympathetic to the nuns. Dr J. Forrest, Rector of St John's University College, and a friend of Quinn, took a 'practical theological view' favourable to the nuns,[46] and asked Quinn to delegate his authority to Father Robert Dunne to enable him to act as circumstances might direct. The bishop refused to do so. Dunne, he said was not to be trusted; he had temporized 'when manly action would have saved these poor ladies'. Besides, 'there is no course to be followed at present, but that traced out—these ladies have deserted their convent without a shadow of reason, they should come back to it.'[47]

Dunne had refused to be his intermediary 'at the commencement of this business' even though Quinn promised him that he would incur no responsibility. But the lack of discretionary power was precisely what made Dunne as reluctant to act as episcopal mouthpiece as Sister M. Vincent before him. However, to the uncomprehending Quinn, his refusal was tantamount to disobedience; and in a disgruntled mood the bishop wrote to Forrest that, though he had made Dunne his Vicar-General, 'he has never yet found me in a difficulty of any magnitude that he did not desert me.'[48]

While thus explaining his unwillingness to delegate authority to Dunne, Quinn professed readiness to trust his brother bishops in the matter, naming Matthew Quinn of Bathurst, his cousin Murray of Maitland, and his close friend Lanigan of Goulburn. Polding, of course, was excluded, since he was predisposed towards the Sisters. 'No one had the same regard for the Sisters that I have', Quinn declared. 'They volunteered to come with me to this extreme part of the world, and here they have laboured very hard on my mission.' But his appreciation was devoid of warmth, since it placed juridical considerations before the personal. 'I regret that they have taken this wrong step, and sown for themselves the seeds of bitter grief. I did what I could to prevent it, and will do all I can to remedy it.'[49]

Father Dunne found his task 'anything but cheerful work'.[50] Both Sisters were ill and miserable. 'I assure you that I cannot help looking on the whole matter as particularly sad,' Dunne told Quinn, 'and of the evils coming out of it, we in Brisbane are not guiltless.'[51] The problem before Dunne was absorbing the attention of everyone: Archbishop Polding, Bishop Murray of Maitland, Archdeacon McEncroe, Dr Forrest, Father M. D. D'Arsey and Father J. Monnier. Some advised the nuns to go to Goulburn, others to Bathurst, but Dunne ruled out the idea of Bathurst for them as posing too many difficulties. The nuns recognized his sympathy, and were therefore ready to listen when he spoke of the generous motives that had made them leave home and country, despite all risks. They in turn told Dunne of their motives for leaving Brisbane, their fear that the bishop would make Sister M. Bridget Reverend Mother,[52] adding her rigour to his own.

Dunne communicated the nuns' thoughts to Quinn who finally agreed to their departure on condition that they first returned to Brisbane. 'In all probability they will settle down here in their own convent greatly humbled and improved', he told Cullen.[53] In writing in similar strain to Baggot Street and to his fellow bishops, moreover, Quinn made clear his wishes should the Sisters apply for acceptance in other houses.

Thus when the nuns headed north to rejoin their community

they were unaware that the bishop was deceiving them. He had no intention of letting them leave. He again enjoined secrecy about the plan, told them to retain their respective titles of Reverend Mother and Mother Bursar, and forbade them to apply to other communities until after Easter, when they might first write to Cullen. Both were still under thirty,[54] and believed they could make a fresh start under happier circumstances. But when July came and they had not yet found a niche, the blow fell. Mother Bridget became Reverend Mother, Mother Benedict was made her Assistant, and Mother Cecilia remained Bursar.

And Sister Mary Vincent? It was all her fault. Mother Benedict, pained by her uneasy impartiality in the matter, believed that Sister M. Vincent had capitulated to the bishop, and 'was acting a part';[55] while Quinn attacked her in a letter to Cullen who must have been surprised to read a condemnation of the person whom Quinn had begged him to release from the Order in Dublin: 'Mrs. Whitty's training is the cause of the irregularity committed by these two excellent young Sisters. They have the most generous natural dispositions but no practical idea of religious life. Mrs. Whitty should not have been in office for years before she left Baggot Street.'[56] But Quinn contradicted himself; 'she is utterly unfit to train or guide others', he claimed denouncing the teaching she had given her nuns; but he immediately went on to praise the fruit of her labours. 'Strange to say, we have a most excellent and strictly observant community, numbering eleven professed, four novices, two postulants, and seven lay-sisters. The good our nuns do here is very great.'

As only the eleven professed had the right to vote, the July elections were so only in name: at the bishop's wish Sisters M. de Sales Gorry, Joseph Murphy and Agnes White were denied a vote, and their voices in Chapter were restored only after the event.[57] Then too, Mothers Benedict and Cecilia and Sister M. Vincent had clear reasons for not voting as the bishop wished, and the Constitutions prevented Mother Bridget from voting for herself. That left only four professed who could have voted for Mother Bridget. Thus the term 'election' meant as little as the title 'Reverend Mother' to Quinn.

Soon after the elections, however, Mothers Cecilia and Benedict no longer served as Bursar and Assistant to Mother Bridget. Just before Christmas of that year, Mother Cecilia fell ill and died. Then in the following year, Mother Benedict resigned from office,[58] and, having knocked in vain at many doors, left in 1870 for the south until her dispensation from vows should arrive from Rome.

Even the removal of these nuns failed to produce the sort of discipline which Quinn sought. For although he was pious, zealous and intelligent, he lacked, in the view of contemporaries, common sense and consistency.[59] His harsh disciplinary measures displayed a lack of common sense. In alliance with Mother Bridget, he introduced public penances in the refectory as an exercise in obedience and submission.[60] Further, novices were kept in suspended trial for long periods (up to nine years), whereas the Church's ruling in this respect was that nuns should wait for only two or at most three years before taking vows. Then too, for trifling reasons, various Sisters were deprived of their vote in Chapter.

On the other hand, Quinn's inconsistency was borne out when in 1872 he restored Sister M. Vincent to office as Assistant, and when, two years later, she was once again entrusted with the lambs of the flock, the novices.[61] This about-turn in the bishop's policy was effected by the change he suffered on attending the Vatican Council of 1870.

Prior to his departure for the Council, Quinn had left the affairs of the community in the hands of Mother Bridget. But he had laid down a policy to be carried out in the minutest detail, and commanded Mother Bridget to record in a diary events of the convents and schools. From Rome he wrote encouragement: 'I have got your diary from January 15 to February 16 inclusive. It is worth twenty letters. Nothing could be more gratifying to me . . . Don't fear being too detailed.'[62] She was also to get the teachers 'young and old' to send accounts of their schools. Sister M. Vincent would have been exasperated by his prescriptions of the type of paper to be used, size of margins and spacing. Not Mother Brigdet; she punctiliously obeyed.

Thus though Quinn could trust her implicitly to respect his smallest wish, he left her no room for initiative during his absence of almost three years. Before departing he made all the appointments to the schools and the various charges, and directed her to make no change until his return.[63]

For Sister M. Vincent he had other plans. She was to follow him to Europe, where he 'anxiously awaited [her] arrival.'[64] At the Vatican Council, she was to learn, he had found that other prelates did not share his ideas on episcopal authority and its application. Indeed, 'they greeted him with cold politeness or passed him by'[65] and when he went to his native land, 'an unenviable fame had already preceded him'.[66] At Maynooth he could not obtain a single volunteer for his diocese. All Hallows', Thurles, Carlow—all the seminaries proved strangely reluctant to free their students for Quinn. 'Now isn't it hard', he complained, 'that through the calumnies, chiefly, of one wicked man, and the credulity of a great many good men, I could scarcely get a priest in Ireland to volunteer for my diocese? I had to turn to France, Italy and Germany to look for priests for an Irish population.'[67]

But there was more than 'one wicked man'. Keating had joined the six priests who left in 1867, and their united voices carried volume. Convents heard the news too, which was to make Sister M. Vincent's task the more difficult. For the bishop selected her rather than Mother Bridget to recruit nuns because her name carried prestige in the Irish and English convents where she was known from her old Baggot Street leadership, whereas Mother Bridget was unknown. Moreover, Sister M. Vincent was believed, not without cause, to be among his victims. Thus he relied on Sister M. Vincent's well-known, singleminded devotion to God's work to help him out of his dilemma.

She found on her arrival in Ireland that an unnamed priest and a layman, called O'Connor, were circulating letters warning convents and parents against allowing anyone to depart for Brisbane.[68] Sisters were driven for shelter to Sydney, it was said, vows were commuted, and the Rule changed.[69] The element of truth in the accusations made Sister M. Vincent's task all the harder. While she was in one county, Reverend Mothers anxious to help her in others found parents 'coming . . . in desperation' lest their daughters should volunteer to go to Brisbane.[70] Also, near panic was caused by embellishment of the story of Mother Cecilia's death. 'Could there be any possibility of clearing up or confuting such terrible calumnies and slanders' as those afoot concerning Brisbane? 'I am exhausted from defending the cause', complained one of Sister M. Vincent's loyal helpers.[71]

Sister M. Vincent's presence alone could calm the disturbed relatives. 'It is most necessary for you to come here *as soon as you can*', wrote the correspondent just mentioned, 'and let us advise together, and have you see the parents and hear from their lips what they have to say and what they mean to do—I think your coming would be better than Dr. Quinn's on this occasion.'[72] But Sister M. Vincent shrank from the encounter and promised to send the bishop, who would be better equipped to cope with rumours about Queensland diocesan conditions. However, the Dungarvan Reverend Mother hastily rejected the offer of a visit from his Lordship, declaring that she could not for the life of her see what the good bishop could do in this matter.[73]

In the end, Sister M. Vincent's presence brought peace, for she admitted difficulties and dangers, risks, doubts and temptations in the service of God. She did not minimize the hard work and sacrifice, nor did she paint a rosy picture of another Eden under southern skies. But while struggle was necessary to the spiritual combat, she pointed out that it did not preclude happiness. 'I would not take Sisters to Queensland if I believed that they could not be as happy there as in Ireland', she said,[74] and stressed the point that any nun seeking Christian perfection and willing to teach could find as deep contentment there as in any part of the world.

Reports spread by dissident priests were not the only obstacle to Sister M. Vincent's quest for Sisters. Cardinal Cullen showed no eagerness to permit religious to go to the colonies. Often Bishop Quinn had written to ask him for certain Baggot Street Sisters; but they had not come. Moreover, one of the volunteer nuns was informed by her uncle that 'the Cardinal . . . does not allow emigration from this diocese without a special examination of the parties by himself or one of his Vicars.'[75]

However, Sister M. Vincent had many friends. Bishop D. Moriarty of Kerry permitted three of his nuns to go with her, and the opposition elsewhere slowly melted away. Some Superiors were frankly glad that she could not call on them: 'you might have charmed away some of my very dear children,' confessed one ingenuously, 'and that would have made me very sad.'[76]

Bishop Quinn, as the Dungarvan Reverend Mother pointed out, was more of a hindrance than a help, and in 1872 he departed for Australia. Given *carte blanche* to act as she thought best, Mother Vincent felt trusted again. In Ireland he had made her Mother Assistant, and left her wide scope for judgment and decision. 'Urge good Dr. Moriarty', Quinn wrote from Brisbane, 'to press some of his fine young men . . . to come here. I say nothing about the number of nuns you are to bring. I know it will be as big as you can make it.'

He sought the division of Queensland into four dioceses, which economic development had made possible; hence the urgent need for more clergy and teachers. 'The colony was never in so progressive a state as it is at present', he wrote to Mother Vincent with rare exuberance. 'The mineral wealth discovered is almost fabulous. The country to the north, almost out to Carpentaria, is traversed and partially occupied by diggers. The want of priests becomes more than ever felt.'[77] Thus priests, Sisters and migrants also were to be her care, and Dr Cani had implored her to bring back some Christian Brothers.

In addition to her recruiting duties, Mother Vincent was responsible for the transport arrangements in the ships *Storm King* and *Silver Eagle* which were to carry her recruits, as well as the migrant laymen and women whom she had encouraged to come to Queensland. By April 1873 they were all on the water. 'May God send her safe', the bishop prayed. 'She brings a precious cargo and she is worth a great part of it herself.'[78] Later, he told a brother bishop of her achievement: 'She brought out in all thirty nuns who are now here safe, well, happy, and ready for hard work.'[79] With her had come priests for the diocese, among them the bishop's nephew, Father Andrew Horan. A party of Italian clerics, recruited by Quinn during the Vatican Council, had preceded her; thirteen of the nineteen new priests were Italian. From Mother Vincent's viewpoint, her most valuable companion was Sister M. Claver Mullany from Dublin, the London-born, French-educated and Irish-trained nun who was her close and faithful friend throughout her life.

But the cargo also included gifts; oil paintings from Lord O'Hagan, a marble bust of Queen Victoria from the Earl of Granard, a printing press from the Dowager Marchioness of Lothian, a statue of Mater Admirabilis from Paris, an altar from Mother Liguori Gibson of Liverpool. Cash donations from all over the United Kingdom came from a galaxy of great names; the Lord Chief Baron Fitzroy Kelly of Connaught Place, Lady Mostyn, Sir Charles Clifford, the Dowager Countess of Newburg, the Duke of Norfolk, Right Reverend Dr Errington—but at the head of the list was the largest gift, from 'Uncle Dick' Devereux of Wexford. The money was for the new cathedral, and Dr Cani joined the bishop in a 'panegyric'[80] to Mother Vincent.

She had acquitted herself brilliantly, but now she was back to the status quo. Gone was Quinn's slightest excuse for keeping his religious community in spiritual babyhood. With over forty members, it should have been allowed to arrange its own affairs according to the Constitutions under the general jurisdiction which is the right of all bishops. Instead, Quinn continued to make transfers, appoint the headships of schools and convents, in short, to continue his paterfamilias role. It was his nature, but his attempted domination in other fields brought him sore trouble; and parallels and contrasts were to appear in his relationship with the clergy and with other religious Orders.

While Quinn's conflict with the Sisters of Mercy remained virtually hidden, reverberations of his clashes with the clergy spread to the southern capitals and even to Rome. For the clergy were responsible for sending to Rome what was termed the 'Syllabus Accusationum'. The relevance of the 'Syllabus Accusationum' of the 1870s is threefold; it contains repeated echoes of the bishop's quarrel with Mother Vincent, it quotes the testimony of clerics of many nationalities on the rigidity of control to which the Sisters were subjected, and it demonstrates that Mother Vincent's response can only be understood against the violent background of protest, unsettlement and change of which the 'Syllabus' was a symptom.

The 1870s, it has been noted, were years of rising population and settlement in new mining areas. They saw the debacle of the education controversy during which sharp sectarian squabbles convinced Catholics of the need to unite to maintain their schools on the withdrawal of state aid. With education the vital issue of the decade, one looks for a clergy intent on a cool appraisal and use of resources, and finds instead a divided Church that squandered its energies on side issues and threw back on Mother Vincent and her nuns the onus of keeping the Catholic system afloat.

Still in force were the 1866 diocesan regulations which exacted a Spartan obedience and exacerbated the problem of maintaining a supply of clergymen for Queensland. In 1868 there were just sixteen priests for the whole colony,[81] a number that would have been adequate had Catholics been concentrated in a small area. Instead they were scattered over thousands of square miles as farmers, miners, road and railway builders, or stockmen. Priests risked their lives ministering to them; while on sick calls, young Father Power was swept to his death on the swollen Burnett River.[82] Then too, the moral hazards to the clergy were intensified by pioneering conditions. Polding, through Benedictine eyes, viewed with distaste the company of 'men coarse and addicted to vulgar habits' which made 'prudence and steadiness as necessary as zeal; and perseverance . . . to travel the live long day, through immeasurable solitude, tedious from the monotonous character of the country, and to work upon characters indifferent to everything except money and drink.'[83] This kind of devotion to 'the religious wants of dwellers in the bush' displayed by clergy in Queensland drew praise from the *Queensland Times*,[84] though it darkly suspected that money or politics furnished the motive.

Queensland thus offered a challenge to appal even men nurtured on penal memories. Its impact was traumatic on Quinn's Italian recruits, who arrived in Brisbane in 1871. Accustomed to churches which combined the glory that was Greece and the grandeur that was Rome, and to the dignity and solemnity of elaborate ritual, they found little wooden buildings with (it seemed scandalous) little wooden tabernacles. Their poverty was embittered by loneliness and an incomplete mastery of English. Soon trouble was brewing.

On his return to Queensland in May 1872, Quinn found among the Italians 'una confusione non mediocre'. One of these, Ricci, according to Quinn a political controversialist 'well known in Rome',[85] had already complained in a letter which Quinn received while in London, that the administrator of the diocese, Dr Cani, was 'crazy, tyrannical, barbarous and ignorant'.[86] Moreover, Ricci, a violent man, had organized a new dissident movement. Following this development, Quinn informed the Roman authorities of his plan to form a committee of priests to make a report of the complaints of the clergy in his diocese and of the causes of their return to Europe. But Ricci, excommunicated for intransigence, compiled his own.[87] The reports were duly assessed and filed by the Sacred Congregation. Later in the decade, an unnamed Brisbane priest discovered them, listed twenty-one charges—the 'Syllabus Accusationum'—and in 1877 circulated them in Queensland.

During the ensuing recrudescence of bitterness, a committee of priests wrote a defence of Quinn and his clergy and asked their brethren to sign it. Most did, although Cani and Dunne considered it unwise and refrained.[88] Rome was puzzled by these now-forgotten troubles, and asked Archbishop Vaughan of Sydney to examine the state of the Brisbane diocese,[89] and Vaughan was not averse to having a finger in the pie. Indeed, one may question the ethics of his inquisitorial probings, and of the mission of inquiry on which he sent Sir John O'Shannassy in 1878.[90]

If the press joined spiritedly in the fray,[91] if Vaughan received complaints from dissident laymen[92] and priests that the bishop embezzled and drank, the cause was Quinn's manner rather than his life. A total abstainer during his last fifteen years, he worked too hard ever to relax himself. As to accusations that he acquired land to enrich his relatives, he admitted to holding large tracts as trustee, but thrice publicly read his will to prove that not a penny, not an acre of ground, was for anything other than Church institutions and education.[93]

Thus calumnies could not be substantiated, but he unwisely despised his opponents and was as overbearing with friend as with foe. 'A Bishop ruling as Quinn rules, is really more autocratic than most kings', commented the *Courier*;[94] but impatience with him so blinded his critics that even the Orange *Evangelical Standard*, no advocate for Quinn, felt they had gone too far.

His indignation filled the rolling Latin periods of the collective clerical protest against the accusations addressed to the Prefect of Propaganda.[95] All the charges were rebutted or exculpation sought because of missionary circumstances. Thus the inadequate provision for the spiritual needs of the Sisters of Mercy, particularly the often-repeated protest that the nuns incurred excommunication if they attempted to confess to any but the cleric assigned them, was countered by the most telling point in the whole defence, namely, the immensity of the Church's task, for even in 1878 there were fewer than thirty priests to serve the widely dispersed 43,000 faithful.

Cardinal Cullen viewed Queensland from afar and, because he was a lover of all things Roman, the Sacred Congregation relied on him for a dispassionate opinion. The Italians, he said, did not realize that Queensland was a poor diocese, and they missed the comforts of home. Quinn, in Cullen's view, had erred in engaging so many without the means to support them but, as several had returned, he could do better by those who remained; if missioners resembled the Sisters of Mercy, all would be well, Cullen added, for the Sisters were content with little, but men had other ideas.[96]

Père Brun's reply to Vaughan's questionnaire also covered both general matters and problems of the Sisters. Brun reported that public opinion was more for the bishop than against him, and that the departure of three particularly imprudent Italian priests had helped the diocese. Dr Cani, while personally excellent, was 'rather imperative' in manner, and not a good administrator. Brun suggested that the court which Quinn was to nominate to consider the complaints should be instead elected by the clergy. He sharply criticized the muzzling of both laymen and priests in Synod, who were 'compelled to let things go according to the wishes of the bishop. Prudence advised them to adopt that course . . . the bishop cannot stand that others have opinions different from his own.' To the query, 'Is there anything undesirable in his mode of dealing with the Sisters of Mercy?' Brun replied that they were entirely under Quinn's thumb; but 'as to certain rumours of a very delicate nature, I consider them as pure fiction, without any foundation at all.'[97]

Finally, Cani's assessment of the Italian priests carries the more weight because he was himself Italian. In Brisbane, he commented, they had complained about Cardinals and bishops at home; it was not surprising that in Rome they complained about Brisbane. As to the alleged persecution of Italians by Irish priests, the reverse was true; Father Denis Fouhy had to flee in peril for his life from his mission and from an Italian cleric. The charge that Irish priests were ignorant was, in Cani's judgment, correct in part; but he considered that if older Irishmen neglected canon law they knew their theology. The bishop undertook too much, and spent perhaps too much time in the schools, but his friendships with Protestants did not compromise the faith, and satisfied the canons of polite society. Moreover, in zeal and courage, Cani considered that Quinn was every inch a bishop. About the Sisters' penance, Cani was non-committal. 'I do not know if it can be said that the bishop is the one and only confessor for the nuns.'[98]

Cani was loyal, yet for refusing to sign the repudiation of the 'Syllabus', Quinn deprived him of his vicar-generalship,[99] and he was by sad irony blamed by some as author of one if not several of the accusations.[1] Dunne was also relieved of his vicar-generalship,[2] and was later removed from his parish of Toowoomba despite the petitions of his people, who asked Vaughan to invite him to his archdiocese lest he be lost to Australia.[3] Thus no one escaped censure who refused complete obedience to Quinn—not even Cani and Dunne who had served him faithfully. Yet in 1882 Rome was to name each a bishop.

Certainly the absence of a common history, institutions and traditions binding clergy and people exacerbated Quinn's problems, yet one must look elsewhere for an explanation of his suspicion of his hitherto trusted Cani, for the bitterness of his attacks on parliamentary librarian Denis O'Donovan, and for his bickering with the Sisters of St Joseph. One is forced to conclude that the bishop's increasing ill-health affected his judgment. The malady of which he complained to Mother Vincent in 1872[4] caused intense pain for which the thermal springs of New Zealand brought only temporary relief, and his sufferings gave his thoughts a sombre hue.

In 1881, feeling 'stricken' by the verdict against him in the Gresley Lukin libel case,[5] he retired to his cottage at Nudgee for several months, more than ever a lonely figure. When in August that year he died, the *Courier* touched on a key aspect of his life. 'Although never abating the high claims of the Roman Church and never failing to assert its dignity, he yet managed to enlist the cordial sympathies and enjoy the warm friendship of numbers of very staunch Protestants.'[6] His indefatigable pursuit of the interests of the Church, as he conceived them, testified that he loved it 'with no common ardour and energy'.[7]

That transcendent quality, despite his failings, attracted back to his diocese even some of the priests with whom he had quarrelled. Father Walsh, who had left in the exodus of 1867, returned in the mid-1870s to work in Townsville;[8] Father McDonough came back from New Zealand to labour in Bowen; Father Renehan wrote from New York asking permission to return, but died suddenly before he could do so; McGahan was dead, but McGahan's brother offered to come.[9] Thus when time had put old troubles in perspective, men could acknowledge a rare quality of zeal in Quinn and work under him, so long as Queensland's open spaces lay in between. He was a brilliant authoritarian ruined by his intolerance of the mediocrity of lesser men.

How did the other religious Orders fare under the enigmatic bishop? How did Mother Vincent compare with others who introduced religious teaching Orders into the colony during Quinn's lifetime?

Mother Vincent's Order obviously had more staying power than the Assumptionists, since the remaining three, D. Tissot, H. Brun, and Brother Polycarp returned to France in the late 1870s.

The Christian Brothers, who came to Queensland from Melbourne in 1875 after much negotiation, made a more lasting contribution than the Assumptionists. Archbishop D. Murray of Dublin had suggested that the wisest form of government for the Christian Brothers was centralization under a Superior-General. They were thus immune from outside interference, though some plain speaking was required to make their position clear in both Western Australia and Victoria.[10] Men of such calibre successfully defended themselves against Quinn's enduring attempts to subject them to his will.[11] Thus the only male teaching Order in Queensland enjoyed a rare freedom.

The Sisters of St Joseph were for a time neither wholly independent like the Brothers, nor wholly dependent like the Sisters of Mercy. As their Constitutions were in a state of flux until finally approved at Rome, Quinn hoped to make them diocesan. However, like the Superiors of the Christian Brothers, their foundress Mother Mary of the Cross resisted diocesan control and also Board control of her schools. Like the Sisters of Mercy, her Order was stultified by paternalism; the Sisters were allotted only one confessor, Dr Cani, who was gruff and uncommunicative, and if Mother Mary sought advice, she wrote, 'he just talks at me as papa used to do.'[12]

But the bishop at last met his match in Mother Mary. The 'sentimental young lady', as he called her, 'the obstinate and ambitious woman' in the words of his brother of Bathurst, was only then thirty-two, 'after having had a most eventful career as Mother General already'.[13] She knew how to counter Quinn's efforts to influence Rome and to win away the Sisters from their allegiance to her. The battle royal lasted through a decade, but by 1875 Quinn had made up his mind. Before he would 'allow any relation of dependence' on a Mother General, he declared that he 'would send back every one of the thirteen Adelaide Sisters in Queensland'. Cani, then in Rome, was instructed to further the bishop's theme: 'I want the Sisters of St. Joseph to come under the same system of government as the Sisters of Mercy, that is that the bishop of the diocese in which they live would be their head superior next to the Holy See. You understand from all that what I want to convey.'[14] As Bishop Matthew Quinn was in Rome at the time he and Cani were told to confer together.

But as for Mother Mary, even if she had not determined on central government already, she might have seen no other alternative after learning of Mother Benedict's cautionary tale.[15] Rome approved her idea, but Quinn could not. Hence there had to be a parting. While forcing out the Sisters he implied that their withdrawal was voluntary. Mother Mary was reluctant to leave Queensland but she accepted Vaughan's invitation to Sydney.

Why did not Mother Vincent act similarly? Why did she not so publicly tell the bishop where he had overstepped his powers, even through the daily newspapers, like the Sisters of St Joseph? Why did she not protect her Sisters by withdrawing altogether?

Mother Vincent had had long experience of the ups and downs of missions. She knew Mother Ursula Frayne who had returned from Newfoundland after trouble with Dr Fleming like her own in Queensland. Dr Fleming had died and the Order had returned to its accustomed tranquillity. But by then Mother Ursula had gone to Perth in Western Australia, and so had lost Fleming only to gain Brady, and after Brady, the even more difficult Serra.[16] In similar fashion, another Dublin friend, Mother Xavier Maguire of Geelong, had been so overwhelmed with missionary disasters that she wrote back to Dublin announcing her return.[17] But suddenly diocesan conditions improved, and she remained.

These human considerations guided Mother Vincent to seek for herself and for her Sisters the strength to do God's work at the cost of temporary upset. Furthermore, this was the attitude suggested by her own spirituality, which assumed that submission to conditions past altering was an expression of trust in God; in his good time all would be well. Her weakness and her strength set Mother Vincent among those whose prayers and accepted sufferings generated rather than exercised power.

With her, the social quality of obedience placed her Sisters at the service of the Church, and therefore made her less tenacious of rights than observant of needs. The search for the will of God in the community was a painful effort, but Mother Vincent clung to the idea that the work that lay closest to hand was most in accord with God's will, and that the bishop was the best judge of the educational needs of the vast diocese which he had traversed and she had not.

Without Quinn's authoritative voice the same pattern of discontinuous action would have marked the educational structure in Queensland as elsewhere. Western Australia had a very large number of teaching Orders, each a more or less self-contained administrative unit; and further fragmentation occurred through Bishop Gibney's policy of encouraging branch convents to become independent, even within the one city, like the West Perth Convent founded from Victoria Square.[18] By contrast, Quinn imposed a co-ordinated policy with himself as liaison with the government. A Central Catholic Education Board might have been more open to points of view, but not as expeditious as the one-man Education Department that was the bishop.

Over-organized as her Sisters consequently were, it is a measure of Mother Vincent's greatness that she could still perceive Quinn's, and a measure of her humility and faith that she could fold her own authority away like a garment in order to continue her work among Queensland children. This was strength of character, not weakness. She might well ask, in the words of a much-tried priest of a later day,

> What would become of our souls, Lord, if they lacked the bread of earthly reality to nourish them, the wine of created beauty to intoxicate them, the discipline of human struggle to make them strong? What puny powers and bloodless hearts your creatures would bring to you were they to cut themselves off prematurely from the providential setting in which you have placed them.[19]

For she endured the tension between her own wish to be free and Quinn's special type of episcopal control, without protest, in the vivid faith that God writes straight even with crooked lines.

6

RELATIONSHIP WITH HER COMMUNITY

Mother Vincent's most demanding task was the creation of a sense of community within the convent, within the wider Church, and within society at large. No one person can create community, which involves shared interests, efforts and sympathies. Mother Vincent endeavoured to use the gifts of others to promote harmony and peace. In order to appraise her achievement in this area, and to see why such large numbers were attracted to the community and remained despite difficulties, one must necessarily examine the factors she had to combat which were inimical to growth and stability.

Nothing could contribute less to the Order's inner health than the combination of Quinn's autocracy and Mother Bridget's severity. Yet growth there was. In 1868 the community numbered two dozen Sisters;[1] thirty more sailed with Mother Vincent in 1873, a further sixty arrived in 1880,[2] and local vocations had increased so much that in 1879 eight girls were received or professed. Thus when Robert Dunne became bishop in 1882, though Queensland was then divided into two dioceses and the Sisters in Rockhampton, Mackay, Townsville and Charters Towers came under the jurisdiction of Bishop John Cani, Dunne had in his own diocese 'some twenty-one priests and probably one hundred and twenty Sisters of Mercy'.[3]

How does one account for this phenomenal growth? It cannot be explained only by the need of nineteenth-century women to work for God and man. For there were two struggling indigenous Orders in Queensland, both badly needing recruits. The Sisters of Perpetual Adoration, established by Father Tenison Woods in 1874, barely survived, through lack of vocations, and even four decades later they had no branch house.[4] Devoted to contemplation, not action, their appeal was limited. The second Order was a small splinter group of the Sisters of St Joseph, who elected to return to Queensland after Quinn's dispute with Mother Mary of the Cross. But the bishop reshuffled appointments made by Tenison Woods;[5] and though the St Joseph Sisters taught for several years in Bundaberg, their Order never struck root. The few remaining by the mid-1890s were advised to join the Bathurst community.[6]

With the work of Mother Vincent's congregation so difficult as to cost the lives of fifteen young nuns in two decades, the growth from 6 in 1861 to 140 in 1882 (counting the twenty-odd in the North) must be explained by causes other than the existence of an outlet for the apostolic zeal of Queensland women.

The greatest single cause of growth was Mother Vincent. Officially, she remained second-in-command, morally she led. The bishop's proneness to reshuffling appointments could have sounded the death-knell of the Queensland Mercy congregation just as effectively as it destroyed the Sisters of St Joseph, when in 1865 he demoted Mother Vincent and assumed her duties. Graver still was the community's predicament when in 1868 he named Mother Bridget Reverend Mother. Yet the years 1865 to 1870, when Mother Vincent was numbered among the rank and file, so proved her virtue, ability, and inescapable leadership, that both the bishop and Mother Bridget ranked her, after themselves, as the person most worthy of confidence and trust.

From 1870 until 1879, during the remainder of Mother Bridget's uncanonically prolonged term of office, Mother Vincent was Assistant, and she continued to be so until, on Mother Bridget's resignation to go overseas, the bishop appointed Mother M. Patrick Potter as the new Reverend Mother. Mother Vincent's life in Queensland thus falls into three phases: her own term of office as Reverend Mother; her period of disgrace from 1865 to 1870; and finally, her role as Mother Assistant from then until her death. The events of the first phase have been recorded in the previous chapter. It is now time to ask why she was never restored to supreme command, and how, nevertheless, her influence remained the vitalizing element in the community.

Under Bishop Quinn Superiors were appointed, not elected. Otherwise Mother Vincent would certainly have been returned to office. For the Sisters whom she had brought out in 1873, and who when elections were due formed the majority of the community, saw her as she was considered in Baggot Street and in the Irish convents generally, a nun of high worth in her own right. Mother Vincent's religious formation by the foundress gave her a degree of prestige enjoyed by no one else in Queensland, and the acknowledged similarity of her spirit to Mother McAuley's imparted a special grace to her words. 'A Pillar of the Order', Mother Vincent had been 'known and praised by the sainted Foundress'.[7] To the new arrivals, the causes of Mother Vincent's removal from office were common knowledge, and served only to enhance her reputation.

Their approval of her defence of the integrity of the Constitutions was made abundantly clear by their action after the bishop's death, when, having met in Chapter, they revoked his ruling concerning vows and religious habit. In the 1860s Mother Vincent had resisted Quinn's impatient wish to curtail the novice's training period, and to deny perpetual vows to Sisters destined for domestic work. For as guardian of the Constitutions, Mother Vincent could not permit such changes without authority from Rome. Moreover, there was a danger of introducing class distinction between Sisters appointed for different kinds of duties, which the grey habit chosen for lay Sisters would further accentuate.

Nevertheless, after the Vatican Council, when Quinn told Mother Vincent that he had received verbal assent from Pius IX to the changes he had made, her opposition ended. One of her letters to the Cardinal Prefect shows that there was an 'ad experimentum' permission for temporary vows and grey habit for lay Sisters,[8] but on Quinn's death the whole question was dropped with much relief.[9]

With respect to Community matters, however, where Mother Vincent resisted the bishop's alterations, Mother Bridget complied. Thus the spiritual turbulence induced by the shipboard novice with no religious formation posed a threat to the continued existence of the Mercy Institute in its old form. But while Mother Bridget at first strongly defended the bishop's point of view, she was later won over to Mother Vincent's different ideas of government. Mother Bridget's character was thus of the first importance.

Brought up in a comfortable home in Kingstown (Dun Laoghaire) Mother Bridget had received the education fashionable for Victorian young ladies, but the family library included such contemporaries as Emerson as well as the older classics. As the professions were closed to women, Emily Conlan found her satisfactions instead in social life until James Quinn turned her thoughts into more serious channels.

For seven years he was her spiritual director, and at twenty-eight she joined his missionary party. Of that group, Emily Conlan had less training as a teacher than any except Jane Townsend and Sister M. Catherine Morgan, neither of whom remained in Queensland more than eighteen months. But Emily's disadvantage was outweighed by her piety, intelligence, and steadfastness of purpose. Furthermore, Quinn knew her home and family background, having been an associate of her brothers, Father Robert, and George, a ship's captain, Frank, who was to accompany them to Queensland and Mary, the only sister. Therefore he had more in common with Mother Bridget Conlan than with Sisters M. Cecilia and Benedict,[10] whom he saw only through his chaplaincy duties.

The closeness of Quinn's relations with Emily Conlan explains his reliance on her rather than on the Baggot Street Sisters, and Emily Conlan's reciprocal trust in Quinn. It explains but does not justify Quinn's calm assumption that Sisters with longer service and higher rank ought to obey Sister Bridget Conlan simply because she was older than they, and in his eyes more capable. His unfortunate attempt to rule through Mother Bridget, while preserving the empty shell of constitutional government, pointed up the difficulties in the way of a return to the Mercy view of community. This included a way of life demonstrated by Mother Vincent's own leadership, a sharing in service and love, according to Mother McAuley's own advice to the Reverend Mother: 'Don't govern too much.' Departure from this idea meant, among other things, that community could not be truly created, and that identity of purpose would be lost.

Mother Bridget, like the bishop, was a dictator. Her complete accord with the revered 'Pater Noster' (her title for Quinn) did not indicate servility or weakness. Rather she is remembered as a grenadier, aristocratic in her bearing, fastidious in her choice of company, and for all her slightness of build, of iron constitution and of iron will. Indeed, 'No General of an Army or Commodore of a Fleet could have issued more laconic epistles' than Mother Bridget in enforcing her wishes. The Cork nuns in forwarding Lord Emly's gift of a clock, addressed her as 'Your Ladyship', with the subtle hint that the title Lady Emily befitted her.[11]

But the force which made Mother Bridget a tyrant gave her a tremendous capacity for hard work. If she expected too much of others, after the manner of the old Irish ascetics, she exhausted herself. Further, Mother Bridget's spirituality was drawn from Irish monasticism, more akin to the ideals of the Eastern cenobites than of St Benedict and the West.[12] But all modern religious rules follow St Benedict's more humane spirit with its keynote of discretion and avoidance of detailed regulation. Lacking this humanity, Mother Bridget's devotion entailed a Spartan enthusiasm for duty as well as for a degree of discomfort repugnant to less hardy souls. Thus she refused an anaesthetic when undergoing surgery for cysts beneath the eyelids, and she continued her work immediately afterwards.[13] Then again, she ordered that during Lent the Sisters should not only stand in silence when taking their vegetarian evening meal, but also go without breakfast if it chanced that they were absent from morning Mass.

Predictably, Mother Bridget's ideas on novitiate clashed with those of Sisters trained in the McAuley ideal. While she admired the blend of mildness and forbearance in Sisters Columbanus, Patrick and Zita, whom she described to Mother Vincent as 'those souls of wonderful longanimity',[14] prayerful, generous and good, the methods she proposed to create future Sisters of the same calibre met with outright condemnation. As an Irish Mistress of Novices told Mother Bridget, 'You will excuse me when I say that I could not for a moment agree with you in desiring that the wills of the Sisters should be crushed so absolutely as you deem necessary.'

It was a pity, therefore, that Mother Bridget knew no Australian Mistresses of Novices who might have curbed her severity; it was one of the disadvantages of lack of contact with other communities which was a great problem in Queensland. In Ireland, however, Mercy novices were 'led very sweetly to resign all freely' and to learn self-abnegation out of love, not compulsion. Hence Mother Bridget's 'severe lesson' gave a very bad impression of religious charity.[15] Just as with novices, she deplored the 'remarkable independence and self-conceit' she found in children, fostered, she believed, by style in dress; and when she became Superior at Nudgee, she set out to correct self-conceit with the drab uniform strongly criticized by Dr Dunne.[16]

She considered that professional training was not enough for aspirant teachers at All Hallows', and it was with disdain that she accepted 'plebeian' Miss Doyle only at the insistence of Père H. Brun.[17] Similarly, young women on entering the Order might find themselves doing menial work. Thus when two applied who were 'talented and humble—rare combination', both with teacher's certificates, she deemed that they should become lay Sisters employed in domestic duties because they were redolent 'of the turf at every turn and intonation.'[18] Mother Bridget was not then Reverend Mother, but declared loftily, 'I regard it as necessary to establish the principle and to insist on it that *position* is to be determined by the Superior,'[19] though the bishop, still virtual director, overruled her wish to restrict the work of these talented teachers.

Even in Mother Bridget's own family, to which she was devoted, George and Robert had to bow to her will like other mortals. Thus when in 1879 Canon Robert Conlan excused himself, because of heavy preparations for Easter, from accompanying her from Dublin to Rome on Quinn's business, Mother Bridget applied to his archbishop to have him excused from parish duties. In the request, Mother Bridget mentioned that she had sought letters of introduction to prelates in the Eternal City, from Cardinal Manning, the Bishop of Ossory (Moran), and the Bishop of Southwark. Then she slipped in her request for Robert's release so that he could be with her in Rome.[20] Meanwhile she had her brother, the captain, comb London for a mislaid book. 'I shall call at Scotland Yard tomorrow to see if the prayer-book has turned up', promised George.[21] While Cardinals, bishops and captains thus helped her in England and Ireland, Dr Cani and Bishop O'Mahoney were already in Rome so that she would be 'sufficiently befriended'.[22]

Mother Mary of the Cross suspected that Mother Bridget, while in the Holy City, intended to use her influence against the Sisters of St Joseph. Indeed she wrote that Mother Bridget 'was a pious earnest Religious, but her views and ours are opposite. I love her as a pious, hard-working sister in religion, but . . . she is not, I fear, our Institute's friend. It is reported that she will do all she can to promote Dr. James Quinn's views with regard to us.'[23]

This was not a surprising opinion, since Mother Bridget had absorbed Quinn's idea of the monarchical character of the episcopacy. Nevertheless, although Mother Mary, like Mother Vincent, accepted wholeheartedly the premiss that bishops enjoy a divine authority, neither could go so far as Mother Bridget in accepting Quinn's notion of episcopal rule. Experience in Queensland had already shown that the monarchical concept could not always be validly applied because it was too hard; for a Church leader failed in the practice of authority if, in the pursuit of ecclesiastical interests, he denied the individual both justice and compassion. Mothers Vincent, Benedict and Cecilia had been sacrificed to ecclesiastical interest in the 1860s, and the St Joseph Sisters were to suffer a similar fate in the 1870s. But here again, Mother Bridget was on Quinn's side.

If Mother Mary of the Cross would not agree to his terms, Quinn expected her to withdraw her nuns from their Queensland schools.[24] The avowed aim of Mother Bridget's overseas visit in 1879 was to find Sisters to replace the Josephites, as the State subsidy to the schools was soon to cease.[25] If, however, Mother Bridget did use her influence as Mother Mary thought, her letters to Mother Vincent make no mention of it. Nevertheless, Mother Bridget's sentiments were expressed by Bishop Quinn who described a letter to the *Courier* from a St Joseph Sister as 'unseemly rebellion', and complained about the efforts of Catholic laymen to retain the Josephite Sisters in Queensland as 'schismatical and rebellious'.[26]

Because Mother Bridget was 'fond of feeling . . . a moral haircloth' about her body,[27] she was not a comfortable person to know. She lacked the ability to delegate tasks to others and trust them to carry them out. She would come to advise and change, until all initiative was dead. 'What is the good of forever worrying them?' reminded Archbishop Dunne,[28] who could be blunt with her, and unlike Quinn held her in no high regard. 'Fussing is terribly her way', he complained.[29]

Shortly after Quinn's death in 1881, Mother Bridget was sent to Dalby as local Superior. There the archbishop restrained her from imposing too severe a fast on the Sisters during Lent. However, fortunately for them, her term was brief, because she could not agree with the parish priest, Father Byrne. After a few years in All Hallows' as Bursar, she was posted to Nudgee where she remained for her last twenty-seven years, supervising the work of the Home, organizing the Holy Family movement, and on the annual Nudgee Day dispensing hospitality lavishly with the aplomb of an accomplished hostess.

The archbishop (Dunne) kept an eye on her Sisters to preserve them from haircloth, and protested when he found that their reading was limited to solemn spiritual books. 'It is absurd for you to assign those little folk at Nudgee nothing for their recreation but Rodriguez', his Grace told her. 'Get a few good cheery books . . . You'll have them cranky or rebellious.'[30] Similarly he asked her to throw open the doors of St Vincent's with genial hospitality to the Sisters from the western houses down for the summer vacation.[31] Mother Bridget had to unbend to make them feel welcome, because her formality hid sterling qualities. This stiffness appeared even in her letters. Her sister Mary's, Dunne reminded her, were 'quite as Christian' as her own, but 'infinitely more human'.[32]

Mother Bridget's most memorable characteristic was loyalty to friends. In death as in life, Quinn was 'our great and good bishop'.[33] Her cold manner to Archbishop Vaughan, her slighting reference to him in correspondence as 'the friar', embarrassed Dunne when the Benedictine prelate journeyed from Sydney for his consecration, for Dunne wished to bury for ever the bitter internecine feuds of the 1870s; this Mother Bridget found hard to do. Declining Cardinal Moran's invitation to her to write about Quinn, she would only say that 'God mercifully rescued him from the painful conflicts of this life'.[34] But she cherished the memory of a holy prelate who had been 'Pater Noster'.

Such was the character of the woman who posed the greatest obstacle to Mother Vincent's ideal of a Mercy community, and who won the bishop's approval by her stern concept of duty and discipline. After Mother Vincent was deposed, what was her relationship with Mother Bridget? Did the one play victim and the other victor? Did divided loyalties divide the Community?

While Mother Vincent was still *persona non grata* with the bishop in the late 1860s, she systematically decided what course to pursue. Whenever she attempted to effect a special good, she said, she found herself in trouble; but she trusted that divine Providence would fructify her pain.[35] Mother Bridget expressed her admiration for Mother Vincent at this time in one pithy phrase: 'She edifies'.[36] On the arrival of the bishop's letter in 1870 summoning Mother Vincent to Europe, Mother Bridget and Dr Cani consulted together, and decided that they could not do without her. Mother Bridget then wrote to the bishop explaining their great need of her, chiefly because 'of her mature protection to the community', but also because she was indispensable in the schools,[37] quoting the testimony of Dean C. Murlay, Fathers J. Horan and R. Dunne in support of her remarks. The clinching reason for not freeing Mother Vincent to go overseas was the then turbulence of Europe.

Thus for a second time, Mother Vincent had the fleeting vision of home before her eyes only, it seemed, to be robbed of the reality. On an earlier occasion the bishop had recalled her from Hobart; but where the bishop had the charism of office to rule, Cani was only his representative, and Cani was actually reversing the episcopal decision. Mother Vincent could have gone to him to argue, to reason and to have her way, for here the Community was not involved, but only herself.

To understand her response, which on the face of it looks passive, even supine, one has to recall the spirit in which a nun makes her vow.[38] If God delegates his authority to man, the nun shows her love for God by obedience. She does not thereby lose her freedom; rather, she makes more room in her heart for God. Only the vision of faith that God works through men can overcome a natural repugnance for accepting his will through frail and imperfect agents. 'I hope', commented Mother Bridget to Cani, 'that it is unnecessary to say that Sister M. Vincent unites with us in being perfectly satisfied with your judgment on the matter.'[39]

But the bishop was far from satisfied. Much as Brisbane needed her, he needed her more. Curtly he countermanded. 'Respecting Mother Vincent Whitty's return to Europe, I have this much to say. It was *settled* by me . . . that she was to come.' Dr Cani had acted according to his lights when the matter was put to him, the bishop's letter continued, but 'it should not have been submitted at all, *I having already decided it*. Let there be no avoidable delay in her departure.'[40]

Suitably contrite, Mother Bridget hurried the preparations, noting that 'dearest Sister M. Vincent's presence' had been 'of solid benefit to the schools and the edification of her community'.[41] Indeed so hastily was a berth booked on the *Royal Dane* that Mother Bridget discovered only when she took the traveller to the ship that Mother Vincent's cabin was completely unfurnished. Mother Bridget expressed her admiration of Mother Vincent in an account of the event: 'A comment upon the unprovided voyage was never heard from her.'[42] A four-month passage lay ahead through the forties south of Cape Horn, and Mother Vincent watched the dangerous manœuvres of the ship through a lane of icebergs, and sent back to All Hallows' a magnificent picture of one taken from on board.[43]

When Mother Vincent had gone, Mother Bridget made an entry in the Chapter Book that Mother Vincent had been elected Assistant, and in the absence of a council, the entry was witnessed by Sister M. Joseph Murphy.[44] On Mother Vincent's return, Mother Bridget welcomed her cordially and, made wiser by the bishop's peremptoriness and Cani's procrastination, leaned heavily on her whenever Quinn's snap decisions irritated beyond measure the Sisters in some outlying convent.

Two tasks assigned to Mother Vincent from 1873 onwards afforded her the ideal opportunity to meet the Sisters and bring them strength and consolation. She was to travel from convent to convent to give retreats and individual and collective counsel; she was also to share her practical experience in fund-raising. Her itinerary was often settled by the bishops, first Quinn, and later Dunne, who recognized her value as liaison officer between the centre and the scattered houses.

Her visits to branch convents were welcomed by isolated Sisters, partly because she was good company. But what made her most sought was that 'she stood alone in charity and sympathy for all who needed either.'[45] She knew how to listen; she was aware of the great difficulties of convents underfinanced and understaffed. Prompt to help both in house and school, she also visited the sick of the parish, and in any crisis she remained serene; Father Byrne of Dalby praised her for never showing fuss.[46] Respect for all that the Sisters were and tried to be found expression in her clear trust in them.

Her experience in the 1860s, when external pressure had driven to flight Mother Benedict and Mother Cecilia, had taught her that over-organization destroys community. However, even in the 1870s, curt unexplained orders still caused distress. Thus Sister M. Agnes of Stanthorpe found herself embarrassed by the bishop's swift changes in house-arrangements when a telegram-like message announcing 'You are to take charge' placed the government of the house in her hands while the former Superior still remained on the staff.[47] At such times, Mother Vincent's charity and tact proved invaluable.

To create true community, a society is only a commencement, even if it involves shared effort and responsibility; on the other hand, the application of iron-clad principles and drastic unilateral action is the danger of absolute monarchy. Mother Vincent's mode of thought and action cushioned the rigour of directives from above, but at the same time brought about the co-operation needed to extend the kingdom of God. In this mode of action she differed from Mother Bridget, for where a Sister failed in mature responsibility, Mother Bridget's letter would convey a blunt warning from the bishop that 'if there was not a total change for the better by the end of the year [the Sister at fault] could not continue with us.'[48] How was Mother Vincent to bridge the gap between society with its laws and the community of grace which was the ideal?

She attempted to reconcile the strictness of superiors with the individual's hunger for freedom and love, and in this succeeded best by her manner. Far from being a good letter-writer, she was rather inarticulate, and found words 'slow and imperfect' to express her deepest thoughts.[49] But when she had to give a correction she included herself among those who made mistakes, and so forged a bond of understanding. However, although she took the sting from the correction, she avoided the over-protectiveness which ends in inaction.

Mother Bridget, on the other hand, still unconvinced of the efficacy of the spoonful of honey, sent letters after her urging sternness. 'Now, in this case—my dearest Mother Vincent—it will be necessary for you to be on your guard against your disposition to justify all delinquents.'[50] Clearly there were two principles at work: the authoritarian, so characteristic of the nineteenth century, and the old gospel freedom.

The transformation Mother Vincent was able to achieve is incalculable. She blended into a genuine united community the disparate elements of the All Hallows' congregation, namely, the Sisters trained in Queensland, the new arrivals from overseas who had been accustomed to slightly different observances, and Sisters like Sister M. Elizabeth Hersey who returned to Brisbane after years in other colonies. The impression of earlier severity under Quinn's autocratic rule had so disappeared by the late 1870s that during the 1879–80 quest for Sisters in Ireland, Mothers Bridget and Claver encountered no repetition of the obstructing tactics which Mother Vincent had so painfully overcome in 1872.

Through gifted young nuns receptive to her ideas, Mother Vincent communicated the urgency of the educational need of the 1870s. To follow the population and reorganize the schools so as to meet the new conditions after 1880 was a need which inspired a phenomenal effort. The cause took on the ringing appeal of a crusade, and the enthusiasm and generosity channelled through many Sisters attracted young girls still at school to answer the call for volunteers to the Order. From All Hallows' alone came Winifrede Trotman, Blanche Byrne, Anne Fitzgerald, and the dux of the school, Nell Ring.[51] Nell at seventeen heard Sister M. Patrick discuss convents to be opened shortly at Charters Towers, Cooktown, Maryborough and Gympie. The staffing of these new schools, the bishop said, 'taxed and perplexed us to the last degree. After passing in review (on paper) over and over again all the members of every community in the diocese looking for a good musician, we were unsuccessful. You know that without a good musician here, any foundation is only half complete.'[52] At this point Nell offered herself. She had studied music for seven years, and the Community accepted her though reluctant to cut off her education a year before due time.

The wide scatter immediately necessary in those days, before regular novitiate studies could be undertaken, took the postulants and novices to the far corners of Queensland. They then came under local Superiors of the stamp of those old champions of Mother Vincent—Sister M. de Sales Gorry, now of Rockhampton; Sister M. Joseph Murphy of Ipswich; Sister M. Kevin O'Brien, Warwick; and Sister M. Agnes White, Stanthorpe, whose names denote the finest qualities of a Sister of Mercy.

Yet more outstanding still is the memory of Mother M. Patrick Potter. Best known and loved among Mother Vincent's disciples was this young principal of All Hallows' school. She came from the house which Mother Vincent had founded in County Kildare, the Athy convent presided over by Mother Teresa Maher. Sister M. Patrick was like Mother Vincent in her genuine interest in persons, and where Mother Bridget's unyielding ways had provoked resentment among the staff, children and parents, Sister M. Patrick smoothed and soothed. She was thus a strong ally of Mother Vincent in preserving peace and fostering vocations to religious life. Bishop Quinn appointed her Reverend Mother while Mother Bridget was overseas (in 1880) with the now ageing Mother Vincent as her Assistant.

Mother Patrick returned the affectionate respect of the older nun. 'I am so grateful to God that I knew her so intimately', Mother Patrick told Mr G. W. Gray, long after Mother Vincent's death, 'for it is well to have one of her spirit before my mind to copy even at a distance.'[53] With the close bonds between them, Mother Patrick turned naturally to her mentor even in such matters as the building of the All Hallows' school; Mother Vincent's ideas decided the height of each storey and the disposition of the concert-hall and music rooms, though Mother Patrick remained principal.[54]

Once the Community had an able leader (Mother Patrick), Mother Vincent longed to be free from routine administration to do more for the poor and the sick. She had plans for a Mater Hospital in Brisbane, and hoped to bring out her cousin, Sister M. Berchmans, Superior of the Dublin Mater, to launch the work. However, Archbishop Dunne told Mother Vincent that she must still act as chief provider for the Community.[55] She thereby remained associated with the Sisters and schools even during her last decade when her health was failing and the task of building Holy Cross Home claimed all her energy. Precisely because one 'could not be near her without loving and revering her', her advice and example made a profound impression. The combination of vision, trust and love made Mother Vincent in her Sisters' eyes a 'great woman' whom they felt privileged to be near.[56]

To create community with the congregation was one thing, but to create it in the wider society was another. The active religious community exists to serve society, a task which requires sensitivity to needs through a bond of understanding. In the turbulent currents of the nineteenth century, to create such a bond was no small task.

How did the presence of the Sisters affect society? Was the attitude of the Queensland people towards the Church notably different in 1890 from what it had been in 1860? If so, can it be demonstrated that through their work the Sisters had penetrated other worlds? Had they entered politics, moral, intellectual and social life? Or on the other hand did they concentrate on education as a way of insulating Catholics from outside influences?

To answer these questions adequately would demand a full-scale social survey. Treating them in the context of Mother Vincent's life work limits the field but provides enough evidence to form an estimate.

Mother Vincent assumed, in common with other religious, that just as the Fall is part of our collective predicament, so must redemption in Christ be collective as well as individual.[57] Thus everyone living in society has some share in the responsibility for the success or failure of others. This religious world-view determined the scope and type of action for her and her Sisters; it was action aimed at making the Redemption permanently effective. The Sisters' goals coincided with some liberal objectives in that they sought to increase the sum of harmony, health and achievement in the world, but this work differed from philanthropy in its religious basis.

The form which Mother Vincent's action took, apart from direct education, was to help immigrants to become part of Australian society, to stem the erosion of religion and family in urban life, and to tide the less fortunate over hard times in benevolent homes.

During Mother Vincent's lifespan in Queensland, 53,000 Irish left home for Queensland,[58] and by 1875 she was able to boast to Monsignor Kirby in Rome that children of many nationalities, Catholic and Protestant, filled her classrooms.[59] In the very year of her arrival, 1861, she described the tents that mushroomed between Brisbane houses to accommodate the steady influx of new colonists.[60] By the following year the bishop's Queensland Immigration Society had chartered ships of the Black Ball line to bring thousands more. Even though the Society was permitted to operate only until 1864, the impetus it gave to the population movement was considerable.

Mother Vincent, too, actively promoted migration through her wide contacts with convents in England and Ireland. Care of unemployed women was everywhere part of Mercy work. To the practical mind of a woman closely associated with charitable work in Dublin, a fresh start in a new land was a solution to both economic and social ills. To draw off the surplus population from the old countries for Queensland's open spaces was to benefit both the new and old lands. 'The Colony offers rare advantages to the poor', she wrote, to publicize Queensland. 'The institutions of the Sisters will be so many depots to receive and provide situations for growing girls of workhouses and Industrial Schools so numerous in Ireland and England', said the printed sheets which she had distributed overseas. 'Any girl trained to domestic service may be sent from London to Queensland for £1.'[61] Enthusiastic about the potentialities of Queensland, she did not neglect to urge that men of substance should come likewise; they 'would increase their own capital and do good by employing the numbers who are coming here'.[62]

The bishop's agents addressed themselves particularly to the rural population, holding out the inducement of land, but Mother Vincent saw the tendency even then for the Australian population to concentrate in towns and noted that 'farmers with money to invest in land do very well about Brisbane, the crops are so abundant.'[63] Her main concern, however, was with women and her letters to convents asked for teachers from the home training colleges, governesses, shop-assistants and domestics,[64] for in Queensland they would be free from the vagaries of casual employment. Mother Vincent felt certain that a fine future lay ahead for them, and prophesied that 'when we are in our graves, this will be a great country'.[65]

Even though Mother Vincent and the bishop actively encouraged migration, the drift of Westerners to Australia had commenced long before their arrival, and was, in fact, the direct cause of their coming. The usual reason given for the high migration figures to Queensland in the early 1860s is the temporary closure of America through the Civil War. But Australia was attractive to migrants even before war broke out.

Neil Coughlan's recent analysis of the migration-trend[66] shows that by the late 1850s there was already a large increase in the numbers turning to Australia. Apart from the land-settlement plan and the gold rushes at this end of the world, powerful magnets both, other factors determined the type, age and status of those choosing the long route to the south. 'In the decade from 1851–1861, nineteen per cent of Munster's population emigrated.'[67] After the lesson of the potato blight, land-owners turned away from the small crop economy and evicted the small farmer. By the 1850s, the old practice of cutting up farms among all the children of a household was abandoned, and primogeniture became the rule. With nothing left for the younger sons, they naturally turned to the rural life they had known at home wherever it could be procured. Australia offered better opportunities than America, already largely settled and to some extent industrialized. Thus Queensland's new migrants were predominantly from the rural class.

Another factor made them extraordinarily of a piece. Father Patrick Dunne was Quinn's main agent in Ireland, and they came chiefly from Dunne's own county, Offaly.[68]

The remittance system accentuated still further the tendency for farmers and labourers to predominate. Money sent home to bring out brothers, sisters or cousins created a concentration of persons from one family or from one area, from the south rather than the north or east, and gave a drum to beat to those Queenslanders who feared racial or religious imbalance.

The culture shock to this rural people was exaggerated by the sectarian feeling stirred up by the different press organs, especially the anti-Catholic *Guardian*. Resulting intolerance made Mother Vincent's task more difficult for the 'startling homogeneity of the Irish' brought discrimination and active sectarianism, since this undifferentiated group was 'projected against an English and Scottish emigration which largely reflected the great variation in age, skill, education, family grouping and wealth to be found in a comparatively advanced society.'[69]

Despite her realism and stability, Mother Vincent was often troubled by this kind of prejudice. She deplored the painful insularity and bigotry then so prevalent.[70] It was a source of discouragement, she said, even to priests and religious; some found it insufferable and returned home.[71] This seemed to Mother Vincent a sad waste, 'with so much to be done'. Fed on Macaulay's idea of inevitable economic and intellectual progress and a Protestant ethic of thrift, frugality and hard work,[72] Protestant colonists tended to profess the optimistic idea which persuaded them that they were the privileged possessors of absolute social and ethical values, and sole heirs to all the centuries.

In Liverpool Mother Vincent had seen the evil effects of similar social and religious imbalance, with immigrants imprisoned in the lower stratum. But there was no need for this inexorable stagnation in Queensland, even though here too the Catholics were 'drawn for the most part from the poorer classes of the Mother Country',[73] for there was no lack of opportunity to carve a future for themselves and their families. Determined to help them to settle in every way she could, Mother Vincent, and the Sisters, met the immigrants at the port,[74] and provided meals and accommodation at Brisbane and Ipswich[75] until the newcomers were ready to depart for Toowoomba, Warwick, the Logan Valley, Beaudesert or Caboolture.

There was a depot for immigrants at Kangaroo Point,[76] but Mother Vincent did her utmost to provide other shelter for unattached girls until they could find work; for this reason she took some school-age girls as boarders without pay, while by 1866 she had a House of Mercy adjoining All Hallows' where young women could stay until they were placed. 'While I have a bed I cannot refuse to give shelter to such persons in a strange land', Mother Vincent wrote.[77]

Regular Sunday classes also helped greatly in the assimilation of adult women, while preserving a certain cohesion which was useful while the fresh arrivals were socially absorbed. In the old country religious culture and tradition had permeated and saturated the civil and social life of society; in Queensland the little convent centres were to carry on that function through the Sodality of the Holy Family, the Children of Mary and other semi-religious, semi-social gatherings.

To find openings for teachers presented no problems because of the number of schools 'so rapidly rising in all parts of the colony', but Mother Vincent found it difficult to place domestics from among the single girls reluctant to go 'up the country'.[78] Where there were small colonies of Irish, however, other Irish immigrants naturally went, and names such as Innisfail, Killarney, Rathdowney and Charleville testify to the Irish origin of the first colonists in centres all over the State.

Nor was Mother Vincent's charity confined to Irishmen. Some Germans were brought out through the bishop's scheme and settled around Laidley, Gatton and Marburg. The better to help these migrants assimilate and to render them all aid possible, spiritual and temporal, German was introduced into the All Hallows' curriculum quite early,[79] and even the Sisters not engaged in teaching the language learned it.

Mother Vincent's personal interest was obvious, even in unstable immigrants whom she could not trust. Frank Conlan, for instance, the ne'er-do-well son of a good family, was a symbol of men she most deeply desired to help, the improvident but good-hearted Irish wanderers, wasting life and substance from job to job. Frank Conlan caused heartbreak to his sister Mother Bridget, so different in character, and from overseas she wrote to 'Darling Mother Vincent' concerning him: 'Thanks for your news of my *dear* brother. There is too little to congratulate him on his present position to admit of my writing to him.'[80]

Mother Vincent and her Sisters encountered two opposing attitudes to wealth among the Catholic colonists, in their extreme forms either utter carelessness or tight-fisted acquisitiveness. Frank Conlan was an instance of the feckless type. Where Methodists and Presbyterians believed in the sober prudence that applied itself industriously to saving and material improvement, most Irishmen believed that the 'money-making faculty is not inseparably associated with intellectual ability or moral worth—rather the reverse.'[81]

This attitude derived from religious outlook and family habits. While not at all a diligent private reader of the Bible, the Catholic had his Sunday readings from Old and New Testament, and had been for years inured to deprivation by contemplating the poverty of Christ. Moreover, the Sermon on the Mount echoed the long tradition of Israel,[82] in which the poor of Yahweh, the humble who trusted God, formed a class apart. Although they were frequently oppressed by the rich and powerful, these were God's chosen ones, the heirs of the promise to Abraham and his posterity. While Mother Vincent appreciated the basic religious concept that saw poverty of spirit as a goal to be won, she set her face against shiftlessness and that penury deriving from laziness and lack of ambition.

Herself a product of Irish middle-class society, Mother Vincent desired to raise the material standards of those under her care. Yet she spoke with admiration of the close bonds even among the poorest Irish, of their unfailing wish to share and to help which was so much part of them that they found it hard to live in isolation. To visit, to converse, to laugh, and to sorrow with friends was for these people the most precious part of daily life.

A corrective for their insouciance was afforded by the English and Scottish portion of the Queensland community to whom an Ipswich lecturer set out to 'show that it is labour which feeds, instructs, enriches and dignifies man; that it is to labour that the Anglo-Saxon race owe their present position in the van of civilization.'[83] Further, the policy of the first two bishops, Quinn and Dunne, was to fight the tendency to the nomad existence of Irish workers by the stability of land ownership. Mother Vincent through the schools sought to blend Anglo-Saxon perseverance with Irish family solidarity in her own theology of work which gave due proportion to matter and spirit.

Mother Vincent was less concerned with the improvident but warmhearted whose interest in the neighbour was basically Christian than with the opposite extreme, of whom she spoke with some discouragement to her brother. 'I don't think you have got a colder, harder and more ignorant people to deal with than we have in this parish, and in Edinburgh', he replied. 'They are like trees, as I tell them, transplanted in a cold dreary soil, and they show abundant signs of the influence of years in such an atmosphere.'[84]

He considered that such men and women fell an easy prey to the more materialistic values when they emigrated. Conformity to new surroundings led some to abandon the faith, while others like Thaddeus O'Kane, editor of the Charters Towers *Northern Miner*, not only apostatized but rejected their national roots.

Mother Vincent saw her main work of education in the context of the wider needs of society. She had a duty to adults as to children, since children accept so many of their fundamental ideas from the adults of their own immediate family. To help the immigrants to absorb all that was good in Australian society while clinging steadfastly to their sense of the immanence and transcendence of God was, in her judgment, to integrate them in the best possible manner. 'Lay the foundation of Brisbane in very fervent and continual *prayer*', her brother wrote. 'No work easy or difficult can bring many souls to God which is not prayed over *hard* and *long*.'[85] Her prayer, shared with the prayer of all the Church—and that meant the prayer of all the Churches—would effect the union and harmony which she so deeply desired.

Her Sisters lived in intimate relationship with the people in every town which had a convent. In the homes they gave counsel, encouraged frequent reception of the sacraments, and helped to build Church and community. After a confirmation of over four hundred in St Stephen's, the bishop declared that the adults included many 'young men from Government offices and whole families from the outskirts of the parish' whom the Sisters had sought out and of whose existence he had been unaware.[86] Mother Vincent was unflagging in visitation of homes, though this involved wearisome journeys on foot.

The strength of the Church, the men and women who threw their weight behind every Catholic project, were neither the improvident nomads nor the tight-fisted individualists. During the first two or three decades the Catholic community produced such outstanding figures as parliamentarians P. O'Sullivan, K. I. O'Doherty, Henry Fitzgerald, J. M. Macrossan and P. Perkins; lawyers A. J. Thynne and P. Real; Inspector N. McGroarty and P. J. McDermott of the public service. However, the majority of Catholics were famous in nothing but their unexampled religious fidelity.

Without the active help of Catholic laymen, Mother Vincent could not have found a foothold in Queensland, let alone initiated her various projects. Thus in her last undertaking, her co-workers as the trustees of the Benevolent Home for Women at Wooloowin were Messrs J. M. Macrossan, G. W. Gray and Burton. John Murtagh Macrossan was well known for his brave and uncompromising stand on Catholic education, but while he was 'a good Donegal Catholic' he was also an enthusiastic Australian and died in the midst of his efforts to realize Federation.[87] G. W. Gray, also a parliamentarian, and very wealthy, was a convert to the faith, and befriended Mother Vincent by standing godfather to most of her plans. Of all men he perhaps appreciated most her concern for the poor and friendless, and he preserved every note she sent him. She needed such friends, for though the immigrants were homogeneous, mainly working-class, and made up a genuinely popular Church, there were obstacles in the path to harmony with the rest of society.

The secret and confidential despatches of Governor Bowen and the correspondence of the first Premier, Herbert, enshrine the sense of racial and religious superiority common among nineteenth-century Englishmen. Brisbane society might have been invoked to prove that the Englishmen shows his ethnic intelligence by repudiating Rome, the Irishman his ethnic inferiority by accepting it.[88] The entanglement of national and religious prejudice was almost inevitable.

Two examples will sufficiently illustrate the way in which hostile pressures impinged directly on Mother Vincent's life. In the 1863 elections education was the chief issue, and Catholics, 25 per cent of the population, hoped to place one representative in parliament. In the event they failed. Herbert, a candidate for West Moreton, saw the whole Church in league against him, including the Sisters of Mercy. 'I have been triumphantly elected by a majority of about ten', he wrote home. 'You never saw such a contest, a Roman Catholic bishop, and even nuns, did all they could against me . . . they have been ignominiously defeated. The Pope must feel very small.'[89] The *Guardian* thundered its partisanship for Herbert so that uninformed readers must conclude that Mother Vincent and her Sisters were political campaigners.

Mother Vincent had reason to believe that there was 'much bigotry against Catholicity and the Irish'[90] and the All Hallows' girls had reason to fear the sulphurous atmosphere where religion and politics were dangerously compounded. During the visit of the Duke of Edinburgh in 1868, at the children's demonstration of welcome, the entry of the All Hallows' girls almost caused 'an exceedingly serious riot . . . attended by the most dire and calamitous results.'[91]

A group of Lang migrants, strong Evangelicals, attempted to prevent the pupils from marching with banners, while a large number of onlookers were 'strongly sympathetic with the children on account of their being girls and having only a few female teachers to look after them.' The result was a clash between hotheads, which frightened the girls and was brought to an end only by police intervention.

Herbert's campaign and the incident at the demonstration for the Prince, which fortunately occurred before the O'Farrell fracas at Sydney, were symptomatic of the tensions in Queensland society in the 1860s. The climate of mistrust was to change considerably before Mother Vincent's death, but not until after the demise of the two papers most hostile to Catholics, the *Guardian*, extinct by 1875, and the *Queensland Evangelical Standard* which lasted into the 1880s.

There was less violence but more persistence in this second paper, which specialized in revelations of the Maria Monk kind, and as such kept Mother Vincent and her Sisters under constant and hostile surveillance.

The *Standard* attacked convents as the stronghold of ultramontanism. Mother Vincent and her Sisters, it implied, were part of the army with which Catholicism fought liberalism. While the *Courier* was not behindhand with anti-Catholic and pro-liberal views, its lively interest in local politics and its support in the anti-Griffith party evoked the *Standard*'s denunciation; for neglect of the Protestant aspect of the world-wide Catholic-Liberal struggle was not to be tolerated.

Since this, in the *Standard*'s view, was the principal historical conflict of the age, 'beyond or perhaps, we ought to say below the province of the secular press', the *Standard* set itself up as watch-dog and called on all Dissenting and Evangelical Protestants to unite.

There was a formidable response, for over thirty Orange Lodges sponsored the paper.[92] No mere parish-pump politics could have rallied so many clergymen. In the opinion of these men, the *Syllabus of Errors*, the struggle to preserve the temporal power of the Papacy, and the Vatican Council were each a sinister aspect of an international plot. Nuns stood for the extreme views of Pio Nono in Church-State relations, and the paper warned of the 'insidious cleverness' of the 'black-draped figures who walk softly, speak softly and have no room in their hearts for any imagery but that of the Holy Father and the Blessed Virgin.'[93]

Significantly the first number appeared in the heat of the controversy concerning the 1875 Education Act. The very success of Mother Vincent's schools and the favour which they enjoyed among Protestants made the attack on the Sisters the more bitter. There schools were, in this hostile view, instruments of 'a policy the most subtle and far-seeing and comprehensive which the world has seen . . . The mot d'ordre is uttered infallibly at Rome and it runs through all the nations of Christendom and ultramontanism makes the possession of the schools a matter of life and death.'[94] The contributors to the *Standard* saw the Church as a monolith and seized on every insignificant event as evidence of their theory with the zeal of the obsessed.

Thus an ordinary meeting of 500–600 Catholic teetotallers at St Stephen's was interpreted as an effort to overturn the post-1875 education settlement, through an alliance between the extreme squatters and the extreme denominationalists, represented by McIlwraith and Macrossan. The fusion of interests of these two men intensified the conflict of the 1870s, and Macrossan was equally hated by Griffith's followers (but not by Griffith) as a bitter partisan of their foe, a McIlwraithite and as a Catholic.

Personal, political, and religious antipathies were mixed in equal proportions, and each intensified the other. Anti-Catholics gravitated to Liberalism as a matter of course; but men who fell foul of some sectional interest of Macrossan were drawn into the same camp and confirmed in hatred of the Pope. Macrossan was all the more identified with Papalism in that he was not only the chief champion of Catholic education in parliament, but was also a diligent worker on Mother Vincent's charities.

But where Macrossan drew fire partly for his share in parish-pump politics, the Catholic priest represented sacerdotalism, which the *Standard* classed with rationalism as a terrible threat. 'We know not which of these two is . . . the more formidable for the liberties of men.'[95] The progressive and enlightened nineteenth century should gradually destroy the Papal superstition, but Catholic schools continued to extend; hence the bewilderment and anger at Mother Vincent and her Sisters and at the Protestant families who befriended them.

The gibes and innuendoes of a hostile press drew no answer from Mother Vincent, even when it was suggested that the convent should be 'inspected or suppressed'.[96] She could not help feeling pain at misrepresentation, but believed that it was better ignored.[97] She did, however, help to sponsor a paper for the guidance of laymen and laywomen.[98] Its title, the *Australian*, is significant, its aim more so. It was to be

> a Catholic family, social, literary, mining and agricultural paper, to disseminate Catholic views on education and all other topics that interest the Catholic body, and to claim for Catholics a fair share of Government patronage in the shape of position and emolument, which is not accorded to them at present.[99]

It discussed Kanaka labour, science and the Bible, urbanization, capital and labour, and all the topics agitating men of the day.

Neither Mother Vincent nor her Sisters wrote for the *Australian*, though they were co-sponsors with the bishop. Nor was the journal invariably temperate, for some of its contributors were no more adept at turning the other cheek than were the men of the *Standard*, but bitterness was the exception rather than the rule.

Its own readers too advised the *Standard* to 'adopt wider views', to 'have less Orangeism', to build up the Church in general and 'not to pull down any section thereof' since 'Roman Catholicism will exist only as long as good men live in it'.[1] The *Australian* gave ecclesiastical news from England, Ireland, America and the Continent.

While the sectarian conflict of the 1870s centred upon the ultramontane and educational claims of the Church, the distinguishing mark of the controversy after 1880 was the political future of Ireland, for during that decade the Irish agrarian question was debated in the press after the visit of Michael Davitt and the foundation of a branch of the Land League. Thus the Irish Catholic fought his battles before 1880 as a Catholic, after 1880 as an Irishman; but in the 1880s the social threat brought Catholics and Orangemen into the one conservative political camp, and so imposed a temporary truce.[2]

The first of these phases involved Mother Vincent deeply, the second not at all, but the third accorded well with the sunset calm of a life whose keynote was fraternal co-operation for spiritual and temporal goals.

Ideas that explain the development of Catholic communities in other States do not always apply in Queensland, and so the generalizations of Austin, O'Farrell and Suttor break down here. O'Farrell sees the nineteenth-century Church committed 'to an outlook on the world which was implicitly hostile, unyielding, uncompromising'. While he concedes that it 'produced a Catholicism which, whatever its faults and limitations, is of firm, self-respecting, and unique character',[3] his evidence of a siege mentality must be drawn from cities like Melbourne where there was a greater concentration of Catholics.

In Queensland, there was no more evidence of a 'mental and spiritual ghetto'[4] among the Catholics than among Evangelicals or Anglicans, who likewise had some religious cohesion, since 'the most effective tie to hold together a community of workers in a strange land is a spiritual one. A common religion . . . has been found to bind families together by fostering that spirit of mutual assistance . . . more than any mere sentiment of kinship or race.'[5] If O'Farrell means that Catholics offered stronger opposition to the currents of secularism and liberalism than others, then New South Wales affords evidence for his statement.

But liberalism was a spent force in Queensland except in so far as it carried the conviction of the need for a universal education system; and secularism was not, in the hands of Griffith and Lilley, contemptuous of religion. Strong sectarian discrimination inevitably strengthened Catholics in their cohesion, but there is no evidence that what Suttor calls 'the orange-green symbiosis' made them huddle together in towns for mutual support. Urban areas were more apt to have sharp politico-religious divisions, and there is some evidence for 'green belts' in Brisbane's Kangaroo Point, Spring Hill and Fortitude Valley; but it is uncertain whether such homogeneous districts were the result of clinging together for security, or of racial liking for togetherness, or for the convenience of a church and school within reasonable distance of the home. While there is no proof of a set policy to encourage Irish social cohesiveness in this way, there is strong evidence of an episcopal policy for scattered land-settlement; and in remote areas 'mateship' and the interdependence of colonists tended to break down barriers between man and man. Indeed, the wide spaces of Queensland made a siege mentality meaningless.

Suttor too would find Queensland disappointingly barren of proof for his theory of the Hibernicization of the Church.[6] Though the Sisters of Mercy from Dublin were virtually the only teaching Order of women until the turn of the century, one looks in vain for any expression of national sentiment in Mother Vincent. From the moment she arrived in Queensland, Brisbane became the centre of her world—'at least after Rome'. She and Mother Bridget 'would no longer condescend to call the Northern Hemisphere "home" '.[7] Dr Whitty, living in England, considered his sister as thoroughly English as her friends Mother Juliana of Birmingham and Mother Liguori of Liverpool. She could equally well have been American or Australian.

The universal fellowship of the Church which she fostered is strikingly illustrated by the state of her own community shortly after her death. Elected to the top three posts after Reverend Mother Patrick Potter were Mother Vincent's life-long friend Sister M. Claver Mullaney, who had been brought up in Boulogne; Sister M. Winifrede Trotman, an English convert; and Sister M. Audeon Fitzgerald, born in New Zealand but brought as a child to Queensland by her father Henry, of parliamentary fame;[8] while the senior members included English Sister M. Elizabeth Hercy, who wore a red rose on her veil on St George's Day.

By 1893 there were 173 Sisters of Mercy in the Brisbane Archdiocese,[9] and the response of Queenslanders justified Dunne's claim that 'only for our Australian-born girls we would have to shut up shop'.[10] This shift to largely Australian composition within three decades showed how thoroughly Mother Vincent comprehended Queensland conditions.

The composition of the clergy of her time displayed the same breadth. Irish priests were in the majority, but about half of those had been educated in Belgium, Paris or Rome. Besides, there were two English, three French and seven Italian priests, and one German. Apart from Western Australia, no other colony could muster such a multi-racial roll-call.

By 1891 census figures show an increasingly large Australian-born element in the Catholic population. While Catholics were then 21.36 per cent of the Queensland people, 12.14 Queenslanders were Irish-born, but this figure included Irish Anglicans and Presbyterians. The great nineteenth-century immigration wave had spent itself. Gone was the sharp differentiation between the different sections of the community which had marked the 1860s. The professions had received a steadily increasing quota of Catholics, especially law and medicine; they began to filter into clerical posts of responsibility, and maintained their exceptional strength in the teaching service. They benefited by the general improvement of living conditions, and if we are to judge by their most articulate representatives, O'Doherty and Macrossan, were at least as interested in Australia as the Empire. The new generation of Catholics, nurtured in Mother Vincent's schools over thirty years, were self-reliant, socially mobile, and deeply Australian.

Brisbane in the 1890s shone in the mellower light, and newspapers noted with relief that by 1893 Orangeman's day was no longer what it had been—'a vast amount of that bitterness and strife had come to an end.'[11] Such a change was the fruit of a continuous effort on the part of many men and women to generate a strong and reasonable good through forgiveness and brotherhood. Mother Vincent pre-eminently sought that goal, both within her own congregation and in wider society through her schools and her contact with men and women in every profession and class.

All fulfilment has a limit, and it troubled Mother Vincent that she could do so little for the Aboriginals. Her earlier plan for them included a developmental centre at Maryborough, where a Catholic, Mr Clery, who was interested in their welfare, had assigned to the Church a piece of land for their use.[12] However, the adults with their nomadic life and different culture were not to be easily reached, and her brother discouraged the project. 'I fear there is but little chance of your doing anything for the natives, they are so timid and wild. Our civilization seems to kill them and destroy them off the face of the earth.'[13]

Still, as some were selling their children for a shilling or sixpence,[14] she would have made a start if she could have secured the bishop's permission. But he was cold to the idea.[15] The attempt of the Passionist Fathers to evangelize them had not been encouraging.[16] Moreover, Quinn was short of priests and religious for the work that lay immediately to hand.[17] When Mother Vincent's longing to engage in this work continued, her brother consoled her, 'Hard as seems the spiritual lot of so many, let us not stretch ourselves out beyond God's own will or strive to get before him.'[18]

Mother Vincent's awareness of social needs made her too full of plans for Archbishop Dunne's cautious temper. He charged her with a proneness 'to make a start anyhow'[19] without thinking her way through, and obstructed her projects for a hospital and for a home for the aged. She was too prodigal to calculate the cost to others and to herself, and she suffered Sisters to be victims of their own generosity. Instead of insisting on adequate time for their full spiritual and professional formation, she assented to a quick novitiate and a swift passage to a busy life, while novices were still young and vulnerable. Of their health she might likewise have taken more care. Though not as ascetic as Mother Bridget, Mother Vincent also needed to be reminded not to impose too severe a Lenten fast. Again, while the schools were centralized under the bishop, she gave insufficient thought to internal planning. Even though the result was wide freedom for Sisters capable of using it wisely, it left room for the haphazard and incompetent to multiply mistakes.

In pioneering social works in Queensland, Mother Vincent was chagrined to discover that the return did not balance the output of effort, expense and care. The industries that she tried to establish at Nudgee, such as small crops and cattle raising, wilted, largely for want of sufficient training for those placed in charge. Moreover, Mother Vincent forgot that not all had exceptional gifts for dealing with the young women at Holy Cross Refuge. Both the Children's and the Women's Homes had more regimentation than was necessary for the good order and well-being of those under the Sisters' care. Mother Vincent was a pioneer, and like all who blaze a trail she left much ground to be cleared by those who followed her.

But to admit her faults is not to deny her greatness. She accomplished much by inspiring others with her own vision and energy. Never a lone worker, she attached to herself 'whole armies of followers, and . . . had the calmness and courage to lead them safely under the most trying and difficult circumstances. Was ever anyone known to resist her gentle sway or disobey her wishes?'[20] Neither domineering nor egotistic, she had a modest estimate of her own gifts.

By taste and by training she acted as one of a group. Her achievements were not in the mould of a strong individualist, to be fossilized with time; rather she gave plastic form and direction to a service for changing society. She acted as a yeast, a leaven, to her Sisters and colleagues, in a greater or lesser degree according to their capacity, with her own sense of commitment to God and her neighbour. Nothing is more striking than her submergence of self to spiritual goals. With it went, paradoxically, the conviction that what we are is the only real test; that the packaging is of small account. This genuineness, together with her concern for persons, reached the heart and made Mother Vincent one whom to know was to love.

The occasion of her golden jubilee, August 1891, brought telegrams, letters and gifts from Ireland, England and Scotland, from North and South America, from New Zealand and every colony in Australia. Her spiritual children recalled her nameless half-forgotten kindnesses to them during her twenty years as Novice-Mistress and Reverend Mother in Dublin, and her thirty-year labours in Queensland. Prelates like the Australian Bishop Byrne of Bathurst dwelt in their letters and commemorative addresses more on the value of Mother Vincent's contribution to the Church; she had formed her community true to the ideal of Mother McAuley, and Bishop Byrne declared himself proud of 'the loving and devoted young Sisters . . . filled with the same sweet spirit of charity, who were to perpetuate her work.'[21] In the eyes of past pupils she was the sainted foundress who had spent herself for others.[22] Her immediate religious family wrote verses and songs in gratitude for her virtues and humanity, and the children who were then at school could remember details of the festivities many decades later.[23]

At seventy-two years of age, Mother Vincent's once erect figure had become somewhat stooped, her step was slower, and increasing frailty curtailed her journeys to branch convents. But on their visits to the mother house the Sisters found her out on 'the walk' to greet them with cordial affection; she gave them a sense of homecoming like no one else. Yet they noted her occasional lapses of memory on matters touching the minutiae of living, such as when to take meals, or when to retire. But she needed no reminder for chapel. She would kneel upright on her prie-dieu, lost to everything but God.[24] She brought the world to God, and God to the world. In the words of Eva O'Doherty's poem for the Jubilee Missa Cantata, she was

> Half veiled in earthly shadows grey,
> Half shining in the light of heavenly day.[25]

She was prepared for death when, six months after the August celebrations, she suffered a severe bronchial attack. During the second week of her illness, her strength so failed that word of her condition alarmed the Community. Sisters hastened down from Warwick, Gympie and other centres to receive her blessing and counsel and bid her a last farewell; and they found that her final prayer for them was that the beauty and holiness of charity might abide in their hearts.

As she lay dying, she made a solemn profession of faith, renewed her vows, and prepared to receive the last rites of the Church. The Sisters now donned their cream-coloured cloaks and, with lighted tapers in their hands, awaited the arrival of the archbishop. He come robed in rochet and stole, his pectoral cross glinting in the candlelight as he moved through the ranks of nuns down the corridor to the sick room. No one was present to hear his final words to the faithful servant, but when death came, it found her tranquil.

Clothed in her religious habit and veil, her crucifix on her breast and the scroll of her vows in her hands, her body was borne to St Stephen's Cathedral. The Requiem Mass was attended by Church and state in the person of the archbishop and his clergy, the Minister for Education and other public figures. A vast congregation paid tribute to her life and works, and afterwards, as carriage after carriage moved into place for the ten-mile journey to Nudgee, crowds lined the streets in reverent silence.

On the day of her death, 9 March 1892, a cable reached her old Dublin convent just before the Community Mass. As Reverend Mother Liguori Keenan read the words, 'Vincent dead', she felt a stab of pain and loneliness. She announced the news to the assembled nuns, then despatched telegrams to other convents in Ireland and England. In press and panegyric both in Ireland and

Australia, the praises were sung of Queensland's 'first and most distinguished Sister of Mercy'.[26] Her deeds were recounted, her qualities described; but her concrete achievements were less impressive than the spirit that inspired them, the grace given to 'an apostle of love'.

7

SYNTHESIS

What conclusions emerge from this study? Did Mother Vincent Whitty's personal decision and activity materially affect education in Queensland? Is her life work overshadowed by Bishop Quinn's, or does it have its own peculiar relevance?

It was initially suggested that as an individual Mother Vincent would not have caught the eye of history, but that time and place combined to sweep her into the vortex of a great nineteenth-century movement and thrust on her the role of leader. It was further suggested that her influence was minor. Real decision in Catholic affairs was vested in the hierarchy. Archbishops Murray and Cullen of Dublin under whom she served as Reverend Mother, and Bishop Quinn of Queensland, were men of outstanding ability, each personally involved in the work of education. Thus her part was to accept directives from above, and she could be regarded as co-founder of Catholic education in Queensland only in the sense that she and her Sisters were instruments of episcopal policy.

But that initial assumption is only partly true: the foregoing chapters prove the need to modify it considerably. New material has shown that Mother Vincent Whitty took her place among those women of vision and strong initiative who did so much to advance the spiritual resurgence of nineteenth-century Ireland. Educational and social work engaged her there for two decades before Queensland claimed her as a pioneer.

The Australian phase of her life has a peculiar relevance, even though Mother Vincent did not strike the same highly individual note as Mother Mary of the Cross or Caroline Chisholm. The tension between authority and freedom which confronted her was essentially the same as for Mother Mary, but the solutions were different. Because background, spiritual formation and personality influenced Mother Vincent's decisions, it has been worthwhile to detach her forcibly from the Community in which she loved to merge herself, and study her as an individual.

It has been argued in the opening chapter that her Dublin experience proved her a person of distinction in her own right. When in 1839 she entered Catherine McAuley's Institute of Mercy only eight years after its origin, she found herself in the midst of young and venturesome members unmoored from the safe traditions of the cloistered Orders of the past. She watched the experimental stage of a stimulating approach to education and imbibed a new concept of how an active Order could help regenerate society.

Few of her letters survive from this period. Contemporary records show, however, that the foundress saw in her a promise of greatness, and the Chapter Book notes that Mother Vincent was rapidly promoted from one responsible position to another until, at thirty-one years of age, she was elected to the highest post of the Order, as Reverend Mother of the Dublin convents. Until she left Ireland in 1860, no one apart from the foundress had enjoyed so long a term in this office and preserved such close contact with communities elsewhere in Ireland, England, America and Australia.

She was 'one of the most distinguished members', 'a Pillar of the Order', according to her Sisters. Her schools under the constant scrutiny of officials from the Lord Lieutenant down, 'under her judicious management . . . became distinguished for the efficiency of their organization' in the eyes of the National Board inspectors. Lord O'Hagan praised the broad unsectarian spirit in her hospitals, which were open to members of every class and creed. W. M. Thackeray observed and publicized the benefit to society of her rehabilitation work for women. Dr Manning of Westminster turned to her when the need arose for nuns to nurse at the Crimea. This new and strange venture she discussed with Newman of the Catholic University, and then crossed to London to settle details with Sidney Herbert, Secretary for War, and with Manning, liaison between the government and the Catholic body. Once convinced that the unconventional presence of Sisters in military barracks would hasten the disappearance of sectarian strife, she acted with promptitude and decision. Her great goal was to replace disunity by community and mutual assistance.

Yet a streak of obstinacy involved her in an occasional conflict. It is hard to understand, for example, why she allowed a dispute with Dean Walter Meyler to drag on for two years. She was no match in a battle of words with the hard-hitting dean, and the uselessness of this quarrel taught her the wisdom of moderating the fiery temper which now and then possessed her. It helped also to make her humble. However, obstinacy had its value, and Archbishop Cullen praised this quality in her when she achieved superior results by insisting that plans which she had carefully thought out should be followed. Tenacity of purpose was a facet of her stability that was to mean much to Queensland.

No more convincing proof can be advanced for Mother Vincent's pre-eminence in the world of religious women than Dr James Quinn's efforts to secure her for his new mission when he was consecrated bishop in 1859. He was a man who aimed high and left nothing undone to achieve his ends. He was well aware of Mother Vincent's work, having been president of a nearby college and Community confessor.

But he could not prevail on the Sisters to free Mother Vincent for Queensland. During the years 1859 and 1860 he travelled through Ireland, England, and the Continent in a vain search for nuns for his diocese. Mother Vincent sought to help and visited various convents, but where Sisters were willing to go, their bishops withheld permission, because the great exodus of the 1840s and 1850s had drained the country of missioners. A week before he was due to sail, Quinn had still found no nuns. He was equally unsuccessful in attempts to secure Christian Bothers, De La Salle Brothers, Vincentians or Cistercians. In desperation he turned to Archbishop Cullen to force the consent of the Mercy Institute. Cullen then issued an order to the Chapter. If Mother Vincent were willing to go, she was to be allowed to do so, and to be given a couple of novices as companions. Thus Quinn's only prospect of introducing a religious Order hinged on Mother Vincent's decision.

From the moment of her arrival in Queensland, she faced a paradoxical situation. Her physical world was immeasurably enlarged, but the scope for her initiative was greatly diminished.

The first check came from the Board of General Education which had assumed a virtual monopoly. Mother Vincent did not understand the cumulative effect of the historical and social circumstances which had thrown on the government the responsibility for effective action in education. She saw that, though the government could allot only a little public money to schools in view of the immediate demands for roads, railways, and public works, the Board was reluctant to enlist the co-operation of the

Churches. Unlike the National Board in Ireland, it did not include official representatives of the Anglican and Catholic bodies. In fact the newly arrived Anglican bishop, Tufnell, was cold-shouldered in his efforts to win recognition for his schools. Further, it became clear that Presbyterians and the smaller Evangelical churches had aligned themselves with the Liberals in a bid to prevent subsidy to denominational schools. Few in number, they were powerful through their control of the press and strong voice in business and in parliament. A few of their ministers like the anti-Catholic Reverend Charles Ogg wished to include religion on a curricular basis, but most did not.

However, while the government was not committed to a purely secular policy in education, the restrictions placed by the Board on the teaching of religion were unacceptable to Anglican and Catholic prelates. Thus they joined battle in a debate which ended only with the passing of the Education Act of 1875. Queensland people gaped at the sight of the two bishops in unprecedented fraternization addressing crowds from the same platform in their tour of south-east Queensland during what was known as 'the bishops' crusade'.

In this public debate Mother Vincent had no part. In fact her position was very different from her bishop's. Far from wishing to connect her schools with the Board, she desired to run an independent system. To limit Christian doctrine to pre-school hours, as the Board insisted its schools should do, was particularly inconvenient in Queensland, where the shortage of labour made the help of children necessary in the home, business and farm. Moreover changes in Board rules in Ireland had made illegal the display of religious symbols, and she feared the Queensland system, based on the Irish, would follow suit.

Mother Vincent's stance in 1861 was identical with that taken by Mother Mary of the Cross when in 1867 she began her work with the Sisters of St Joseph in South Australia. Mother Vincent saw no exclusiveness or divisiveness in thus standing apart, because her schools were open to any child who sought education from her, Protestant or Catholic. From 1861 to 1866 she was free to implement her scheme. The result was three primary schools in Brisbane and Ipswich and the first girls' high school in the colony.

But from the beginning she foresaw that the bishop would in the long run achieve his objective and connect her primary schools with the Board, as the crucial state of colonial finance eventually forced the government to take the Churches into temporary partnership. The severe mid-1860s depression told on Church as well as state effort to expand educational facilities.

Other factors persuaded her to surrender her former position. She had noted the large number of Catholic parents who sent their children to the public schools, and saw that their desire for learning exceeded their wish for religious education. The cure was to prove to them that the convent schools could impart at least an equally good secular education while affording, in addition, the moral, religious, and character formation consonant with full Catholic life. She could assure parents that their children were missing nothing essential if she allowed government inspectors to measure her schools by public-school standards. She must make the Church's most durable protection against loss, education, as efficient as possible.

This modification in Mother Vincent's views explains the three phases in the history of her school system noted in chapter 1: complete independence to 1866; alliance with the Board until the dissolution of the non-vested system in 1880; and finally, the preservation of links with the Department of Education through inspection and examination. During her lifetime Mother Vincent was criticized by laymen for allegedly traducing Catholic principles in allowing a measure of state control and in admitting Protestants. But her solution to the tension between state authority and freedom of conscience in education was vindicated by a group of bishops who made an official examination of her schools and declared that they combined all-round secular knowledge with a sound religious formation.

The 'tyranny of distance' was the second great challenge to Mother Vincent's aims. The frontier State needed time to build roads and railways, to find and develop its resources. Mother Vincent's pioneering problems were accentuated by the vastness over which a few thousand Catholics were scattered, the poverty of the Church, and isolation not only from the home country but from colonies farther south and from other teaching Orders.

With the inventiveness of the pioneer she quickly devised a method to combat distance and dispersal. Because families living inland in pastoral homesteads were often a full day's ride from the nearest neighbour, and even the grasslands of the Darling Downs and of the Burnett River were remote from the small towns springing up near the coast, she resolved to establish boarding schools in the larger centres to accommodate children from the distant settlements, while her day schools provided for all who could ride in on horseback or buggy. Within a few months of her arrival she turned St Stephen's into a mixed boarding and day school.

Parents welcomed the supervision and close attention to education thus afforded to their daughters, and within two decades the main towns north to Townsville and inland to Roma and Dalby were similarly served. Because girls often remained to their middle or late teens, such schools early showed a trend towards secondary education. The most outstanding was All Hallows', whose excellent standards of music and choral work allowed the school to contribute greatly to the cultural life of Brisbane. Languages, art in the Romantic tradition, and attention to the social graces made it popular with the elite society of the day, including Protestant families, who gave friendship and support. Other high schools were distantly modelled on All Hallows', and they were among Mother Vincent's best means of furthering social harmony.

Boarding schools also provided teachers and supplemented the funds available for poorer schools. Girls were encouraged to prepare themselves for a profession and, as teaching was the most open avenue, many of the students took the teacher's certificate and either passed on to government schools or remained in the Catholic system. In 1863 the first Queenslander joined the Sisters, starting a trickle of vocations to the religious life that became in time a goodly stream. Pensions from the boarding schools helped to support the parish schools where very few children, particularly those of migrants, were able to pay anything towards their education. Fees from music lessons supplemented by occasional art unions and bazaars were other sources of finance. Fund-raising was always distracting, time-consuming and wearisome, and Mother Vincent was saddled with it for life. Despite her efforts, she and her Sisters knew sharp poverty and hardship in providing for the upkeep of parish schools.

Extension northwards for a thousand miles made the Mercy schools by 1882 the largest and most highly centralized network of the Australian dioceses. For the field strategy credit must go to the first bishop. Quinn decided which settlements were most likely to become permanent centres of population and Mother Vincent's Sisters acted as a kind of flying corps ready to go at his bidding. In the work of education their efforts complemented one another. Without the bishop Mother Vincent would not have been able to extend so far and so fast. When difficulties from the dispersal and cultural indifference of their flocks made priests on the Darling

Downs slow to push ahead with school buildings, episcopal authority was needed to overcome their reluctance. But when in 1880 the government subsidy was withdrawn, the value of central organization was proved.

The deep and broad cultural formation which is today's ideal was beyond the reach of Mother Vincent's schools. Rapid expansion made great demands on her resources, both personal and financial. Hard living conditions sent many nuns to a premature grave. The institutional weakness of giving primacy to buildings rather than to persons, to quantity rather than quality, meant that the time and money which should have been devoted to spiritual and professional formation of the nuns were absorbed by immediate needs.

Intellectual excellence for its own sake was not one of Mother Vincent's goals. It could be argued that the period did not call for specialists, scholars or intellectuals. It was nevertheless true that Catholics were slow to come forward as leaders in any sphere. But in Mother Vincent's view there was no choice. The dominion of the immediate was the price she paid to assist an impoverished people to acquire the essentials of worship and doctrine, and such literacy as could be achieved in their years of schooling.

She perpetually regretted that her achievements fell short of her aim. Though her contacts with Irish and English convents provided an ever-flowing source of Sisters and teachers, and Australian girls joined her in larger numbers as the years went on, by the end of her life her schools were still able to teach only 60 per cent of the Catholic girls of school age in Queensland. The vastness of the colony posed an insuperable problem.

From the point of view of sheer survival as an Order, the most significant theme of this work is the third—the tension between Mother Vincent's individual responsibility and the authority of Dr James Quinn. As Superior of the Sisters of Mercy, she was subject to the bishop in all concerning the works of the diocese, but she was bound to preserve the autonomy of the Institute. Friends of many years' standing, she and Quinn shared the same broad vision of a strong and vigorous Church in Queensland. She viewed his leadership in education in a tolerant and affirmative spirit, modified her views and adapted her methods to circumstances. But appointed head of the Community by the Dublin Chapter and by Archbishop Cullen, she had a duty to arrange internal matters with her Sisters, to protect them from the harmful effects of the bishop's impatient drive to realize his dream, and to safeguard the Constitutions by which the Sisters of Mercy everywhere had vowed to live.

The tension became apparent when Mother Vincent met Quinn's excessive demands for control with her old obstinacy. Her Dublin companions, Mothers Benedict and Cecilia, openly resented his autocracy and believed that flight to another diocese was the only solution. Sister M. Bridget, on the other hand, adopted the attitude that the bishop could do no wrong. Mother Vincent, isolated from all sources of counsel and support, was in a perplexing situation. To leave Queensland would be to abandon the great work of education for which she had come and to forsake thousands of children without a knowledge of their faith. To regard the bishop as sole interpreter of the Rule was equally impossible.

The course which she followed was of questionable wisdom. Privately she expostulated with him, but to prevent open revolt she defended him with her Sisters. She only succeeded in annoying Quinn to the point where he removed her from office and assumed the direction of the Community, and she alienated her Sisters by seeming to condone what she did not. Her self-sacrifice, so open to misinterpretation, can be understood only in the light of her own spirituality. It saved the day for Queensland Catholic schools.

To underline the seriousness of the challenge to Mother Vincent and her Sisters, it has been necessary to show Quinn as he was, warts and all; and to demonstrate that under the same stress the Assumptionist Fathers withdrew, the Sisters of St Joseph were forced out, the clergy repeatedly protested, the Vicars-General were removed from office, and Archbishop Vaughan, at Rome's request, instituted an inquiry into the administration of the diocese. For Quinn pushed to its ultimate the principle that there can be no co-ordination without subordination; and he thereby limited his achievement. He, only, was to rule in matters temporal as well as spiritual within his diocese; he was not the man to use the wisdom of others.

His refusal to heed even their just complaints won him ill-will. Polding called him a globule of oil that failed to mingle with the water into which it dropped. It would be more accurate to think of him as an explosive. In the raw living conditions and the mixture of nationalities among the clergy—Irish, French, Italian, German, Scottish and English—the most sagacious of bishops could hardly have avoided faction; with Quinn it was inevitable.

In this area of tension, qualities of character counted for more than brilliance or organizing ability. Mother Vincent's temper was essentially moderate, conciliatory and unassuming. She combined respect for established custom and a dislike of extremes. It was not possible calmly to hear and debate arguments as to what was just and expedient; but her endurance and fidelity to what she regarded as God's hidden ways of achieving his purpose, enabled her to weather the difficult years. In her own life she demonstrated the 'enduring love, forgiving love' which she counselled her Sisters to practise; and when the bishop, overseas, met with cold refusal in his appeals for help, he sent for Mother Vincent, and she went to his aid as if there had been no difference between them.

The discussion of the final theme—the tension between the Mercy ideal and the new elements in the community—affords an opportunity of considering the integrating idea of Mother Vincent's life, her ambition to strengthen community, to build up a strong closely knit group, competent to aid, fortify, and elevate Catholic lay society, and to lessen the gulf separating class from class and one religion from another.

Her first task lay within the religious community itself; she had to stem the effect of a new rigid approach to spirituality introduced by a young Sister who made observance of the letter of the law the test of goodness. On the point of leaving Ireland Mother Vincent had accepted Emily Conlan as a candidate for the religious life. The hurried and imperfect formation of a novitiate partly undergone on board ship and partly in the confusion of settling in, and still further curtailed at the bishop's wish, did little to impart the McAuley breadth of vision to Sister M. Bridget. Yet her automatic and unquestioning obedience won the admiration of Quinn, and she became his voice in the convent. Her streak of hardness, of unbending righteousness, allied to an impeccable exterior observance of the order of the day, both dismayed and repelled. Appointed by the bishop to form spirited young Sisters, her machine-like precision seemed to them inhuman.

To see Mother Bridget in action, suddenly by contrast is to feel in Mother Vincent a breadth, a balance, a humanity, a distinction; one discovers what a precious gift was the self-restraint, the striving to understand, which made her slow to take sides, and which won for her the devoted attachment of the new Sisters from overseas. Gradually the fidelity of members won to the Mercy ideal rather than to a lifeless formalism restored moral leadership to Mother Vincent, and among the conquests of her genuine attractiveness was Sister M. Bridget Conlan herself.

In attempting to show the change which Mother Vincent aimed at effecting in the wider society, one facet of particular importance was examined—her role in the absorption of immigrants of different nationalities, but chiefly those who came through or as a result of the Queensland Immigration Society. Their poverty and the absence of male religious Orders (the Christian Brothers were established in Queensland only in 1875) demanded that Mother Vincent adapt to Queensland needs and accept boys as well as girls in her classrooms. Further, to promote such economic independence as would free the adult for spiritual goals and to give the submerged Irish quarter of the population a voice in civil life, became the concerted policy of bishop and Sisters; and Mother Vincent's strong drive towards unity spurred social integration; her schools helped to break down barriers of class and creed.

Her life was no easy journey. The themes of this work highlight the struggle and drama, the tragedy and success of her ventures. But in the effort to establish an independent school system, to meet the challenge of Queensland's vastness, to counter the episcopal bid for undue control, and to demolish the obstacles to harmony, she did not stand alone; she relied on the strength of her community, merged herself with it, and acted as one with it. Her solution to the tension between authority and responsibility was not fight or flight; it was to live with ambiguity, to submerge the spontaneous impulse to a good here and now, in view of a more remote but higher spiritual value. She grafted a fully Catholic system on to the state's. She acquiesced to some but not all of the bishop's demands and accepted demotion rather than suffer breach of principle; yet even then she remained to guide her community past the rocks and shoals of uncharted waters. In her positive efforts to build up the Church and to create harmony, her own courage, humility and realism were of the first importance. Her life was her best lesson in synthesis between temporal things and the eternal.

As an educationist, she was no genius, no great theorist or innovator. Yet her contribution to Queensland was considerable. At the time of her death 222 Sisters managed twenty-six schools with about seven thousand pupils. She commenced secondary education for girls fifty years before the first state high school was built. Her schools were efficient by colonial standards. She met the child in the family setting and sought through education to improve his environment. Without her Bishop Quinn, however magnificent his dream, could have accomplished little. Yet when all is said and done, her reticence makes it impossible to pluck out the heart of her mystery. She did not altogether succeed in bridging the discontinuity between the secular world and the world of faith, because her highest goals lay beyond history.

ABBREVIATIONS

A.C.R.	*Australasian Catholic Record*
A.H.A.	All Hallows' Convent Archives
B.A.A.	Brisbane Archdiocesan Archives
C.P.A.	Carysfort Park (Dublin) Archives
D.L.	Dixson Library, Sydney
M.L.	Mitchell Library, Sydney
O.M.L.	Oxley Memorial Library, Brisbane
Parl. Deb.	*Parliamentary Debates*
Prop. Arch.	Archives of the Sacred Congregation for the Propagation of the Faith (Rome)
Q.S.A.	Queensland State Archives
S.A.A.	Sydney Archdiocesan Archives
V. & P.	*Votes and Proceedings*

REFERENCES

INTRODUCTION

1 *Australia, the Catholic Chapter.*

2 *Catholic Education in Australia, 1806–1950.*

3 'Critical appreciation of the educational system of All Hallows' congregation', unpubl. M.Ed. thesis, University of Queensland.

4 *Hierarchy and Democracy in Australia, 1788–1870*, p. 308.

1 MOTHER VINCENT'S BACKGROUND

1 T. L. Suttor, *Hierarchy and Democracy in Australia, 1788–1870*, p. 15.

2 *Australian*, 19 March 1892.

3 Dr Whitty to Sister M. Claver, [?] August 1892, A.H.A.

4 Ibid.

5 R. Burke-Savage, *Catherine McAuley*, p. 77.

6 6 January 1839, C.P.A.

7 M. Austin Carroll, *Annals of the Sisters of Mercy*, vol. 2, p. 541.

8 To Mother Vincent, 24 July 1862, A.H.A.

9 Oral testimony, Baggot Street Sisters.

10 Mother Vincent, Sketch of Mother Catherine McAuley, C.P.A.

11 Ibid.

12 Catherine McAuley, *Familiar Instructions*, p. 122.

13 Mother Vincent, Sketch of Mother Catherine McAuley, C.P.A.

14 McAuley, op. cit., p. 122.

15 Ibid., p. 170.

16 Ibid., p. 97.

17 E. E. Y. Hales, *The Catholic Church in the Modern World*, pp. 95–113; E. L. Woodward, *Three Studies in European Conservatism*, pp. 248–75.

18 MS. copy of Rule, A.H.A.

19 Burke-Savage, op. cit., p. 270.

20 Ibid.

21 Certificate held in A.H.A.

22 Mother Catherine to Mother Aloysius, Birr, 30 June 1841, C.P.A.

23 Sister M. Bertrand Degnan, *Mercy unto Thousands*, p. 343.

24 Years later, a Passionist retreat-master sought details about the foundress. In the confessional Mother Vincent related the incident, which he declared should no longer be kept secret. (Testimony of Mother M. Liguori Keenan: 'I heard this from Mother Vincent's own lips.')

25 MS. Annals, St Ethelburga's, Liverpool.

26 David Mathew, *Catholicism in England*, p. 184.

27 Meriol Trevor, *Newman: The pillar of the cloud*, p. 365.

28 Register, C.P.A.

29 Canon Conlan to Mother Vincent, 30 August 1891, A.H.A.

30 T. P. O'Neill, 'Rural life' in R. B. McDowell (ed.), *Social Life in Ireland, 1800–1845*, p. 43.

31 Letter of Mother Ursula Frayne, 25 March 1848, C.P.A.

32 A. G. Austin, *Australian Education 1788–1900*, pp. 87–9.

33 25 March 1848, C.P.A.

34 The correspondence lasted from September 1849 to August 1851, A.H.A.

35 Burke-Savage, op. cit., pp. 116, 222ff.

36 Carroll, op. cit., vol. 2, p. 541.

37 M. Russell, *Three Sisters of Lord Russell of Killowen*, p. 26.

38 Carroll, op. cit., vol. 3, p. 328.

[39] E. Bolster, *The Sisters of Mercy at the Crimean War*, pp. 49–51.
[40] Full text in the *Australian*, 19 March 1893.
[41] Bolster, op. cit., p. 52.
[42] 18 November 1854, Cullen Papers, D.A.A.
[43] Minutes of the Board of the Jervis Street Infirmary; copy, A.H.A.
[44] E. T. Freeman (ed.), *1861–1961*, p. 8.
[45] Quoted in Tyr-Owen, *Sketch of the Life and Labours of the Right Rev. Dr. O'Quinn*, p. 14.
[46] Peader MacSuibhne, *Paul Cullen and his Contemporaries*, vol. 3, p. 278.
[47] *Cornhill Magazine*, vol. 3 (1861), pp. 424–32.
[48] Menia Page to Sister M. Claver, 27 March 1892, A.H.A.
[49] McAuley, op. cit., p. 104.
[50] Letter to Sister M. Claver, n.d., A.H.A.
[51] Mother Joseph Sherlock, Melbourne, 17 August 1892, A.H.A.
[52] Carroll, op. cit., vol. 3, p. 388.
[53] 2 October 1865, A.H.A.
[54] 10 February 1872, A.H.A.
[55] Stated by his cousin, Mother Catherine, Carlow, 7 July 1891, A.H.A.
[56] Mother Xavier Maguire to M. of Mercy, 22 February 1861, C.P.A.
[57] To Mother M. of Mercy, 15 November 1860, C.P.A.
[58] Baggot Street convent, 20 November 1860, Chapter Book, C.P.A.
[59] 28 November 1860, A.H.A.

2 THE EDUCATION QUESTION

[1] J. S. Gregory, 'Church and state, and education in Victoria to 1872' in E. L. French (ed.), *Melbourne Studies in Education 1958–1959*, p. 6.
[2] Mother Vincent to Dublin, 13 May 1861, C.P.A.
[3] Ibid.
[4] Ibid., 19 October 1863, C.P.A.
[5] A. G. Austin, *Australian Education 1788–1900*, p. 109.
[6] Mother Vincent to Dublin, 13 May 1861, C.P.A.
[7] Ibid.
[8] Ibid., 16 May, 18 June 1863.
[9] *Queensland Times*, 5 May 1866.
[10] *North Australian*, 28 July 1864.
[11] Sister M. Ita Nolan, recollections (written and oral), A.H.A.
[12] Misses Sheldon, recollections (oral).
[13] *Queensland Times*, 5 May 1866.
[14] Ibid.
[15] Ibid.
[16] *Freeman's Journal*, 26 October 1867.
[17] *Queensland Times*, 15 July 1869.
[18] *Australian*, 25 September 1880.
[19] Mother Vincent to Dublin, 18 May 1864, C.P.A.
[20] *North Australian*, 2 August 1864.
[21] *Queensland Times*, 15 July 1869.
[22] Mother Ursula Lavery, Notebook, A.H.A.
[23] J. Griffin, review of T. L. Suttor, *Hierarchy and Democracy in Australia 1788–1870* in *Australian Journal of Politics and History* (December 1966), p. 485.
[24] For Mother Vincent and secondary education, see chapter 3.
[25] To Dublin, 13 May 1861, C.P.A.
[26] Cf. C. Roberts, 'Bishop James Quinn', *A.C.R.*, vol. 37, nos 1, 2 (January, April 1960).
[27] *North Australian*, 2 August 1864.
[28] Ibid., 1 October 1861.
[29] See J. Barrett, *That Better Country: The religious aspect of life in eastern Australia, 1835–1850*.
[30] Mother Vincent to Dublin, 9 October 1863, C.P.A.
[31] *North Australian*, 9 October 1863.
[32] 14 March 1862.
[33] J. S. Gregory, 'Church and State in Victoria to 1872' in E. L. French, op. cit., p. 6.
[34] *North Australian*, 17 August 1864.
[35] *Australian*, 21 May 1879.
[36] *Moreton Bay Courier*, 4 September 1860.
[37] *North Australian*, 8, 12 February 1861.
[38] Governor Sir George Bowen, despatch, 15 December 1864, O.M.L.
[39] H. Bryan, 'The political career of John Murtagh Macrossan', unpubl. M.A. thesis, University of Queensland, p. 29.
[40] To Dublin, 18 May 1864.
[41] C. A. Bernays, *Queensland Politics during Sixty Years, 1859–1919*, p. 10.
[42] H. Bryan, 'The political career of John Murtagh Macrossan', unpubl. M.A. thesis, University of Queensland, p. 26.

43 Despatch, 15 December 1864, O.M.L.
44 Memorandum of R. G. Herbert and the Ministry, attached to Bowen, despatch, 15 December 1864, O.M.L.
45 Bowen, despatch, 15 December 1864, O.M.L.
46 Austin, op. cit., p. 174.
47 *V. & P.* (Qld), 1867, vol. 1, p. 194.
48 See chapter 4.
49 To Dublin, 17 May 1864, C.P.A.
50 Ibid., 18 May 1864, C.P.A.
51 To Mother M. of Mercy Norris, 15 November 1860, C.P.A.
52 To Dublin, 22 March 1861, C.P.A.
53 Ibid., 13 May 1861, C.P.A.
54 MacNab to Vaughan, n.d. [*c.* 1878], S.A.A.
55 Rosenstengel to Father Kaercher, 5 July 1878, S.A.A.
56 S.A.A.
57 Plaint of O'Donovan and other laymen to Rome, 1879, Prop. Arch.
58 Quoted by J. S. Gregory in French, op. cit., p. 29.
59 Pastoral of 1868, S.A.A.
60 *V. & P.* (Qld), 1873, vol. 1, p. 297.
61 Ibid., 1861, vol. 1, p. 720.
62 Ibid., 1874, vol. 1, p. 296.
63 Royal Commission evidence, ibid., 1875, vol. 2, p. 246.
64 Mother Bridget, Reminiscences, pt 2, p. 3, A.H.A.
65 *Courier*, 5 July 1873.
66 See S. Gilley, 'Catholic social and political attitudes in Queensland, 1870–1900', unpubl. B.A. (Hons) thesis, University of Queensland, pp. 106–10.
67 *Parl. Deb.* (Qld), 8 May 1874, vol. 16, p. 439.
68 Macrossan's phrase, *Parl. Deb.*, 1875, vol. 19, p. 782.
69 C. K. Clark, 'The Royal Commissions of Queensland, 1859–1901', unpubl. B.A. (Hons) thesis, University of Queensland, p. 202.
70 H. Bryan, 'The political career of John Murtagh Macrossan', unpubl. M.A. thesis, University of Queensland, p. 138.
71 C. M. H. Clark, *Sources of Australian History*, pp. xl, 355, 359.
72 E. R. Wyeth, *Education in Queensland*, p. 134.
73 *Legislative Council Journal*, 1875, vol. 2, pt. 1, p. 677.
74 Ibid., p. 679.
75 *Australian*, 24 January 1880.
76 *Legislative Council Journal*, 1875, vol. 2, pt 1, p. 678.
77 Sister M. Xaverius O'Donoghue, *Beyond Our Dreams: A review of the Mercy Order in Queensland over one hundred years*, pp. 71–2.
78 *Parl. Deb.* (Qld), 1875, vol. 15, p. 423.
79 Joint Pastoral of 1879, S.A.A.
80 Letter to Quinn, 10 October 1880, signed jointly by Mother Vincent and Mother Patrick, A.H.A.
81 Austin, op. cit., p. 200.
82 *Queensland Evangelical Standard*, 5 August 1876, which also prints an acid retort.
83 A. Barcan, 'History of Australian education' in R. Cowan (ed.), *The Australian Tradition in Education*, p. 11.
84 His description to Canon Kennedy, 10 February 1891, B.A.A.

3 VASTNESS AND ISOLATION

1 Mother Vincent to Dublin, 17 June 1863, C.P.A.
2 Ibid., 13 May 1861.
3 *North Australian*, 17 September 1864.
4 Dunne to Byrne, 5 March 1874, Letterbook, B.A.A.
5 Quinn to Byrne, 14 July 1876, B.A.A.
6 Dunne to Mother Bridget, 3 February 1873, B.A.A.
7 Non-vested Schools, inward files, 13 March 1875, Q.S.A.
8 Ibid., outward files, 18 March 1875, Q.S.A.
9 Ibid., 7 April 1875, Q.S.A.
10 Annals, Convent of Mercy, Crumlin Road, Belfast.
11 Dunne to Mother Bridget, 3 February 1873, B.A.A.
12 Samples of his examinations in Yvonne McLay, 'Critical appreciation of the education system of All Hallows' congregation', unpubl. M.Ed. thesis, University of Queensland, pp. 563–5.
13 Ipswich and Brisbane were not then connected by rail.
14 Dunne to Mother Bridget, 3 February 1873, B.A.A.
15 Dunne to Quinn, 22 February 1875,

B.A.A.

[16] Letters, February 1874 to March 1875, B.A.A.

[17] Mother Vincent to Dublin, 13 May 1861, C.P.A.

[18] Ibid., 17 June 1873, C.P.A.

[19] K. Rayner, 'The attitudes and influence of the Churches in Queensland in matters of social and political importance, 1859–1914', unpubl. M.A. thesis, University of Queensland, pp. 65–6.

[20] *Legislative Council Journal*, 1871, vol. 18, no. 1, p. 975.

[21] E. R. Wyeth, *Education in Queensland*, p.123.

[22] *Courier*, 27 July 1877.

[23] Memorandum, Quinn's Letterbook, 1867, B.A.A.

[24] Programme among Griffith Papers, D.L.; Quinn to O'Donohoe, 23 March 1868, B.A.A.

[25] For a sketch of Diggles's work, see Elizabeth Marks, *Queensland Naturalist*, vol. 17, nos 1, 2 (July 1963), vol. 19, nos 5, 6 (June 1965).

[26] Vida Lahey, *Art in Queensland 1859–1959*, pp. 6, 45.

[27] Quoted by Father Andrew Quinn to Archbishop Cullen, 27 December 1861, C.P.A.

[28] Mother Vincent's letters, 1861–3.

[29] 28 March 1879, B.A.A.

[30] Quinn's speech, *North Australian*, 27 December 1864.

[31] Mother Vincent to Dublin, 18 February 1863, C.P.A.

[32] Mother Bridget, Reminiscences, pt 1, p. 16, A.H.A.

[33] *Queensland Daily Guardian*, 1 January 1863.

[34] K. Rayner, op. cit., p. 154.

[35] Mother Bridget, Reminiscences, A.H.A., pt 1, pp. 16–17.

[36] Mother Bridget, Diary, 19 October 1871, A.H.A.

[37] K. Rayner, op. cit.

[38] Ibid.

[39] Mother Bridget, Reminiscences, pt 2, p. 29, A.H.A.

[40] Notice on St Anne's School, *Australasian Catholic Directory*, 1893.

[41] *Courier*, 21 September 1880.

[42] Mother Vincent to Dublin, 9 June 1861, C.P.A.

[43] Ibid., 13 May 1861, C.P.A.

[44] Ibid., 9 June 1861, C.P.A.

[45] Ibid., 9 June 1861, C.P.A.

[46] Ibid., 13 May 1861, C.P.A.

[47] Sister M. Evangelist to Mother Vincent, 4 July 1879, A.H.A.

[48] Dunne to Mother M. Rose, 9 September 1873, B.A.A.

[49] Dunne to Cani, 3 March 1873, B.A.A.

[50] Quinn to Dunne, 24 February 1873, B.A.A.

[51] Quinn to Father O'Connell, 9 March 1881, B.A.A.

[52] Signed by Denis O'Donovan *et al.*, Prop. Arch.

[53] To Cani, 16 March 1879, B.A.A.

[54] To Mother M. Regis, [?] 1888, B.A.A.

[55] Dunne to Cardinal Moran, 'Draught of some matters which the undersigned thinks might be usefully brought under the consideration of the Australian Synod of 1885. In five chapters', 24 October 1884, S.A.A.

[56] Ibid.

[57] Extract from the Proceedings of the Diocesan Synod, 1880, A.H.A.

[58] *Australian*, 3 May 1879. American Father Henneberry had advocated pew rents during his temperance campaign.

[59] Dunne, personal letter to Synod, 13 November 1879, B.A.A.

[60] *Australian*, 7 February 1880.

[61] Dunne, Letterbook, October 1880, B.A.A.

[62] Dunne to Father Renehan, 3 October 1872, B.A.A.

[63] Ibid., inward files, 11 April 1878, Q.S.A.

[64] Ibid., outward files, 12 April 1878, Q.S.A.

[65] Ibid., 12 April 1877, Q.S.A.

[66] Non-vested Schools, outward files, Q.S.A.

[67] Geoffrey Blainey, *The Tyranny of Distance*, p. 168.

[68] Sister M. Vincent Donovan, testimony, A.H.A.

[69] Dunne to Father Byrne, 5 March 1874, Letterbook, B.A.A.

[70] Wyeth, op. cit., p. 105.

[71] Extract from the Proceedings of the Diocesan Synod, 1880, A.H.A.

[72] Sister M. Agnes to Mother Bridget, 15 February 1877, A.H.A.

[73] Dunne to Davadi, 20 August 1891, Letterbook, B.A.A.

[74] Quinn to Sister M. Claver, 4 May 1876, A.H.A.
[75] Dunne to Mother Vincent, [?] 1882, Letterbook, B.A.A.
[76] *Week*, 15 July 1867.
[77] Dunne to Mother Vincent, [?] 1876, B.A.A.
[78] Quinn to Mother Bridget, 27 January 1880, B.A.A.
[79] Dunne to Mother Vincent, January, February 1882, B.A.A.
[80] *Australian*, quoting the *Telegraph*, 16 August 1879.
[81] *Queensland Evangelical Standard*, 4 August 1878.
[82] *Australian*, 24 January 1880.
[83] Dunne to Mother M. Regis, 22 October 1891, B.A.A.
[84] Sister M. Benedict to editor, *Queensland Times*, 14 December 1865.
[85] Quinn to Gentlemen of the Committee, April 1866, B.A.A.
[86] Dr Whitty to Mother Vincent, 24 August 1863, A.H.A.
[87] G. C. Bolton, *A Thousand Miles Away: A history of north Queensland to 1926*, p. 174.
[88] Sister M. Gabriel, Moate, to Mother Vincent, August 1871, A.H.A.
[89] Mother Bridget to Anderson and Anderson, London, 9 April 1879, A.H.A.
[90] Blainey, op. cit., p. 168.
[91] Quinn to Secretary of the Sacred Congregation for the Propagation of the Faith, [?] 1880, A.H.A.
[92] MS. Annals, St John's, Tralee.
[93] Sister M. of St Phillip Lescher to Mother Vincent, 7 October 1871, A.H.A.
[94] P. F. Connole, 'The Christian Brothers in secondary education in Queensland, 1875–1965', unpubl. M.A. thesis, University of Queensland, p. 60.
[95] Memorandum, 5 July 1871, Non-vested Schools files, Q.S.A.
[96] Quinn to Bishop Murray, 18 September 1875, B.A.A.
[97] Quinn to Father Andrew Quinn, 11 August 1868, B.A.A.
[98] Quinn to Cani, 12 August 1875, B.A.A.
[99] Quinn to Dunne, 12 January 1876, B.A.A.
[1] Ibid.
[2] n.d., Quinn's Letterbook, B.A.A.
[3] Ibid.
[4] Yvonne McLay, 'Critical Appreciation of the educational system of All Hallows' congregation', unpubl. M.A. thesis, University of Queensland, pp. 571ff.
[5] Dunne in home mail, 3 December 1899, B.A.A.
[6] Mother Bridget, Diary, 20 April 1877.
[7] Non-vested Schools, outward files, 23 April 1877, Q.S.A.
[8] 6 December 1879.
[9] Non-vested Schools files, 10 February 1881, Q.S.A.
[10] A recurring theme in letters, 1889–90, Dunne's Letterbooks, B.A.A.
[11] To Sister M. Kevin, Warwick, [?] 1889, Letterbook, B.A.A.
[12] *North Australian*, 12 February 1861.
[13] Alan Barcan, 'Education and Catholic social status', *Australian Quarterly*, vol. 34, no. 1 (March 1962).
[14] Blainey, op. cit., p. 171.
[15] Memorandum to Dalby head teacher, 25 July 1877, Non-vested Schools, outward files, Q.S.A.
[16] Quinn to Rome, n.d., A.H.A.
[17] Mother Bridget, Diary, 25 August 1870, A.H.A.
[18] Mother Vincent to Dublin, 18 May 1864, C.P.A.
[19] To Mother Patrick, August 1882, Letterbook, B.A.A.
[20] J. J. Barrett, 'Queensland', *Christian Brothers' Educational Record* (1894), p. 180.
[21] Ibid.
[22] *Australian*, 17 May 1879.
[23] Ibid., 29 November 1879.
[24] Dunne to Mother Vincent's secretary, Sister M. Mel Mayne, 2 June 1881, Letterbook, B.A.A. Also *Queensland Evangelical Standard*, 25 March 1882.
[25] Dunne to Mother Vincent, 2 April 1888, Letterbook, B.A.A.
[26] To Mother Vincent, June 1890, Letterbook, B.A.A.
[27] Dunne to Cardinal Moran, 2 April 1888, Letterbook, B.A.A.
[28] *Courier*, 30 July 1887.
[29] Figures from *Australasian Catholic Directory*, 1893.
[30] Anne Prentice to Sister M. Claver, 4 March 1892, A.H.A.

4 EPISCOPAL CONTROL (1)

[1] T. L. Suttor, *Hierarchy and Democracy in Australia, 1788–1870*, p. 284.
[2] Letter to Newman, quoted in F. McGrath, *Newman's University: Idea and reality*, p. 445.
[3] To Cardinal Barnabo, 24 February 1869, Letterbook, B.A.A.
[4] Mother Vincent to Mother M. of Mercy, 13 May 1861, C.P.A.
[5] Suttor, op. cit., gives much space to this story, pp. 284–92.
[6] A. A. Morrison in 'Town "liberal" and squatter', *Journal of the Historical Society of Queensland*, vol. 4, no. 5 (December 1952), shows the skill of the Lang migrants at bringing 'pressure to bear on the Government by agitation, public meeting and outspoken press.'
[7] R. McDowell, *Social Life in Ireland, 1800–1845*, p. 66.
[8] C. A. Bernays, *Queensland Politics during Sixty Years, 1859–1919*, p. 15.
[9] *Queensland Times*, 5 June 1863.
[10] *North Australian*, 10 June 1862. John Lawry's article on Tufnell reveals a similar attitude in the Anglican bishop, which partly accounted for the failure of the joint 'crusade'. See E. L. French, *Melbourne Studies in Education, 1966*.
[11] Suttor, op. cit., p. 309.
[12] Testimony of Father Kevin O'Sullivan, S.J., grandson.
[13] A. A. Morrison, 'Religion and politics in Queensland', *Journal of the Historical Society of Queensland*, vol. 4, no. 4 (December 1951).
[14] Suttor, op. cit., p. 309.
[15] Sister M. Gonzaga to Sister M. Claver, 11 March 1892, A.H.A.
[16] To Mother M. of Mercy, 9 June 1861, C.P.A.
[17] Sister M. Benignus to Mother Vincent, 14 April 1891, A.H.A.
[18] To Mother M. of Mercy, 9 June 1861, C.P.A.
[19] 13 February 1863, C.P.A.
[20] 26 June 1863.
[21] 30 June 1863.
[22] To Dublin, 18 July 1863, C.P.A.
[23] Ibid.
[24] Sister M. Vincent Donovan, oral testimony.
[25] To Dublin, 17 April 1863, C.P.A.
[26] To Mother M. of Mercy, 15 May 1863, C.P.A.
[27] Ibid., 17 June 1863, C.P.A.
[28] H. J. Schroeder, *Canons and Decrees of the Council of Trent*, p. 224.
[29] Mother Vincent to Dublin, 13 June 1861, C.P.A. Compare Polding's comment on Quinn's missioners: 'A queer lot of clergy he has brought . . . one of them [Cusse] between sixty and seventy.' *A.C.R.*, vol. 37, no. 2 (April, 1960), p. 126.
[30] Quinn to Barnabo, 16 July 1862, Prop. Arch.
[31] Père d'Alzon to Barnabo, 13 November 1865, Prop. Arch.
[32] Mother Vincent to Dublin, 19 October 1863.
[33] Sister M. Cecilia to Father Renehan, 3 February 1865, Prop. Arch.
[34] Mother Vincent to Mother M. of Mercy, 18 February 1863, C.P.A.
[35] Dunne to Quinn, 6 February 1868, Letterbook, B.A.A.; copies of the Sisters' letters to Father Renehan in Italian in Prop. Arch.
[36] August 1862, A.H.A.
[37] To Dublin, 17 February 1864, C.P.A.
[38] 19 October 1863, C.P.A.
[39] 18 September 1863, C.P.A.
[40] 17 February 1864, C.P.A.
[41] 17 June 1863, C.P.A.
[42] Ibid.
[43] To Mother M. of Mercy, 18 August 1864, C.P.A.
[44] Her itinerary and expenses in her own handwriting, A.H.A.
[45] Mother Ursula and Mother Xavier had founded houses at Perth, Melbourne and Geelong.
[46] Tasmanian State Archives shipping-list announces her arrival on the *Derwent* and Dunne's on the *Tasmania*, 31 January 1865.
[47] Copies of their letters in Italian in Prop. Arch.
[48] Polding to Barnabo, 14 March 1866, Prop. Arch.
[49] M. Shanahan, *Out of Time, Out of Place*, pp. 91–111.
[50] Chapter Book, 11 March 1865, A.H.A., states the event without giving a reason. Quinn's letters giving his ostensible motives are quoted from in this chapter.
[51] *Queensland Times*, 18 November 1865.

52 Dunne to Quinn, 2 September 1868, Letterbook, B.A.A.

5 EPISCOPAL CONTROL (2)

1 J. H. Newman, *The Idea of a University*, discourse 3.
2 To Archdeacon McEncroe, 12 May 1866; quoted in Eris O'Brien, 'Some McEncroe letters', *A.C.R.*, vol. 7, no. 3 (1930).
3 24 April 1866, ibid.
4 22 February 1865, ibid.
5 27 July 1866, Letterbook, B.A.A.
6 13 August 1866, Letterbook, B.A.A.
7 1 March 1867; quoted in Eris O'Brien, 'Some McEncroe letters', *A.C.R.*, vol. 7, no. 3 (1930).
8 Quinn's report of his diocese to Barnabo, 1865, Prop. Arch.
9 Père d'Alzon forwarded this letter to Barnabo with his own; Prop. Arch.
10 Mother Bridget, Reminiscences, pt 1, p. 17, A.H.A.
11 To Dublin, March 1892, Letterbook, B.A.A.
12 Mother Vincent to Mother M. of Mercy, 9 June 1861, C.P.A.
13 Mother Bridget, Reminiscences, pt 1, p.17, A.H.A.
14 Ibid.
15 Letter dated January 1867; copy in A.H.A.
16 Mother Bridget, Reminiscences, pt 1, p. 17, A.H.A.
17 4 October 1867, Letterbook, B.A.A.
18 'It was worked principally by Protestants', he said, many of whom Mother Vincent had won.
19 Mother Bridget, Reminiscences, pt 1, p. 17, A.H.A.
20 Ibid.
21 8 June 1866, Letterbook, B.A.A.
22 20 June 1866, Letterbook, B.A.A.
23 20 July 1866, Letterbook, B.A.A.
24 July 1865, Letterbook, B.A.A.
25 John L. McKenzie, *Authority in the Church*, p. 90.
26 Bishop Matthew Quinn to the Sacred Congregation for the Propagation of the Faith, 1865, Prop. Arch. Professor O'Farrell, *The Catholic Church in Australia*, refers to the 'Irish junta' (p. 140) and 'Irish ecclesiastical imperialism'. A close study of Quinn reveals no trace of 'a vision of spiritual empire' (p. 133). Quinn's chief friend and counsellor was always Cani, the Italian priest who came out with him in 1861 (not in 1870 as O'Farrell states, p. 147). There is, in fact, more evidence for Molony's theory of *Roman* influence on Quinn than for the Suttor–O'Farrell myth of a grand Hibernian dream of spiritual glory; see J. N. Molony, *The Roman Mould of the Australian Catholic Church*.
27 Letters from Renehan, 19 September, 19 November 1865, Prop. Arch.
28 Copy of Queensland diocesan regulations, Sydney Archdiocesan Archives.
29 Tyr-Owen, *Sketch of the Life and Labours of the Right Rev. Dr. O'Quinn*, p. 15.
30 Quinn to Rome lists the dissident priests, 18 October 1869, Prop. Arch.
31 Renehan to Rome in the name of his group, 28 July 1867, Prop. Arch.
32 Tyr-Owen, op. cit., p. 15.
33 Dunne to Quinn, 8 December 1868, Letterbook, B.A.A.
34 To Reverend Mother, Hull Convent, 28 December 1867, Letterbook, B.A.A.
35 Dunne to Quinn, 6 February 1868, Letterbook, B.A.A.
36 Ibid.
37 Ibid.
38 30 January 1868, Letterbook, B.A.A.
39 Ibid.
40 6 February 1868, Letterbook, B.A.A.
41 To Cullen, 30 January 1868, Letterbook, B.A.A.
42 To Matthew Quinn, 10 February 1868, Letterbook, B.A.A.
43 20 January 1868, Letterbook, B.A.A.
44 22 January 1868, Letterbook, B.A.A.
45 1 February 1868, Letterbook, B.A.A.
46 Quinn to Matthew Quinn, 10 February 1868, Letterbook, B.A.A.
47 Quinn to Rev. Dr Forrest,, 10 February 1868, Letterbook, B.A.A.
48 Ibid.
49 Ibid.
50 To Mary [?], 1 February 1868, Letterbook, B.A.A.
51 23 January 1868, Letterbook, B.A.A. See 'The syllabus of accusations', no. 11, quoted in P. O'Farrell, *Documents in Australian Catholic*

History, vol. 1, pp. 341–3.
[52] Dunne to Rose Mayne (later Sister M. Mel), 17 June 1868, Letterbook, B.A.A.
[53] 23 March 1868, Letterbook, B.A.A.
[54] To Robert Dunne, 1 February 1868, Letterbook, B.A.A.
[55] Dunne to Quinn, 6 February 1868, Letterbook, B.A.A.
[56] To Cullen, 2 March 1868, Letterbook, B.A.A.
[57] Chapter Book, n.d., A.H.A.
[58] Chapter Book, 19 March 1869, A.H.A.
[59] In letters to the Roman authorities concerning Quinn, particularly from Père d'Alzon of Nîmes who knew the bishop personally, and members of whose Order withdrew from Queensland in the 1870s.
[60] Chapter Book, 19 March 1869, A.H.A.
[61] Chapter Book, 28 February 1872, 1 January 1874, A.H.A.
[62] 20 April 1870, Letterbook, B.A.A.
[63] Père Brun, in answer to questions, n.d., Prop. Arch.; see p. 114.
[64] Mother Bridget, Reminiscences, pt 1, p. 34, A.H.A.
[65] Tyr-Owen, op. cit., pt 2, p. 16.
[66] Ibid.
[67] To Bishop Delany of Cork, 10 June 1873, Letterbook, B.A.A.
[68] Letters from Thomas O'Connor, 1, 18 October 1871, A.H.A.
[69] Quoted in a letter from Mother Vincent, Tullamore, 26 November 1871, A.H.A.
[70] Mother Vincent of Dungarvan to Mother Vincent Whitty, 16 November 1871, A.H.A.
[71] Mother Catherine of Cappoquin to Mother Vincent, 5 December 1871, A.H.A.
[72] Mother Vincent of Dungarvan to Mother Vincent Whitty, 17 December 1871, A.H.A.
[73] Ibid.
[74] To Mother Catherine of Cappoquin, 12 November 1871, A.H.A.
[75] Michael Scally to Sister M. de Sales, 25 May 1872, A.H.A.
[76] Sister M. de C. Coleman, Bantry, [?] 1872, A.H.A.
[77] 4 August 1872, Letterbook, B.A.A.
[78] To Canon Andrew Quinn, 16 April 1873, Letterbook, B.A.A.
[79] To Bishop Delany, 10 June 1873, Letterbook, B.A.A.
[80] Mother Bridget, Reminiscences, pt 1, p. 49, A.H.A.
[81] Robert Dunne gives names and locations, Letterbook, 1868, B.A.A.
[82] *Queensland Times*, 16 November 1865.
[83] K. Inglis, 'Catholic historiography in Australia', *Historical Studies, Australia and New Zealand*, vol. 8, no. 31, p. 245.
[84] 28 January 1864.
[85] Quinn to Rome, 11 July 1872, Prop. Arch. Translation from Italian mine.
[86] Ibid.
[87] Not only Ricci, but other Italians also. See Dunne in home mail, 21 January 1880, Letterbook, B.A.A. J. N. Molony, *The Roman Mould of the Australian Catholic Church*, is generally correct in stating (p. 83) that Bishop James Quinn governed his diocese on Roman lines of law and theology, but the Italian clerics charged repeatedly that he failed to preach the doctrine of papal infallibility.
[88] Vaughan to Cani, 30 April, 17 May 1878, Prop. Arch.
[89] Dunne, home mail, 21 January 1880, Letterbook, B.A.A.
[90] Quinn to Bishop O'Mahony, 15 June 1878, Letterbook, B.A.A.
[91] *Courier*, 12, 17, 19 January 1880.
[92] Including Rosenstengel, Crofton and O'Donovan; S.A.A.
[93] Tyr-Owen, op. cit., p. 18.
[94] 26 January 1880.
[95] n.d., Prop. Arch.
[96] Cullen to the Sacred Congregation for the Propagation of the Faith, 11 October 1873, Prop. Arch.
[97] n.d., Prop. Arch.
[98] To Rome, 5 January 1875, 10 May 1879, Prop. Arch. Translation mine.
[99] Vaughan to Cani, 17 May 1878, Prop. Arch.
[1] *Courier*, 7 April, 8 May 1882.
[2] MacNab to Vaughan, first letter n.d., also 29 July 1878, S.A.A.
[3] *Darling Downs Gazette*, 4 January 1881; *Toowoomba Chronicle*, 6 November 1881; petitions and signatures, S.A.A.
[4] 4 August 1872, Letterbook, B.A.A.
[5] Mother Bridget, Reminiscences, pt 2, p. 34, A.H.A.

[6] 18 August 1881.
[7] *Queensland Evangelical Standard*, 10 December 1881.
[8] Quinn to Andrew Quinn, 18 June 1875, Letterbook, B.A.A.
[9] *Australian*, 20 March 1880.
[10] P. F. Connole, 'The Christian Brothers in secondary education in Queensland, 1875–1965', unpubl. M.A. thesis, University of Queensland, p. 62.
[11] *Australian*, 24 January 1880.
[12] G. O'Neill, *Life of Mother Mary of the Cross*, pp. 66, 83.
[13] To Cani, 2 March 1875, Letterbook, B.A.A.
[14] Ibid.
[15] Mother Bridget to Mother Benedict, 20 February 1870, Letterbook, A.H.A.
[16] P. D. Tannock, 'A history of Catholic education in Western Australia, 1829–1929, unpubl. M.Ed. thesis, University of Western Australia, p. 50.
[17] Mother Vincent to Dublin, 18 February 1863, C.P.A.
[18] P. D. Tannock, op. cit., p. 131.
[19] Teilhard de Chardin, 'Pensees' in *Hymn of the Universe*, p. 88.

6 RELATIONSHIP WITH HER COMMUNITY

[1] Quinn to Cullen, 23 March 1868, Letterbook, B.A.A.
[2] Quinn to Monsignor Kirby, Rome, 5 September 1880, B.A.A.
[3] Dunne to Madame Blumenthal, London, 17 July 1882, Letterbook, B.A.A.
[4] Ian Hoyle, S.J., in the *Catholic Leader*, 9 September 1959.
[5] To Woods, 27, 24 July 1880, Letterbook, B.A.A.
[6] Dunne to the Sacred Congregation for the Propagation of the Faith, 12 May 1897, B.A.A.
[7] Sister M. Aloysius, Orange, to Sister M. Claver, 13 April 1891.
[8] Mother Vincent to Cardinal Franchi, Rome, 18 May 1879, Prop. Arch.
[9] Sister M. Vincent Donovan, written testimony, A.H.A.
[10] To his brother Matthew, Bishop of Bathurst, he complained that Mother Benedict refused to obey Mother Bridget. Mother Benedict was then Reverend Mother. 10 February 1868, Letterbook, B.A.A.
[11] Letter from Sister M. Baptist ruefully laughing at Mother Bridget's style, n.d., A.H.A.
[12] See J. Decarreaux, *Les Moines et la civilisation en occident.*
[13] Mother Bridget to Mother Vincent, 23 July 1879, A.H.A.
[14] Ibid., 26 November 1879, A.H.A.
[15] Mother Michael Longford to Mother Bridget, 1879, A.H.A.
[16] To Mother Bridget, 30 June 1890, Letterbook, B.A.A.
[17] Diary, 20 June 1870, A.H.A.
[18] To Mother Vincent, 21 August 1879, A.H.A.
[19] Ibid.
[20] To Archbishop McCabe, Tuesday in Holy Week 1879, A.H.A.
[21] 19 March 1879, A.H.A.
[22] To McCabe, Wednesday in Holy Week 1879, A.H.A.
[23] Quoted in G. O'Neill, *Life of Mother Mary of the Cross*, p. 271.
[24] Quinn to Tenison Woods, 2 July 1875, Letterbook, B.A.A.
[25] Quinn to Monsignor Kirby, 5 September 1880, Letterbook, B.A.A.
[26] *Australian*, 29 November 1879.
[27] Dunne to Mother Bridget, 16 January 1890. Letterbook, B.A.A.
[28] 13 May 1889, Letterbook, B.A.A.
[29] To Mother Regis, 28 March 1890, Letterbook, B.A.A.
[30] 24 December 1889, Letterbook, B.A.A.
[31] 31 December 1889, Letterbook, B.A.A.
[32] 10 December 1889, Letterbook, B.A.A.
[33] Mother Bridget, Reminiscences, pt 2, p. 34, A.H.A.
[34] To Cardinal Moran, 26 August 1890 S.A.A.
[35] Reminiscences, pt 1, p. 31, A.H.A.
[36] Diary, 17 August 1870, A.H.A.
[37] To Quinn, 9 September 1870, Letterbook, A.H.A.
[38] Catherine McAuley, *Familiar Instructions*, pp. 39–46.
[39] Passion Sunday 1870, Letterbook, A.H.A.
[40] Quoted in Mother Bridget to Cani, 7 September 1870, Letterbook, A.H.A.

[41] To Mrs Lucas, September 1870, Letterbook, A.H.A.
[42] Reminiscences, pt 1, p. 19, A.H.A.
[43] Ibid.
[44] Chapter Book, n.d., A.H.A.
[45] Sister M. of Mercy, Warwick, to Sister M. Claver, 20 March 1892, A.H.A.
[46] Sister M. Benignus to Mother Vincent, 14 April 1891, A.H.A.
[47] Mother Bridget to Sister M. Agnes, Palm Sunday 1875, Letterbook, A.H.A.
[48] Mother Bridget to Mother Vincent, 21 March 1879, Letterbook, A.H.A.
[49] Mother Vincent, Sketch of Mother Catherine McAuley, C.P.A.
[50] 9 March 1877, Letterbook, A.H.A.
[51] Quinn to Cani, 28 April 1879, Letterbook, B.A.A.
[52] Ibid.
[53] 14 July 1905, A.H.A.
[54] Mother Patrick to G. W. Gray, chairman of the Building Committee, 1881, A.H.A.
[55] Lent 1887, Letterbook, A.H.A.
[56] Sister M. Livinus St Ledger to Mother Patrick, 6 May 1891, A.H.A.
[57] St Paul, Romans, ch. 12; Ephesians, ch. 2.
[58] S. Gilley, 'Catholic social and political attitudes in Queensland 1870–1900', unpubl. B.A. (Hons) thesis, University of Queensland, p. 9.
[59] Quoted by Kirby in a memorandum to the Sacred Congregation for the Propagation of the Faith, n.d., Prop. Arch.
[60] To Dublin, 13 May 1861, C.P.A.
[61] Copy in A.H.A.
[62] To Dublin, 17 March 1863, C.P.A.
[63] Ibid., 16 May 1863, C.P.A.
[64] Ibid., 9 June 1861, 17 March, 17 April 1863, C.P.A.
[65] Ibid., 16 May 1863, C.P.A.
[66] *Historical Studies, Australia and New Zealand*, vol. 12, no. 45 (October 1965), p. 68.
[67] Ibid., p. 73.
[68] T. P. Boland, 'The Queensland Immigration Society', *A.C.R.*, vol. 40, no. 3 (July 1963), pp. 196–7.
[69] Coughlan, op. cit., pp. 83–4.
[70] To Dublin, 9 June 1861, C.P.A.
[71] Ibid.
[72] Macaulay, *Critical and Historical Essays*, vol. 2, p. 66.
[73] Mother Vincent's printed sheet on immigration to Australia, etc. [1871–3], A.H.A.
[74] Ibid.
[75] Mother Bridget, Reminiscences, pt 1, p. 16; *Queensland Times*, 13 March 1863.
[76] Dunne to Father Renehan, 16 February 1867, Prop. Arch.
[77] Mother Vincent to Dublin, 17 April 1863, C.P.A.
[78] Ibid., 17 March 1863, C.P.A.
[79] Mother Bridget, Reminiscences, pt 1, pp. 15–16.
[80] 26 September 1879, A.H.A.
[81] Massy Morton to Cardinal Moran, 2 July 1905, S.A.A.
[82] Cf. the *Tablet*, 10 January 1885. The note was familiar to readers of the *Dublin Review*.
[83] *North Australian*, 4 January 1859.
[84] Dr Whitty to Mother Vincent, [?] January 1867, A.H.A.
[85] Ibid., 23 June 1861, A.H.A.
[86] Bishop Dunne to Mother Vincent, [?] 1884, Letterbook, B.A.A.
[87] H. Bryan, 'The political career of John Murtagh Macrossan', unpubl. M.A. thesis, University of Queensland.
[88] Mr Tapp in *Melbourne Review*, January 1881, p. 121.
[89] 18 June 1863, Letterbook, O.M.L.
[90] To Dublin, 17 June 1863, C.P.A.
[91] General correspondence records (1868), no. 1835, col. A/107, Q.S.A.
[92] 8 July 1876.
[93] 17 June 1875.
[94] Ibid.
[95] 10 June 1875.
[96] *Standard*, 29 July 1875.
[97] Mother Vincent to Sister M. Magdalen, 10 August 1876, A.H.A.
[98] *Age*, 11 March 1893. Crofton, the editor, states that the *Australian* was partly owned by the Sisters.
[99] Prospectus for the *Australian*, S.A.A. Promotion in the civil service was by patronage until 1889.
[1] *Standard*, 16 September 1875.
[2] See S. W. Gilley, 'Social and political attitudes in Queensland, 1870–1900', unpubl. M.A. thesis, University of Queensland.
[3] 'Lay intellectuals in the Church', *Catholic Leader*, 15 January 1967.
[4] *Australian*, 16 September 1967.

[5] *Courier*, 22 January 1881.
[6] See T. L. Suttor, *Hierarchy and Democracy in Australia, 1788–1870.*
[7] To her sister Mary, September 1870, A.H.A.
[8] Dunne to Mother Liguori, Dublin, 1897, Letterbook, B.A.A.
[9] Dunne to Benedictine Abbot 30 June 1893, Letterbook, B.A.A.
[10] To Mother Liguori, 1897, Letterbook, B.A.A.
[11] *Age*, 22 July 1893.
[12] Mother Vincent to Dublin, 8 September 1863, C.P.A.
[13] Dr Whitty to Mother Vincent, 22 June 1861, A.H.A.
[14] Mother Vincent to Dublin, 8 September 1863, C.P.A.
[15] Mother Bridget, Reminiscences, pt 1, p. 41, A.H.A.
[16] P. Moran, *History of the Catholic Church in Australasia*, vol. 1, p. 408.
[17] Quinn to Rome, 21 October 1867, Prop. Arch.
[18] February 1862, A.H.A.
[19] 2 April 1888, Letterbook, B.A.A.
[20] *Australian*, 19 March 1892.
[21] Bishop Byrne to Mother Vincent, 16 August 1891, A.H.A.
[22] Ida, Dalby, to Sister M. Claver, 17 August 1891, A.H.A.
[23] In the memory of living people, Mother Vincent is shadowy in comparison with Mother Bridget, who out-lived her by thirty-five years. The late Archbishop Sir James Duhig barely recollected Mother Vincent while he revered Mother Bridget and attributed his priestly vocation to her. (See his preface to the writer's *Beyond Our Dreams.*) He thus felt that she was the most important of the pioneers, and signified his preference by falling asleep during Rev. Dr T. P. Boland's excellent centennial panegyric on Mother Vincent.
[24] Even when a stray kitten toyed with her shiny black rosary beads, she was too absorbed to be aware of it, until an edified and amused Sister handed her a drawing of her oblivious self and the vainly pirouetting Felix.
[25] 'Eva' of the Dublin *Nation* in the *Sydney Catholic Home Annual*, 1891.
[26] Newspaper cuttings, A.H.A.

BIBLIOGRAPHY

MATERIALS RELATING TO IRELAND

MANUSCRIPT

Carysfort Park Convent Archives
Chapter Book.
Register.
Letters to the Baggot Street convent from Mothers Vincent Whitty, Ursula Frayne, Xavier Maguire, Anne Xavier, and the New York Sisters.

Dublin Archdiocesan Archives
The Cullen Papers, unclassified, include letters from Mother Vincent Whitty, Bishop James Quinn, Dr Andrew Quinn, Sister M. Catherine Morgan, and Sister M. Ignatius McQuoin.

National Library Dublin
Minutes of the Commissioners of the Board of National Education.
Typescript of O'Donovan's O.S. Letters.
Statistical Survey of Co. Wexford, 1840 (2 vols).

Conventual Archives
Convent of Mercy, Crumlin Road, Belfast.
St Ethelburga's, Liverpool.
St John's, Tralee, Co. Kerry.
St Leo's, Carlow, Co. Carlow.
St Michael's, Athy, Co. Kildare.

OFFICIAL SOURCES

Dublin Almanac, Registry and Directory. Pettigrew and Oulton, 1840.

Minutes of Evidence of the Select Committee of the House of Lords (1854). National Library, Dublin.

Official Report of the Inspector General of Prisons, 1860. Dublin Castle.

Powis Commission Report, 1870. National Library, Dublin.
Report on the Council of Education. Government Printer, Dublin, n.d. (*c.* 1855).

BOOKS AND ARTICLES

Contemporary

Carroll, M. Austin, *Annals of the Sisters of Mercy.* 4 vols. New York, 1881–8.
Fitzpatrick, W. J., *Memoirs of Richard Whately, Archbishop of Dublin.* London, 1864.
Lewis, Samuel, *Topographical Dictionary of Ireland with Historical and Statistical Description.* Dublin, 1816.
Lucas, Edward, *The Life of Frederick Lucas, M.P.* London, 1858.
McAuley, Catherine, *Familiar Instructions.* St Louis, 1927.
Taylor, F. M., *Irish Homes and Irish Hearts.* London, 1867.
Thackeray, W. M., 'The Irish penal system', *Cornhill Magazine,* vol. 2 (1861).
Ward, Wilfrid, *Life and Times of Cardinal Wiseman.* London, 1900.
Whately, Jane, *Life and Correspondence of Richard Whately, D.D.* London, 1866.

Modern

Albrecht-Carrie, Rene, *A Diplomatic History of Europe since the Congress of Vienna.* London, 1958.
Bolster, E., *The Sisters of Mercy at the Crimean War.* Cork, 1964.
Burke-Savage, R., *Catherine McAuley.* Dublin, 1950.
Chauvire, R., *History of Ireland.* Dublin, 1960.
Decarreaux, J., *Les Moines et la civilisation en occident.* Paris, 1962.
Degnan, Sister M. Bertrand, *Mercy unto Thousands.* Baltimore, Md, 1957.
Geyl, Pieter, *Debates with Historians.* London, 1962.
Inglis, K. S., *Churches and the Working Class in Victorian England.* London, 1963.
McGrath, Fergal, *Newman's University, Idea and reality.* Bristol, 1951.
McDowell, R. B., *Social Life in Ireland, 1800–1845.* Dublin, 1957.
MacSuibhne, Peader, *Paul Cullen and his Contemporaries.* 3 vols. Dublin, 1961–5.
Mathew, David, *Catholicism in England.* London, 1955.
Newman, J. H., *The Idea of a University.* London, 1899.

Norman, E. R., *The Catholic Church and Ireland in the Age of Rebellion, 1859–1873*. London, 1965.

Rafferty, T., 'Mixed education and the Synod of Ulster, 1831–1840', *Irish Historical Studies* (1956).

Russell, M., *Three Sisters of Lord Russell of Killowen*. London, 1912.

Trevor, Meriol, *Newman: The pillar of the cloud*. London, 1962.

Woodward, E. L., *Three Studies in European Conservatism*. London, 1964.

MATERIALS RELATING TO AUSTRALIA

MANUSCRIPT

All Hallows' Convent, Brisbane

Chapter Books.

Registers.

Letters from, to and concerning Mother Vincent Whitty.

Manuscript copy of the early Rule.

Letters from Bishop Quinn and Archbishop Dunne to Mother Vincent.

Typescript of Mother Vincent Whitty's Sketch of Mother McAuley.

Sister M. Bridget Conlan's Reminiscences (recorded about 1925), her Diary, and Letterbooks.

Notebooks of Mother Ursula Lavery, Sister M. Vincent Donovan and Sister M. Ita Nolan.

Printed memorial of the clergy to the Bishop, 1867.

Proceedings of the 1880 Brisbane Synod.

Memoirs of Sister M. Agnes Fitzgerald.

Account Books, Invoices, and School Returns.

Copies of Papers of Jervis Street hospital.

Archivio della S. Congregazione De Propaganda Fide, Rome

Under the heading 'Scritture referite della Sacra Congregazione' are reports of diocesan progress, and letters making requests or lodging complaints from Oceania to the Secretary of the Congregation for the Propagation of the Faith. Materials from Brisbane are classified 'S.R.C.O.' in the Archives, but in this work are indicated by 'Prop. Arch'.

Collegio Irlandese, Rome

The Kirby Papers include letters from Mother Vincent and Bishop Quinn. Archbishop Kirby, Rector of the Irish College, was agent at Rome for the Queensland Mission.

Jesuit Archives, Borgo Santo Spiritu, Rome
The Whitty letters held here supplement material in the Archives of the English Province of the Society of Jesus, and provide matter on the family background, education and friendships of Dr Whitty and Mother Vincent.
Sydney Archdiocesan Archives, St Mary's Cathedral
Letters from Messrs Crofton and O'Donovan to Archbishop Vaughan; also from Fathers MacNab and Kaercher, and Dr Cani.
Letters from Mother Bridget and Archbishop Dunne to Cardinal Moran; also from Massey Morton.
Material relating to National Synods and Councils.
Brisbane Archdiocesan Archives
Formerly the 'Wynberg Archives', these include the Letterbooks of Bishop Quinn and Archbishop Dunne. Unless otherwise mentioned, all letters quoted from these prelates are in the letterbooks.
Oxley Memorial Library
Microfilms of the Governors' confidential despatches 1864–76, held in the Public Records Office, London.
R. G. Herbert's Letterbook.
Queensland State Archives
General correspondence records.
Governors' despatches.
Letterbooks of the Board of General Education 1860–75.
Non-vested Schools files.
Dixson Library, Sydney
The Samuel Griffith Papers, unclassified.
Tasmanian State Archives
Shipping List.

OFFICIAL SOURCES

Australasian Catholic Directory, Official Year Book of the Catholic Church in Australia, New Zealand and Oceania, various publishers, Wm Brooks, Cusa House, E. J. Dwyer.
Board of General Education, *Report,* 1860–81 printed in *Votes and Proceedings* of the Queensland Legislative Assembly for the year following.
Pastoral Letters of Bishop James Quinn, 1862 and 1875; and combined Pastoral of 1879 (Sydney Archdiocesan Archives).
Acta et Decreta concilee primi provinciae Australiensis, 1884. F. Cunninghame, Sydney, 1847.

Acta et Decreta secundi concilii provincialis Australiensis, 1869.
Acta et Decreta concilii plenarii Australasiae, 1885. F. Cunninghame, Sydney, 1898.
Brisbane Diocesan Regulations of 1866 (Sydney Archdiocesan Archives).
Parliamentary Papers and *Debates* as cited.
Pugh's Almanac (various years).

NEWSPAPERS

A paper hitherto neglected by Queensland historians is the *North Australian,* published in Ipswich until 1863 and in Brisbane 1863–5. Copies to 1859 are available in the Mitchell Library in Sydney; thereafter in La Trobe Library, Melbourne. It provides a corrective to the bias of the *Guardian* and the *Courier.* Newstead House, Brisbane, and the Mitchell Library hold copies of the *Queensland Evangelical Standard.* A complete set of the *Age* is available at the office of the *Catholic Leader,* and of the *Australian* (except an odd issue) in the parliamentary library, Brisbane.

Catholic

Age, 1892–8.
Australian, 1880–92.
Catholic Leader, 1867.
Catholic Weekly, 1867.
Freeman's Journal, 1867.
North Australian, 1859–65.
Sydney Catholic Home Annual.

Other

Brisbane Courier, scanned 1861–92.
Cornhill Magazine, 1861.
Darling Downs Gazette.
Guardian (also known as the *Queensland Guardian* and, from 1863, the *Queensland Daily Guardian*), 1861–8.
Melbourne Review.
Moreton Bay Courier, 1860.
Queensland Evangelical Standard, 1875–82.
Queensland Times, 1861–9.
Sydney Morning Herald, 1861.
Toowoomba Chronicle, 1881.
Week, 1870–80.

BOOKS AND ARTICLES

Contemporary

Bernays, C. A., *Queensland Politics during Sixty Years, 1858–1919*. Government Printer, Brisbane, n.d.

Brown, Spencer, *A Journalist's Memories*. Brisbane, 1927.

O'Malley, *Secular Education and Christian Civilization*. Melbourne, 1875.

'Tyr-Owen' [? Father James Breen], *Sketch of the Life and Labours of the Right Rev. Dr. O'Quinn*. Printed at the *Australian* office, Brisbane, 1881.

Modern

Austin, A. G., *Australian Education, 1788–1900*. Melbourne, 1961.

Barcan, A., 'The Australian tradition in education' in T. W. T. Cowan (ed.), *Education for Australians*. Melbourne, 1964.

———, 'Education and Catholic social status', *Australian Quarterly* (March 1962), vol. 34, no. 1.

Barrett, J., *That Better Country: the religious aspect of life in eastern Australia 1835–1850*. Melbourne, 1966.

Boland, T. P., 'The Queensland Immigration Society' in *Australasian Catholic Record* (1962; 1963), vols 39, 40.

Bolton, G. C., *A Thousand Miles Away: A history of north Queensland, to 1926*. Canberra, 1963.

Border, Ross, *Church and State in Australia*. London, 1962.

Blainey, Geoffrey, *The Tyranny of Distance*. Melbourne, 1966.

Butts, R. F., *Assumptions Underlying Australian Education*. Australian Council for Educational Research, Melbourne, 1955.

Clark, C. M. H., *A Short History of Australia*. Sydney, 1963.

———, *Select Documents in Australian History, 1851–1900*. Sydney, 1955.

———, *Sources of Australian History*. Melbourne, 1957.

Cleary, P., *Australia's Debt to the Irish Nation Builders*. Sydney, 1933.

Coughlan, N., 'The Coming of the Irish to Australia', *Historical Studies of Australia and New Zealand* (October 1965), vol. 12, no. 45.

Cowan, R. (ed.), *The Australian Tradition in Education*. Melbourne, 1964.

Fogarty, Ronald, *Catholic Education in Australia, 1806–1950*. 2 vols. Melbourne, 1957.

Greenwood, Gordon, *A Social and Political History*. Sydney, 1955.

Gregory, J., 'Church and State, and education in Victoria to 1872' in E. L. French (ed.), *Melbourne Studies in Education 1958–1959*. Melbourne, 1960.

Griffin, review of T. L. Suttor, *Hierarchy and Democracy in Australia, 1788–1870* in the *Australian Journal of Politics and History* (December 1966), vol. 12, no. 3.

Horne, Donald, *The Lucky Country*. Adelaide, 1964.

Inglis, K., 'Catholic historiography in Australia', *Historical Studies, Australia and New Zealand* (November 1958), vol. 8, no. 31.

Kelly, J., 'Catholic schools and Catholic education', *Twentieth Century* (Winter, 1962).

Lahey, Vida, *Art in Queensland, 1859–1959*. Brisbane, 1959.

Leslie, Shane (ed.), *From Cabin Boy to Archbishop*. London, 1953.

Levy, Mary Raphael, 'The relevance of St Thomas Aquinas for Australian education' in E. L. French (ed.), *Melbourne Studies in Education, 1963*. Melbourne, 1964.

Linz, C. C., *The Establishment of a National System of Education in New South Wales*. Melbourne, 1938.

Marks, Elizabeth, 'Sylvester Diggles', *Queensland Naturalist* (July 1963; June 1965), vol. 17, nos 1–2; nos 4–5.

Molony, J. M., *The Roman Mould of the Australian Catholic Church*. Melbourne, 1969.

Morrison, A. A., 'Religion and Politics in Queensland (to 1881)', *Journal of the Royal Historical Society of Queensland* (December 1951), vol. 4, no. 5.

———, 'Town "liberal" and squatter', ibid. (December 1952), vol. 5, no. 4.

O'Brien, Eris, 'Some McEncroe Letters', *Australian Catholic Record*, (1930), vol. 7.

O'Donoghue, Sister Mary Xaverius, *Beyond our Dreams: A review of the Mercy Order in Queensland over one hundred years*. Brisbane, 1961.

O'Farrell, Patrick, *The Catholic Church in Australia*. Sydney, 1968.

———, *Documents in Australian Catholic History*. 2 vols. London, 1969.

O'Neill, G., *Life of Father Julian Tenison Woods*. Sydney, 1930.

———, *Life of Mother Mary of the Cross*. Sydney, 1931.

Roberts, C., 'Beginnings of the Church in Queensland', *Australasian Catholic Record* (1959; 1960), vols 36, 37.

———, 'Bishop James Quinn', ibid. (1960), vol. 37.

Roe, Michael, *Quest for Authority in Eastern Australia, 1788–1870*. Melbourne, 1965.

Shanahan, M., *Out of Time, Out of Place*. Canberra, 1970.

Suttor, T. L., *Hierarchy and Democracy in Australia, 1788–1870*. Melbourne, 1965.

'Tyr-Owen' [? Father James Breen], 'Obituary notice on Dr. James O'Quinn', *Australian* Office, Brisbane, 1881.

Wyeth, E. R., *Education in Queensland*. Australian Council for Educational Research, Melbourne, n.d.

Zain'uddin, A., 'England and Australia: national education in two pluralist societies' in E. L. French (ed.), *Melbourne Studies in Education, 1961–1962*. Melbourne, 1964.

THESES

Unless otherwise indicated these are held in the history department, University of Queensland.

Boland, T. P., 'The Queensland Immigration Society'. Doctoral thesis, Gregorian University, Rome; summarized in *Australasian Catholic Record*, 1962 and 1963 (see above).

Bryan, H., 'The political career of John Murtagh Macrossan'. 1954.

Burke, K., 'All Hallows' Curriculum: first fifty years, 1860–1911'. Research project in comparative education, Education Methods Library, University of Queensland, 1960.

Connole, P. F., 'The Christian Brothers in secondary education in Queensland, 1875–1965'.

Clark, C. S., 'The Royal Commissions of Queensland, 1859–1901'. 1962.

Dignan, D., 'Sir Thomas McIlwraith'. 1951.

French, E. L., 'Secondary education in the Australian social order, 1788–1898'. Doctoral thesis, University of Melbourne.

Gilley, S. W., 'Catholic social and political attitudes in Queensland, 1870–1900'. 1967.

Hunt, J., 'Church and State in Queensland'. 1959.

Jobson, J. X., 'Aspects of Brisbane society in the 1860s'. 1959.

Lawson, R., 'Secular education in Queensland, 1963'.

Low, M., 'Relations between the Churches and Labour, 1885–1895'. 1963.

McLay, Y:. 'Critical appreciation of the educational system of All Hallows' Congregation'. 1963.

Rayner, K., 'The attitudes and influence of the Churches in Queensland in matters of social and political importance, 1859–1914'. 1951.

Tannock, P., 'A history of Catholic education in Western Australia, 1829–1929'. University of Western Australia.

ECCLESIASTICAL HISTORIES

Altholz, Josef, *The Liberal Catholic Movement in England.* London, 1962.
'A Sister of the Church', *Emily Aycbown: A Valiant Victorian Woman.* London, 1964.
Daniel-Rops, Henri, *The Church in an Age of Revolution. 1822–1870.* London, 1965.
Gray, V., *Catholicism in Queensland: Fifty years of progress.* Brisbane, 1910.
Hales, E. E. Y., *The Catholic Church in the Modern World.* London, 1958.
Moran, Patrick Cardinal, *History of the Catholic Church in Australasia.* Oceanic Publishing Co., Sydney, n.d. [*c.* 1898].
Murtagh, J .G., *Australia, The Catholic Chapter.* Sydney, 1955.
Watkin, I., *Roman Catholicism in England From the Reformation to 1950.* London, 1957.

GENERAL

Barrett, J. J., 'Queensland', *Christian Brothers' Educational Record,* 1894.
Encyclopaedia Britannica (11th edition).
Ferguson, John Alexander, *Bibliography of Australia.* Sydney, 1945.
McKenzie, John L., *Authority in the Church.* London, 1966.
Marcel, Gabriel, *Being and Having.* London, 1965.
Maritain, J., *On the Philosophy of History.* London, 1954.
Murray, John Courtney, *We Hold These Truths.* New York, 1960.
Schroeder, H. J., *Canons and Decrees of the Council of Trent.* London, 1960.
Teilhard De Chardin, *Hymn of the Universe.* London, 1965.

INDEX